Historical Dictionary of Nuclear, Biological, and Chemical Warfare

D1450789

Benjamin C. Garrett
John Hart

*Historical Dictionaries of War,
Revolution, and Civil Unrest, No. 33*

The Scarecrow Press, Inc.
Lanham, Maryland • Toronto • Plymouth, UK
2007

SCARECROW PRESS, INC.

Published in the United States of America
by Scarecrow Press, Inc.
A wholly owned subsidiary of
The Rowman & Littlefield Publishing Group, Inc.
4501 Forbes Boulevard, Suite 200, Lanham, Maryland 20706
www.scarecrowpress.com

Estover Road
Plymouth PL6 7PY
United Kingdom

British Library Cataloguing in Publication Information Available

Library of Congress Cataloging-in-Publication Data

Garrett, Benjamin C., 1949–
  Historical dictionary of nuclear, biological, and chemical warfare / Benjamin C.
Garrett, John Hart.
      p. cm. — (Historical dictionaries of war, revolution, and civil unrest ; no.
33)
  Includes bibliographical references.
  ISBN-13: 978-0-8108-5484-0 (hc : alk. paper)
  ISBN-10: 0-8108-5484-8 (hc : alk. paper)
   1. Weapons of mass destruction—Dictionaries. 2. Weapons of mass
destruction—History—Dictionaries. I. Hart, John, 1967– II. Title.

U793.G37 2007
358'.303—dc22   2007005487

Contents

Editor's Foreword

Unlike other volumes in the series of Historical Dictionaries of War, Revolution, and Civil Unrest, this volume does not deal with specific wars or branches of the armed forces but with certain categories of weapons that are of particular interest at present. On the face of it, there is little in common among nuclear, biological, and chemical weapons. Nuclear weapon programs require vast resources in terms of know-how and finance. Yet there is concern that the hurdles for developing a nuclear weapon have substantially diminished in recent years, partly because of a continuing diffusion of scientific and technological expertise and capabilities around the world. Chemical and biological weapons, by comparison, are relatively cheap and, in principle, easy to acquire. But all three weapon types are particularly nasty in the eyes of the general public, so much so that efforts have been made repeatedly over the past decades to ban or at least contain their spread. While some progress has been made to this end, great challenges remain in an age when warfare can be waged by nonstate actors, as well a world in which terrorism is a constant threat. Control of these weapons is therefore more vital than ever.

So *Historical Dictionary of Nuclear, Biological, and Chemical Warfare* has a double purpose: first, to describe the various sorts of weapons, their origins and characteristics, and their military uses; second, to show what has been done and what remains to be done to bring them under control. This is primarily the task of the dictionary section, with numerous entries on the weapons themselves, persons who helped create them, programs and installations that developed them, and the many states and sometimes individuals who used them, often to devastating effect, as well as the various agreements and organizations, which it is hoped can provide a modicum of control. The introduction offers an overview of the situation, clearly and succinctly, and the chronology traces the milestones in both efforts—to create and to contain. The list of acronyms and abbreviations, always helpful, is this time almost indispensable, since it is quite impossible to read up on the topic without knowing what they all mean. Obviously, this book is intended as just a starting point or a point of reference to which one can return later, but the bulk of the information lies in countless other books, the more important of which are included in an extensive bibliography.

This latest, and rather unique, addition to the series was written by Benjamin C. Garrett and John Hart. While they are both strongly interested in the same field, they have quite different backgrounds and approach it from different angles, which is obviously to the good. Dr. Garrett is a scientist, with training in chemistry, who spent the past two decades working on defense and intelligence programs before joining the Federal Bureau of Investigation, where he serves as a senior scientist. John Hart is presently a researcher at the prestigious Stockholm International Peace Research Institute, after having worked previously at the Verification Research, Training and Information Centre and the Monterey Center of Nonproliferation Studies, among other places. He has already written on many of the topics in this book. While this experience provided an excellent base on which to work, it is obvious that they had to put in countless hours tracking down the basic facts and figures, thereby facilitating the process for any who consult this book.

Jon Woronoff
Series Editor

HISTORICAL DICTIONARIES OF
WAR, REVOLUTION, AND CIVIL UNREST
Jon Woronoff, Series Editor

Preface

In selecting the entries for this volume, attempts have been made to provide an overview of historical, legal, technical, and political aspects of nuclear, biological, and chemical (NBC) weapons. We have endeavored to maintain a balance within the entries in terms of coverage devoted to noteworthy events, notable individuals, nations, fundamental research, and the testing and fielding of NBC weapon systems. We hope that the dictionary contains information that those who closely follow NBC-related developments will find unusual as well as useful.

This work also attempts to provide insight into the behavior and concerns of individuals and organizations. It is hoped that this work will assist readers in gaining an enhanced understanding of how the NBC field has both evolved and remained unchanged over the years. We also hope that it can help to inform consideration of issues of continuing international concern, including determining the purpose for which dual-use/dual-purpose materials, technology, and equipment that can support NBC weapon programs will be used. For example, information is included about the main technological stages necessary to develop a nuclear weapon (e.g., definition of the nuclear fuel cycle, enrichment of nuclear material, fission, fusion, the characteristics of a peaceful nuclear energy program, verification concepts). Future consideration of such issues can be at least partly informed by how they were handled in the past.

The country entries contain unavoidable information gaps. This situation is due in part to space constraints in a work such as this one. By necessity, a choice had to be made regarding content, creating certain gaps in coverage. These holes are also a consequence of the fact that most primary-source research in the NBC field has focused on a limited number of states, mainly in the West. To a certain extent, this Western focus reflects the states that have been most active in the NBC field.

Other contributors to this focus include our language constraints and the availability of reliable primary or otherwise authoritative source material from non-Western sources. It is nevertheless reasonable to suppose that a great deal of research remains to be carried out using primary historical sources from and about countries in Africa, Asia, Latin America, and the Middle East. Activities carried out in these regions might include NBC threat assessments, defensive chemical and biological warfare (CBW) programs, the development of standby NBC weapon capacities, and perhaps the use of CBW agents for assassination purposes.

The information contained in this work is based on unclassified primary or other authoritative sources. While some of the information or phrasing might be considered politically sensitive in some circles, this work contains no sensitive technical information. It is hoped that this work will also assist to correct the occasional error in fact that may have found its way into the literature. In addition, while states are generally able to find out for themselves the information they require to evaluate NBC threats, individuals often cannot. If individuals were to have better understanding of possible threats posed by such weapons, they would be better able to judge the appropriateness and effectiveness of measures taken to meet such threats. We hope that the present work will assist in this regard as well.

Finally, we would like to thank Jon Woronoff, the series editor, for his patience and great assistance. Any errors or omissions are, however, our responsibility.

Acronyms and Abbreviations

ABACC	Brazilian-Argentine Agency for Accounting and Control of Nuclear Materials
ABM	Antiballistic Missile System
AChE	Acetylcholinesterase
ACW	Abandoned Chemical Weapon
ADM	Atomic Demolition Munition
AEC	Atomic Energy Commission
AEF	American Expeditionary Forces
AFB	Air Force Base
AG	Australia Group
AHG	Ad Hoc Group
AviaKhim	Volunteer's Society of the Friends of Aviation and the Chemical Industry
AWE	Atomic Weapons Establishment
BDA	Bilateral Destruction Agreement
BII	BioIndustry Initiative
BND	Bundesnachrichtendienst [Germany's Federal Intelligence Service]
Bq	Becquerel
BTWC	Biological and Toxin Weapons Convention
BTX	Botulinum Toxin
BW	Biological Warfare; Biological Weapon
BWC	Biological Warfare Committee
BWPP	BioWeapons Prevention Project
BZ	Hydrochloride salt of 3-Quinuclidinyl benzilate
CAIS	Chemical Agent Identification Set
CBIAC	Chemical and Biological Information Analysis Center
CBM	Confidence-Building Measure
CBRN	Chemical, Biological, Radiological, and Nuclear

CBW	Chemical and Biological Weapons; Chemical and Biological Warfare
CD	Conference on Disarmament
CDC	Centers for Disease Control and Prevention
CEP	Circular Error Probable
CG	Phosgene
CHASE	Cut Holes and Sink 'Em
Ci	Curie
CIA	Central Intelligence Agency
CmlC	Chemical Corps
CN	Chloroacetophenone
CNS	Central Nervous System
COCOM	Coordinating Committee for Multilateral Export Controls
CTBT	Comprehensive Nuclear Test Ban Treaty
CTR	Cooperative Threat Reduction
CS	2-Chlorobenzilidene malonitrile
CSP	Conference of the States Parties
CUA	Catholic University of America
CW	Chemical Warfare; Chemical Weapon
CWC	Chemical Weapons Convention
CWPF	Chemical Weapon Production Facility
CWS	Chemical Warfare Service
DAS	Diacetoxyscirpenol
DDA	Department of Disarmament Affairs
DF	Methyl phosphonic difluoride
DIA	Defense Intelligence Agency
DobroKhim	Volunteer's Society of the Friends of Chemical Defense and Chemical Industry
DOD	Department of Defense
DOE	Department of Energy
DPG	Dugway Proving Ground
DPRK	Democratic People's Republic of Korea (North Korea)
DSTL	Defence Science and Technology Laboratories
DU	Depleted Uranium
EC	Executive Council
EMP	Electromagnetic Pulse

EMPTA	O-Ethyl methylphosphonothioic acid
ERDA	Energy Research and Development Administration
EUISS	European Union Institute for Security Studies
eV	Electron-volt
FBI	Federal Bureau of Investigation
FMD	Foot-and-Mouth Disease
FSB	Federal Security Service
FSU	Former Soviet Union
GA	Tabun
GB	Sarin
GB2	Binary sarin
GD	Soman
GF	Cyclosarin
GI	Gastrointestinal
GLP	Good Laboratory Practice
GMP	Good Manufacturing Practice
GosNIIOKhT	State Scientific Research Institute for Organic Chemistry and Technology (Moscow)
GPC	General-Purpose Criterion
GWS	Gulf War Syndrome
Gy	Gray
HD	Sulfur mustard
HELCOM	Helsinki Commission
HEU	Highly Enriched Uranium
HL	Sulfur mustard–lewisite mix
HN	Nitrogen mustard
IAEA	International Atomic Energy Agency
ICBM	Intercontinental Ballistic Missile
ICI	Imperial Chemical Industries
IIBR	Israel Institute for Biological Research
IMS	International Monitoring System
IND	Improvised Nuclear Device
INFCIRC	Information Circular
INVO	Iraq Nuclear Verification Office
IPEN	Institute of Energy and Nuclear Research (São Paulo, Brazil)
IRBM	Intermediate-Range Ballistic Missile
ISG	Iraq Survey Group

ISU	Implementation Support Unit
IUPAC	International Union of Pure and Applied Chemistry
JRDB	Joint Research Development Board
kg	Kilogram
km	Kilometer
L	Lewisite
LAC	Large Area Coverage
LEU	Low-Enriched Uranium
LTBT	Limited Test Ban Treaty
LWR	Light-Water Reactor
MADM	Medium Atomic Demolition Munition
MCTL	Militarily Critical Technologies List
MED	Manhattan Engineering District
MIRV	Multiple Independently Targetable Reentry Vehicle
MIT	Massachusetts Institute of Technology
Mk	Mark
MOD	Ministry of Defense
MOPP	Mission Oriented Protective Posture
MOU	Memorandum of Understanding
MTCR	Missile Technology Control Regime
MUF	Materials Unaccounted For
NAM	Nonaligned Movement
NAS	National Academy of Sciences
NATO	North Atlantic Treaty Organization
NBC	Nuclear, Biological, and Chemical
NDRC	National Defense Research Committee
NE	Polymeric sulfur mixture
NEST	Nuclear Emergency Search Team
NIE	National Intelligence Estimate
NNSA	National Nuclear Security Administration
NNWS	Non–Nuclear Weapon State
NORAD	North American Aerospace Defense Command
NORM	Naturally Occurring Radioactive Material
NPT	Nonproliferation Treaty (Treaty on the Nonproliferation of Nuclear Weapons)
NRC	National Research Council
NSG	Nuclear Suppliers Group
NTS	Nevada Test Site

OCW	Old Chemical Weapon
OPA	Isopropyl alcohol–isopropylamine mixture
OPCW	Organization for the Prohibition of Chemical Weapons
OsoAviaKhim	General Society for Aviation and Chemistry
OSRD	Office of Scientific Research and Development
OSS	Office of Strategic Services
PAL	Permissive Action Link
PMR	Proximity Measuring Radar
PNE	Peaceful Nuclear Explosions
POW	Prisoner of War
PPE	Personal Protective Equipment
PRC	People's Republic of China
PrepCom	Preparatory Commission
PSI	Proliferation Security Initiative
PSP	Paralytic Shellfish Poisoning
QL	O-Ethyl O´-(2-diisopropylaminoethyl) methylphosphonite
R	Roentgen
Rad	Radiation Absorbed Dose
RADIAC	Radioactivity Detection, Indication, and Computing
RAF	Royal Air Force
RCA	Riot-Control Agent
RDD	Radiological Dispersal Device
Rem	Roentgen Equivalent (in) Man
SA	Stürm Abteilung
SAB	Scientific Advisory Board
SADM	Special Atomic Demolition Munition
SBU	Sensitive but Unclassified
SHAD	Shipboard Hazard and Defense
SI	Système International d'Unités [metric system]
SIPRI	Stockholm International Peace Research Institute
SLBM	Submarine Launched Ballistic Missile
SNM	Special Nuclear Material
SORT	Strategic Offensive Reduction Treaty
SPRU	Science Policy Research Unit
SQP	Small Quantities Protocol
SS	*Schutzstaffel*

Sv	Sievert
T-2	12,13-Epoxytrichothec-9-ene-3,4,8,15-tetrol-4,15-diacetate 8-(3-methylbutanoate)
TIC	Toxic Industrial Chemical
TIM	Toxic Industrial Material
TNT	Trinitrotoluene
TS	Technical Secretariat
TTBT	Threshold Test Ban Treaty
UK	United Kingdom
UN	United Nations
UNGA	United Nations General Assembly
UNMOVIC	United Nations Monitoring, Verification, and Inspection Commission
UNSC	United Nations Security Council
UNSCOM	United Nations Special Commission on Iraq
U.S.	United States
USAMRIID	United States Army Medical Research Institute of Infectious Diseases
USSR	Union of Soviet Socialist Republics
VX	O-Ethyl S-(2-diisopropylaminoethyl) methylphosphonothiolate
VX2	Binary VX
W	Ricin
WHO	World Health Organization
WMD	Weapon(s) of Mass Destruction
WRS	War Research Service

Chronology

429 B.C. Spartans forces use an early form of chemical warfare (CW) by burning wood soaked with pitch and sulfur at the siege of Plataea, thereby choking defenders.

A.D. 670 Approximate date Greek fire invented.

1854 British chemist Lyon Playfair proposes that artillery shells be filled with cacodyl cyanide as a way to help British and French forces to capture Sevastopol from the Russians. The proposal is rejected.

1861–1865 During the U.S. Civil War, John Doughty proposes filling chlorine into artillery shells, Joseph Lott proposes spraying chloroform onto Confederate troops using a fire engine, and Capt. E. C. Boynton proposes using cacodyls-filled grenades against Confederate ships. None of these chemical warfare (CW) proposals appears to have been followed up.

1874 **27 August:** The International Declaration Concerning the Laws and Customs of War (the Brussels Declaration) is signed at the Brussels Conference of 1874. The declaration, which never entered into force, condemned the use of chemical weapons (CW) and banned the use of poison as a method of warfare.

1899 The Hague Gas Projectile Declaration is issued.

1915 **22 April:** Germany initiates the modern age of chemical warfare (CW) by releasing chlorine against French colonial and Canadian troops outside Ypres, Belgium. The release is successful and spawns a protracted period of CW use by all combatants during World War I.

1917 **12 July:** In fighting outside Ypres, Germany introduces use of weapons containing sulfur mustard. Its persistency and delayed effects cause sulfur mustard to be labeled the "king of chemical weapons."

1919   28 June: The Peace Treaty of Versailles is concluded with Germany, ending the hostilities of World War I. Article 171 of this treaty states in part: "The use of asphyxiating, poisonous or other gases and all analogous liquids, materials or devices being prohibited, their manufacture and importation are strictly forbidden in Germany. The same applies to materials specially intended for the manufacture, storage and use of the said products or devices." **August–September:** British forces operating in the White Sea region of northern Russia use chemical warfare (CW) against Bolshevik troops during the Russian Civil War.

1921   November: Spanish forces begin using chemical weapons (CW) in their fight against rebels in Morocco, which Spain claims as a colony. Chloropicrin, phosgene, and sulfur mustard will be used, with some of the weapons coming from stockpiles left over from World War I and others from a specially constructed factory outside Melilla, Spain.

1922   Germany and the Union of Soviet Socialist Republics (USSR) sign the Treaty of Rapallo, pledging cooperation on economic and military matters. Germany provides technical expertise on chemical warfare (CW) and equipment to the USSR in exchange for laboratory space and permission to carry out CW field trials at Shikhany, Russia. **6 February:** The Treaty of Washington of 1922 Relating to the Use of Submarines and Noxious Gases in Warfare is opened for signature in Washington, D.C. Five nations will sign, but the treaty fails to enter into force. **18 April:** Germany issues patent number 351,894 to chemist Ferdinand Flury for a method of pest control. The patent covers a group of chemicals given the trade name Zyklon. The most infamous of these, Zyklon B, will be used extensively to exterminate humans in Nazi Germany's concentration camps.

1928   8 February: The Protocol for the Prohibition of the Use in War of Asphyxiating, Poisonous, or Other Gases, and of Bacteriological Methods of Warfare, more popularly known as the 1925 Geneva Protocol, enters into force.

1935   American chemist Kyle Ward Jr. publishes a scientific article on *tris*(2-chloroethyl) amine, the first of a novel chemical warfare (CW) group known as the nitrogen mustards. **3 October:** Italy attacks Abyssinia (present-day Ethiopia and Eritrea). Fighting will continue for several years, with repeated uses of CW by Italy.

1936   23 December: German chemist Gerhard Schrader discovers tabun, which becomes the first member of a new class of chemical warfare (CW) agents called organophosphorus nerve agents. Schrader will later discover sarin.

1937–1945   Japanese forces occupying Manchuria and portions of China establish a network of chemical warfare (CW) and biological warfare (BW) facilities centered on Unit 731, Harbin, Manchuria, and repeatedly make use of CW and BW, including lewisite, sulfur mustard, and plague.

1938   December: German scientists Otto Hahn and Fritz Strassmann bombard uranium with neutrons, breaking the uranium apart into two smaller atoms and releasing energy.

1939   11 February: The journal *Nature* features an article by Lisa Meitner and Robert Otto Frisch providing mathematical proof that the Hahn-Strassmann experiments conducted the previous December resulted in a process that Frisch names "nuclear fission." **2 August:** Physicist Albert Einstein addresses the first of several letters to U.S. president Franklin Delano Roosevelt in which he describes how uranium, through a chain fission reaction, could be used as a powerful energy source and expresses concern that Germany might be able to harness this energy as a weapon.

1940   The United Kingdom establishes the Military Applications of Uranium Disintegration or "MAUD" Committee to study the possibility of developing a nuclear weapon.

1941   Britain establishes the Directorate of Tube Alloys, a cover name for its secret nuclear weapon development program. **July:** The Military Applications of Uranium Disintegration or "MAUD" Committee releases its report in which it estimates that 10 kilograms (22 pounds) of uranium-235 would be sufficient to produce a nuclear explosion.

1942   June: The U.S. War Department tasks the Army Corps of Engineers to establish the Manhattan Engineering District (MED), a secret effort to develop a nuclear weapon. MED will become more popularly known as the Manhattan Project. **2 December:** The first self-sustaining chain fission reaction takes place in a nuclear pile at the University of Chicago.

1943   June: President Roosevelt states that the United States will not initiate use of chemical warfare (CW), but reserves the right to retaliate in kind if attacked with such weapons. **16 November:** The ALSOS Mission begins. This U.S.-led scientific intelligence field mission is tasked to determine the extent of Germany's nuclear weapon program. That mission will later be expanded to include Germany's CW and biological warfare (BW) programs. **2 December:** German bombers sink the USS *John Harvey* in the harbor of Bari, Italy, causing extensive injuries from the ship's secret cargo of chemical weapons.

1944   German chemist Konrad Henkel discovers the organophosphorus nerve agent soman.

1945   16 July: "Gadget" detonates successfully at the Trinity Test Site, near Alamogordo, New Mexico, becoming the first man-made nuclear explosion. **6 August:** U.S. Army Air Forces plane *Enola Gay* drops the "Little Boy" nuclear bomb over Hiroshima, Japan. **9 August:** The United States drops the "Fat Man" nuclear bomb over Nagasaki, Japan. **24 October:** George W. Merck submits his final report (the Merck Report) to U.S. secretary of war Robert P. Patterson, describing the U.S. World War II biological warfare (BW) program and concluding that the United States should continue BW development. **15 November:** The ALSOS Mission concludes.

1946   6 September: The U.S. Army Chemical Corps (CmlC) is created out of the Chemical Warfare Service.

1947   January: The Manhattan Project ceases its work, with the transfer of its activities to the newly established Atomic Energy Commission (AEC).

1949   29 August: The Union of Soviet Socialist Republics (USSR) conducts its first successful detonation of a nuclear weapon, dubbed "Joe" by U.S. intelligence.

1951   25 November: William A. Boyles dies following an accidental exposure to anthrax in a laboratory at Fort Detrick, Maryland. The laboratory harvests his organs, using them as the basis for culturing a novel strain of anthrax, V1B, which will be used in U.S. biological weapons.

1952   3 October: The United Kingdom conducts its first successful detonation of a nuclear weapon.

1953   3 December: U.S. president Dwight D. Eisenhower proposes the Atoms for Peace plan.

1954   1 March: The United States conducts its first successful explosion of a deliverable thermonuclear device, "Bravo."

1955   January: The journal *Chemistry and Industry* carries a report by two industrial chemists entitled "A New Class of Organophosphorus Pesticides." The featured chemical is Amiton, which becomes the basis for the novel V-type organophosphorus nerve agents, such as VX.

1960   3 December: France explodes its first nuclear weapon.

1962   26 September: Civil war erupts in Yemen (Sanaa). Periodic claims come forward of chemical warfare (CW) use, mainly sulfur mustard and phosgene, supposedly supplied by Egypt and possibly the Union of Soviet Socialist Republics (USSR). **16–28 October:** The Cuban Missile Crisis occurs.

1963   10 October: The Treaty Banning Nuclear Weapon Tests in the Atmosphere, in Outer Space, and Under Water (Partial Test Ban Treaty) enters into force.

1964   16 October: China conducts its first successful detonation of a nuclear weapon.

1966   17 January: A U.S. B-52 bomber and K-135 tanker collide over Palomares, Spain, resulting in the breakup of the two planes and the release of four unarmed hydrogen bombs.

1968   13 March: The accidental release of VX during an open-air chemical warfare (CW) test kills more than a thousand sheep in Skull Valley, east of Dugway Proving Ground, Utah. **1 July:** The Treaty on the Nonproliferation of Nuclear Weapons (Nonproliferation Treaty, NPT) is opened for signature.

1969   25 November: The United States renounces first use of lethal or incapacitating chemical agents and the use of biological warfare (BW) under any circumstances. U.S. president Richard M. Nixon issues a directive saying the United States will cease the development, procurement, and stockpiling of the weapons.

1970   14 February: The United States extends the biological warfare (BW) renunciation to include toxins and directs that all toxin stocks held for offensive purposes be destroyed. The destruction is completed in 1973.

1972   18 May: The Treaty on the Prohibition of the Emplacement of Nuclear Weapons and Other Weapons of Mass Destruction on the Seabed and the Ocean Floor and in the Subsoil Thereof (Seabed Treaty) enters into force.

1974   18 May: India detonates a nuclear device that it characterizes as a peaceful nuclear explosion (PNE) test.

1975   26 March: The Convention on the Prohibition of the Development, Production, and Stockpiling of Bacteriological (Biological) and Toxin Weapons (Biological and Toxin Weapons Convention, BTWC) enters into force. **10 April:** The United States accedes to the Geneva Protocol of 1925, 50 years after the treaty had opened for signature.

1976   The Peaceful Nuclear Explosions (PNE) Treaty is concluded.

1978   11 September: Georgi I. Markov, a Bulgarian dissident writer living in London, dies. An autopsy reveals a tiny pellet in his leg. Analysis of the pellet reveals it contained ricin, a toxin derived from seeds of the castor-oil plant. Prior to his death, Markov commented that he had been jabbed in the leg by an umbrella near London's Waterloo Bridge days earlier.

1979   The World Health Organization (WHO) certifies that smallpox has been eradicated. **3 April:** At least 64 people die from anthrax in Sverdlovsk, Russia. Following the fall of the Union of Soviet Socialist Republics (USSR), the outbreak is shown to have been the result of an accidental release from a biological warfare (BW) production facility. **22 September:** The "Vela Incident" occurs, in which satellite Vela 6911 detects a double flash of the type known to occur during a nuclear explosion.

1980   May: A panel convened by U.S. president Jimmy Carter concludes that the flash detected by the Vela satellite on 22 September 1979 was likely to have been caused by dust from a meteorite rather than a nuclear explosion. **22 September:** The Iran-Iraq War begins when Iraq attacks Iran. It will last eight years, with repeated Iraqi use of chemical warfare (CW).

1981 The U.S. Department of State issues a report saying it believes the Union of Soviet Socialist Republics (USSR) has supplied mycotoxins to Laos that have been used against anti-Communist insurgents since the late 1970s. South Africa approves Project Coast to carry out research, development, and production of selected chemical and biological weapons (CBW). Israeli planes destroy a nuclear reactor under construction at Osiraq, near Baghdad, Iraq, fearing it might be diverted to nuclear weapon activities.

1983 **2 November:** Able Archer 83, a North Atlantic Treaty Organization (NATO) exercise simulating the use of nuclear weapons, begins, sparking speculation that the Union of Soviet Socialist Republics (USSR) believed the exercise was a prelude to an actual nuclear strike.

1984 **26 March:** Referring to a 1983 incident, United Nations (UN) document S/16433 concludes that chemical weapons had been used during the ongoing Iran-Iraq War. **September:** The Rajneeshee cult spreads *Salmonella enteritica* serotype typhimurium at restaurants in The Dalles, Oregon, causing more than 700 to become ill; no fatalities result. A U.S. Public Health Service official subsequently declares the incident the result of poor hygiene.

1987 The Treaty on the Elimination of Intermediate-Range and Shorter-Range Missiles (INF Treaty) is concluded by the United States and the Union of Soviet Socialist Republics (USSR). The United States begins production of binary chemical weapons (CW). **10 April:** Soviet leader Mikhail Gorbachev announces that the USSR has halted producing CW and had never deployed them outside the territory of the Soviet Union. **30 November:** The United Nations General Assembly (UNGA) passes resolution A/RES/42/37, which empowers the United Nations (UN) secretary-general to investigate alleged use of CW or biological weapons (BW). The legal authority to do so is partly based on the 1925 Geneva Protocol.

1988 **March:** Iraqi forces use chemical warfare (CW) against their own citizens in the Kurdish region around the northern city of Halabja.

1989 Soviet microbiologist Vladimir Pasechnik defects to the United Kingdom and provides extensive information to Britain and the United

States about a secret Soviet offensive biological warfare (BW) program, including the role played by a network of civilian research institutes called Biopreparat.

1990   24 April: The United Kingdom declares Gruinard Island, Scotland, free of anthrax contamination and reopens it to civilian visitors following nearly 50 years of quarantine resulting from its World War II biological warfare (BW) tests. **11 December:** The Threshold Test Ban Treaty, setting a threshold for underground tests of nuclear explosives, enters into force.

1991   The Treaty on the Reduction and Limitation of Strategic Offensive Arms (START I Treaty) is concluded by the United States and the Union of Soviet Socialist Republics (USSR). The Nunn-Lugar Cooperative Threat Reduction (CTR) program is established on the initiative of U.S. senators Richard Lugar and Sam Nunn. **February:** A U.S.-led international coalition ejects Iraqi forces from Kuwait. Iraq agrees to a cease-fire. **3 April:** The United Nations Security Council (UNSC) adopts Resolution 687 requiring Iraq to verifiably dismantle its chemical, nuclear, and biological weapon programs and destroy any stockpiles of such weapons. **19 April:** The UNSC approves the formation of the United Nations Special Commission on Iraq (UNSCOM) to verify Iraq's compliance with its Resolution 687 obligations in the field of chemical warfare (CW) and biological warfare (BW).

1992   Russia, the United States, and the United Kingdom conclude a Trilateral Agreement under which each country agrees to receive on-site inspections of biological sites. There is suspicion that the Russian military is conducting activities without the full consent and knowledge of higher political officials. **January:** Russian president Boris N. Yelstin acknowledges that there has been a delay in his country's implementation of its Biological and Toxin Weapons Convention (BTWC) obligations. **19 February:** Russian decree no. 160 is passed, establishing the Presidential Committee for Convention-Related Chemical and Biological Weapon Matters. **11 April:** President Yeltsin signs presidential decree no. 390, entitled "On Ensuring Fulfillment of International Obligations in the Areas of Biological Weapons."

1994   June: The Japan-based religious cult Aum Shinrikyo purchases a helicopter from Russia, planning to equip it with aerosol dispersal devices for distributing biological agents. Although cult members never use the helicopter for this purpose, they do disperse sarin from a specially modified van in Matsumoto, Japan, outside the homes of three judges who are involved in a legal case involving the cult; seven people die as a result. **21 October:** In Geneva, representatives of North Korea and the United States conclude an "Agreed Framework," which the two parties are careful not to characterize as an "agreement," that aims to achieve peace and security on a nuclear-free Korean Peninsula partly by allowing North Korea to replace its older graphite-moderated reactors with more proliferation-resistant light-water reactors and reaffirming a commitment by both sides to work toward strengthening the international nonproliferation regime, including adherence to the Nonproliferation Treaty (NPT).

1995   South Africa's Project Coast ends. **20 March:** Aum Shinrikyo releases sarin in the Tokyo subway. Twelve people die as result, while another 500 require medical attention or hospitalization. Approximately 5,500 people are examined for ill effects. **7 August:** Iraqi leader Saddam Hussein's son-in-law, Gen. Hussein al-Kamal, defects to Jordan, where he provides the United Nations Special Commission on Iraq (UNSCOM) with evidence that Iraq has produced VX. His defection helps prompt Iraq to admit having had an offensive biological weapons program.

1996   6 September: The Comprehensive Nuclear Test Ban Treaty (CTBT) is opened for signature.

1997   29 April: The Chemical Weapons Convention (CWC) enters into force.

1998   28 May: Pakistan explodes its first nuclear weapon. Earlier, neighboring India had conducted test firings of six nuclear weapons and declared itself to be a nuclear weapon state. **8 June–31 July:** South Africa's Truth and Reconciliation Commission holds hearings on chemical warfare (CW) and biological warfare (BW) activities previously carried out by the country. The activities carried out under Project Coast are a major focus of the commission's hearings. **20 August:** A U.S. air strike destroys the al-Shifa Pharmaceutical Industries factory in Sudan, prompted by fears that the facility was designed to produce precursors for VX.

1999   22 April: The United States announces it will retain its stockpile of smallpox virus, rather than destroy it on 30 June as previously decided. The U.S. position responds to intelligence suggesting supplies of the virus are possessed outside the two agreed-upon repositories in the United States and Russia.

2001   31 May: On-site inspections under the Treaty on the Elimination of Intermediate-Range and Shorter-Range Missiles (INF Treaty) end. **September–October:** Letters containing anthrax spores are mailed anonymously to politicians and members of the media in the United States. Five deaths and another 17 cases of confirmed exposure result, along with massive disruption, including the closing of congressional offices.

2002   27 June: The G8 Global Partnership Against the Spread of Weapons and Materials of Mass Destruction is formally launched at a meeting of the Group of Eight leaders in Kananaskis, Canada. **23 October:** Chechen rebels take approximately 800 hostages at the Dubrovka Theater in Moscow. **26 October:** Russian troops assault the Dubrovka Theater, dispersing what is described as "sleeping gas" into the theater. All rebels perish in the assault, along with 129 hostages.

2003   10 January: North Korea submits a letter to the United Nations announcing its withdrawal, effective the following day, from the Nonproliferation Treaty (NPT). **1 June:** The Strategic Offensive Reductions Treaty (SORT) enters into force. **19 December:** Libya, the United Kingdom, and the United States issue coordinated announcements to the effect that Libya has agreed to renounce nuclear, biological, and chemical (NBC) weapons and longer-range ballistic missile weapons and that the country will adhere to the relevant international treaties prohibiting such weapons.

2006   31 July: The United Nations Security Council (UNSC) adopts Resolution 1696, which notes, with "serious concern," that gaps in knowledge continued to exist regarding the nature of Iran's nuclear program despite more than three years of efforts by the International Atomic Energy Agency (IAEA). The resolution "demand[s]" that Iran suspend all enrichment-related and nuclear fuel reprocessing activities, including research and development. **9 October:** North Korea announces that it has exploded a nuclear weapon. The yield is approximately 500 to 1,000 tons of TNT, and this low yield fuels speculation that the detonation was a fizzle. **14 October:** The UNSC unanimously adopts Resolution 1718, which condemns North Korea's nuclear test and imposes sanctions on the country. **12 December:** Israeli prime minister Ehud Olmert is quoted in a German television interview as admitting that his country possesses nuclear weapons.

Introduction

Human experience with nuclear, biological, and chemical (NBC) warfare has been limited by comparison with conventional forms of warfare. Our experience with nuclear warfare is confined to a period of less than one week during what turned out to be the end of World War II, when the United States successfully used two nuclear weapons (then popularly called "atomic bombs") against targets in Japan. The necessity for dropping of those weapons continues to be debated, although Japan's nearly immediate decision to surrender is certain to have limited the loss of life, other injuries, and the destruction of the landscape and infrastructure that would have accompanied a military invasion by conventional arms.

The emergence of nuclear warfare paralleled the development of nuclear physics. As understanding of the fundamental nature of the atom and its components improved, the prospects of releasing energy from the atom and for harnessing that energy became increasingly apparent to scientists, political figures, and the public. As early as World War I, science-fiction writers were crafting stories featuring atomic energy as sources for good and evil. The notion of a nuclear weapon developed more slowly. The scope of World War II proved important to marshalling the political will, the proper cadre of scientists and engineers, and the financial resources to succeed in first demonstrating that nuclear chain reactions could be controlled and then constructing weapons using such reactions as the principal element in the explosion.

Those scientists who contributed to the growth of nuclear physics in the late 19th century and first half of the 20th century set the stage for nuclear warfare. Some of the major contributors to the new field of nuclear physics became direct participants in developing or attempting to develop nuclear weapons. Examples include Niels Bohr, Albert Einstein, Enrico Fermi, Werner Heisenberg, Otto Hahn, and Andrei Sakharov.

Several of these same scientists would later become forceful advocates against the use of these weapons. Such advocacy occasionally came at a significant personal price relative to their freedom to continue pursuing scientific research.

By the end of the 20th century, the development of nuclear weapons had become an engineering challenge, and the emphasis on addressing fundamental scientific issues lessened. This change brought with it an increased prospect for the spread of nuclear weapons, as success in engineering developments often yields more willingly to time, money, and a trial-and-error approach than do breakthroughs in basic research. An international trade in nuclear weapon technology has emerged, brought to light by discoveries in Iraq and Libya and by the news of the activities of Pakistani scientist A. Q. Khan. This trade has increased the risk that the world might witness another episode of nuclear warfare.

The course of biological warfare and modern use of biological weapons (BW) are difficult to track. By contrast to nuclear warfare, no fundamental scientific breakthroughs appear to have facilitated the development of BW. It is difficult to credit any eminent biologist with contributing directly to the development of such weapons. Rather, biological warfare appears to be an outgrowth of the recognition that biological organisms cause diseases in humans and other animals and that these diseases can be used to advantage during war. This recognition was made possible partly by the development in the 19th century by German biologist and physician Robert Koch of four postulates— Koch's Postulates—which specify the conditions that must be met in order to determine whether a given pathogen is the causative agent for a given disease. Prior to this achievement, the causes of diseases were often ascribed to "bad humors" or "miasmas."

Disease caused by pathogens such as those responsible for anthrax, cholera, plague, and smallpox has long been an inescapable element of war, both among the combatants and within civilian populations. Prior to the availability of prompt medical care and antibiotics in the latter half of the 20th century, wartime deaths and injuries from noncombat causes such as these diseases routinely were greater in numbers than were those from combat causes. Tying such disease outbreaks to deliberate use of these pathogens during war or at any other time is difficult, owing to the challenge of differentiating deliberate use from natural outbreaks, obscuring our ability to determine whether biological warfare has occurred and, if so, its effectiveness. Furthermore, the usefulness of such weapons as a means of warfare is questionable, given the existence of natural and acquired resistance to pathogens in any large human population and the possibility that any deliberate release could affect one's own military forces and civilian population.

Use of BW in acts of terrorism and against civilian targets seems more likely to produce results that might be deemed satisfactory by military analysts and planners. The fall 2001 experience in the United States with the release of anthrax through the U.S. postal system demonstrates the keen potential for biological materials to cause mass disruption, although the casualties incurred were limited to five deaths and 17 confirmed injured. This experience, however, showed that BW could be exceedingly simple in design—in this case, an envelope loaded with anthrax spores. This simplicity and the natural availability of pathogens contrast sharply with the skills and technology required for successful construction of nuclear weapons.

The modern age of chemical warfare might be dated to Germany's 22 April 1915 use of chlorine against French territorial and Canadian troop positions near Ypres, Belgium. That use provoked immediate condemnation from the Allies, but they promptly and successfully undertook efforts to retaliate in kind, making World War I notable as the only major conflict in which both sides used chemical weapons (CW). The course taken by chemical warfare during World War I involved many of the most eminent chemists of the time, including future chemistry Nobel Laureates Fritz Haber and Walther Nernst. The chemicals selected for use in weapons were a mix of well-known substances commonly used by industry, such as chlorine, phosgene, and chloropicrin, and little-known substances previously discovered but overlooked until the needs of the war for novel toxic materials caused scientists to widen their search. The most notorious substance in this latter category is sulfur mustard, which some observers dubbed the "king of chemical weapons" for its ability to cause large numbers of painful, long-lasting blisters. Although sulfur mustard was not introduced to the battlefield until 1917, it was responsible for more than half of all the war's CW casualties.

More generally, knowledge of how toxic chemicals and biological substances might be employed as a method of warfare evolved in conjunction with the industrial and scientific infrastructure that brought about the large-scale production of chemicals, foodstuffs, and the like.

Such an infrastructure provided equipment, production protocols, and analytical techniques from, for example, the chemical industry and its research laboratories for CW production. Prior to these developments, chemical and biological warfare (CBW) essentially consisted of poisoning by persons who had little or no understanding of the underlying physiochemical processes.

CW surfaced occasionally in the decades following World War I, often in conflicts where one adversary had major advantages in terms of protection and defense against such weapons. Notable examples of this situation are the use of CW by Spain during the conflict in Morocco (1921–1927), Italy in Ethiopia (1935–1937), and Japan during its fighting on the Asian mainland (1932–1945). Chemical weapons were stockpiled but never used on any measurable scale by the major combatants during World War II in Europe (1939–1945). Major developments in novel CW, especially the organophosphorus nerve agents, took place during and immediately after that war. The nerve agents grew out of industrial research into pesticides and became a unique class of toxic substances, offering perceived advantages in terms of effects if used in combat. Large stockpiles of the nerve agents accumulated in the United States and the Union of Soviet Social Republics (USSR), and more modest stockpiles were produced by other nations. Although none saw use in combat except during the Iran-Iraq War in the 1980s, the mere existence of these stockpiles may have exerted a significant effect on military planning and strategy.

Despite this limited experience, NBC warfare continues to exert a certain fascination among states, especially in states lacking democratic governments. This situation is illustrated by the repeated attempts made by Iraq during the regime of Saddam Hussein to develop NBC weapons. Fears that such weapons existed or were being developed were confirmed in the aftermath of the 1991 Gulf War. Persistent concerns that Iraq was continuing to pursue such weapons fueled the 2003 invasion. In October 2006, the dictatorial regime of the Democratic People's Republic of Korea (North Korea) captured the world's attention when it exploded a nuclear device, although the explosion was widely viewed as a fizzle.

Repeated efforts have been made to restrict or prohibit the development, stockpiling, and use of NBC weapons, reflecting the nearly universal revulsion with which such weapons are viewed. These efforts have met with some success, as witnessed by the ongoing destruction of the CW stockpiles in accordance with the Chemical Weapons Convention (CWC) and under the auspices of the Organization for the Prohibition of Chemical Weapons (OPCW). But failures of international treaties and arms control agreements were highlighted by the discoveries of the United Nations Special Commission on Iraq (UNSCOM), the International Atomic Energy Agency (IAEA), and the United Nations Monitoring, Verification, and Inspection Commission (UNMOVIC) during their work in Iraq.

Attempts to restrict or prohibit these weapons have been carried out on ad hoc, unilateral, bilateral, and multilateral bases. In 1989, for example, the United States and the Soviet Union concluded a memorandum of understanding meant to facilitate agreement on the eventual destruction of the two countries' respective CW stockpiles. In the early 1990s, the United Kingdom and United States engaged in a secret trilateral process with the USSR (and later with Russia) to ascertain the status of the former Soviet BW program. Results were mixed.

In 2003 Britain and the United States engaged in a similar process with Libya in which the two countries, with the later involvement of the IAEA and OPCW, verified Libya's renunciation of NBC weapons and longer-range missiles. Measures taken to restrict or prohibit NBC weapons may also be divided according to whether they are "demand side" or "supply side." Supply-side measures essentially consist of the development and effective implementation of export controls, while demand-side measures consist of effectively implementing multilateral agreements that prohibit or restrict such weapons. Finally, ad hoc arrangements of like-minded states (such as the Proliferation Security Initiative, PSI) have been developed.

The principal international legal instrument against the acquisition or use of nuclear weapons is the 1968 Nonproliferation Treaty (NPT). Signatories to the NPT fall into two categories: non–nuclear weapon states (NNWS) and those states that possessed nuclear weapons at the time the treaty entered into force. The treaty affirms the right of all its members (currently totaling 142) to develop nuclear energy for peaceful purposes, such as for medical research, food safety, and electricity generation. The treaty obliges the nonpossessor states to conclude safeguards agreements with the IAEA, located in Vienna, and to allow the organization to verify these states' compliance with the treaty in order to prevent the diversion of nuclear energy from peaceful purposes to nuclear weapons or other nuclear explosive devices. For their part, the nuclear weapon possessor states that are signatories—China, France, Russia, the United Kingdom, and the United States, referred to as the "P-5"—are obliged to work in good faith toward complete and final nuclear disarmament. These five nations have periodically reiterated their commitment to work toward achieving this goal.

The regime has nevertheless been under severe strain since the beginning of the 1990s. This is partly because the Cold War ended, thus, in the view of some, reducing the political pressure on the P-5 to continue to remain firmly committed to eliminating their nuclear stockpiles for the forseeable future. Another setback to the regime occurred in 1991 when the extent of Iraq's clandestine nuclear weapon program became apparent following intrusive inspections carried out in that country by the IAEA under the terms of United Nations Security Council Resolution 681, under which hostilities from the first Gulf War were ended. Finally, the withdrawal of North Korea from the NPT in the early 1990s following strong indications that that country was secretly reprocessing and diverting nuclear fuel for use in a possible clandestine nuclear weapon program prompted widespread international concern.

A series of more recent nuclear tests carried out by India (1998), Pakistan (1998), and North Korea (2006), none of which are currently party to the NPT, has reinforced the view that the regime is under severe strain. The United States has also effectively ended sanctions and most restrictions on nuclear-related technology and equipment transfers for India and, to a lesser extent, Pakistan. Moreover, the 2006 U.S.-India Peaceful Atomic Energy Cooperation Act requires changes to the export control regulations of the members of the Nuclear Suppliers Group (NSG), an organization that attempts to prevent the spread of nuclear weapons by coordinating export control policies and regulations. Other NSG members and observers have expressed concern that an exemption for India would particularly undermine the NPT and would adversely affect the viability of the international nonproliferation regime generally. India maintains that it considers the NPT to be inherently discriminatory in that it allows for nuclear weapon "haves" and "have-nots" and reiterates that it is not a member of the treaty. Other states in the region, including Pakistan, will also consider further how their political and security interests might be affected. A state may conclude, for example, that, once achieved, the possession of nuclear weapons can assist in facilitating a broadening and deepening of international economic and military cooperation and will promote a consolidation of its domestic and regional political standing.

The IAEA has taken steps to strengthen its safeguards system, partly by concluding with NPT member states special agreements that allow for more frequent routine inspector access to undeclared facilities and areas adjacent to declared facilities as well as environmental sampling. The IAEA also continues to implement a verification system that includes the placing of seals at key points in the nuclear facilities of NNWS to help detect possible diversion of nuclear materials and video monitoring of nuclear facilities in the NNWS. The P-5 states do not place their military nuclear facilities under IAEA safeguards except in a limited number of instances in order to serve as a confidence-building measure (CBM). The IAEA has also taken measures to address a major loophole in the traditional verification system, namely, how to capture activities where no nuclear materials are present. The loophole is due to the fact that traditional IAEA safeguards have been structured to verify that declared nuclear materials do not go unaccounted for. The IAEA currently has greater authority to use open-source information and information provided by member states to perform countrywide analyses of individual NPT member states. Another key challenge for the IAEA is to try to ensure that it conducts its work in a manner that does not undermine the principle of equal treatment of member states that are in good standing of their treaty obligations. Otherwise the moral, political, or legal legitimacy of the NPT regime might be questioned.

The main international legal instrument against BW is the 1972 Biological and Toxin Weapons Convention (BTWC). The treaty's weak mechanisms for verifying compliance were underlined by allegations in the late 1970s and 1980s that the USSR employed "Yellow Rain" mycotoxins in Afghanistan and Southeast Asia (which have since been largely discounted) and confirmation that the Soviets pursued an offensive BW program after the BTWC had entered into force. There have also been periodic unfounded allegations of BW use. In December 2006 the Sixth Review Conference of the BTWC agreed on a series of annual meetings to be held in 2007–2010. The meetings will, among other things, consider measures to promote effective implementation of the treaty, to improve biosafety and biosecurity at biological facilities, and to improve national capabilities for disease surveillance, detection, and diagnosis. These goals will be achieved partly through the establishment of a temporary treaty implementation support unit (ISU). The BTWC, together with other international mechanisms, can be effectively used to clarify BW-related concerns provided there is sufficient political interest and will by states.

The primary international legal instrument against CW is the CWC, which is implemented by the OPCW, based in The Hague. No compliance concern against other member states has been formally raised within the treaty regime. Some compliance concerns, often of a technical (as opposed to "fundamental") nature have, however, been informally raised and addressed under the CWC provisions for consultations, cooperation, and fact-finding. Much of the compliance-related discussion relates to the broader question of how much of a nation's past offensive CW program and current CW defense establishment activities should be declared and verified by on-site inspections. Member states ("States Parties") to the CWC have also expressed concern about the fact that the two states with the largest CW stockpiles (the United States and Russia) will be unable to meet their CWC-mandated destruction deadlines, which require the stockpiles to be destroyed by no later than April 2012. The CWC States Parties are also considering how the treaty's verification regime should be structured once CW destruction operations have been essentially completed (old and abandoned chemical weapons will continue to be periodically recovered for the foreseeable future). This includes the level of intrusiveness and scope of chemical industry inspections.

The principal verification challenge in the NBC field is how to evaluate accurately and precisely the intended purpose for materials, technologies, and equipment that can support either a peaceful or a prohibited military program. For example, nuclear fuel cycle technologies have legitimate and peaceful applications in the field of generating power, but these same technologies might be used to support a nuclear weapon program. This sort of problem surfaced when it became clear that India had diverted nuclear technologies, know-how, and materials provided to it by the United States under the "Atoms for Peace" program, using them for its national program to develop a nuclear weapon. Because of such experiences, there is a view that no state should be allowed to develop a full nuclear fuel cycle and that some key elements of the cycle should be placed under some form of international control.

A related challenge is determining whether a national program is solely defensive in nature or supports the offensive use of NBC weapons. Arms control and disarmament agreements provide some guidance, but few specifics. The BTWC has a general-purpose criterion (GPC) banning all microbial or other biological agents or toxins except for nonprohibited purposes. The CWC, which also has a GPC, defines a CW as consisting of one or more of three elements:

1. Toxic chemicals and their precursors, except where intended for purposes not prohibited by the treaty (i.e., not as a "method of warfare")
2. Munitions and devices specifically designed to cause death or harm through the use of such toxic chemicals
3. Any equipment specifically designed to be used directly in connection with such chemicals, munitions, and devices

The GPC is the means by which the two conventions ensure that future technological and scientific developments are covered by the treaty regime. Uncertainties about ambiguous CBW program indicators stem partly from the consideration of how to apply the GPC in practice.

Difficulties that have been encountered in implementing export controls designed to stop NBC weapon programs include agreeing on guidelines for achieving an internationally harmonized and politically acceptable set of guidelines to inform the drafting of national export control regulations and ensuring that "end user" certificates are accurate (i.e., that a declared end user is in fact the recipient of the shipment and will use the materials and equipment for nonprohibited purposes). Export control arrangements, such as the NSG, have been criticized for placing undue restrictions on the rights of all nations to chemical-, biological-, and nuclear-related materials and equipment that can be used either for peaceful purposes or to support NBC weapon programs. Whether a given shipment of material is to be used to support an NBC program is usually the subject of classified intelligence and law enforcement information that often cannot be fully shared among states. Such information may also be ambiguous or open to political interpretation.

A major historical theme of continuing relevance is how work to develop or protect against NBC weapon programs can or should be justified in legal and political terms. It is hoped that this dictionary will help to provide a historical context to the consideration of these issues, as well as to the broader political and technical challenges of the future.

Dictionary

– A –

ABANDONED CHEMICAL WEAPONS (ACW). The 1993 **Chemical Weapons Convention (CWC)** defines *abandoned chemical weapons* as **chemical weapons (CW)** (including **old chemical weapons (OCW)**) abandoned by a State Party after 1 January 1925 on the territory of another state without the consent of the latter. Official declarations to the effect that a state "does not possess chemical weapons" sometimes cause confusion because the treaty makes distinctions among the terms *abandoned chemical weapons*, *old chemical weapons*, and *chemical weapons*.

ABLE ARCHER '83. The code name given to a 10-day Europe-wide North Atlantic Treaty Organization (NATO) exercise that began on 2 November 1983 and included a full-scale simulated release of **nuclear weapons**. Scholars disagree about whether the Soviet Union believed the exercise was the prelude to an actual nuclear strike and the event was comparable to the **Cuban Missile Crisis**.

ABSOLUTE DUD. A **nuclear weapon** that fails to explode. *See also* DWARF DUD; PREINITIATION.

ACETYLCHOLINESTERASE. *See* CHOLINESTERASES.

ACONITINE. A potent **neurotoxin** occurring naturally in plants of the *Aconitum* genus of the Ranunculaceae or buttercup family. **Germany** tested aconitine during World War II as a potential **chemical weapon (CW)**. Details of these tests came to light during the "Doctors' Trial," part of the Nuremberg Tribunal following World War II. German defendants claimed the testing was inspired by fears that the partisan forces from the Soviet Union were using aconitine-laced bullets in areas occupied by Germany. According to testimony at the trial, tests included firing aconitine-laced bullets into Soviet prisoners of war. Several defendants were convicted for their complicity in these tests and were executed for this crime and others.

ADAMSITE. The common name for 10-chloro-5,10-dihydrophenarsazine. Its chemical formula is $C_{12}H_9AsClN$. This yellow crystalline solid is both a sternutator (a substance causing intense sneezing) and a **vomiting agent**. It has been used as a chemical warfare (CW) agent. The name given this substance honors U.S. chemist Roger Adams (1889–1971), who was involved in its synthesis by the **United States** during World War I. Although the synthesis of adamsite was perfected by the United States in May 1918, developing methods for its dispersion proved difficult. Consequently, the United States did not have adamsite munitions (mostly in the form of **smoke** candles) ready until after World War I had ended.

At the same time as the U.S. group under Adams was investigating adamsite, a group in the **United Kingdom** was conducting similar studies. As often happens in scientific research, each group was unaware of the work of the other—and both groups were unaware that **German** scientists had already patented a process for adamsite preparation prior to the war. Various German accounts report that adamsite was studied during World War I at the Kaiser Wilhelm Institute of Physical Chemistry and Electrochemistry near Berlin. According to these accounts, results were deemed insufficiently encouraging for the Germans to pursue adamsite as a CW agent. In addition to interest in adamsite in the United States, Britain, and Germany during World War I, the Italians also investigated it and developed an alternative synthesis procedure that proved highly attractive, and adamsite was used by **Japanese** forces in China in 1937–1945.

Although it was also stockpiled by some states as a **riot-control agent (RCA)**, the Scientific Advisory Board to the **Organization for the Prohibition of Chemical Weapons (OPCW)** has recommended that this agent not be used for this purpose.

ADJUVANT. In the context of **chemical weapons (CW)**, an adjuvant is a substance added to a chemical warfare agent to enhance the military effectiveness of the agent. Adjuvants might be separated into four categories based on the desired effect: **carrier**, **freezing-point depressant**, **stabilizer**, and **thickener**. Some adjuvants serve more than one purpose, while a few appear to have served no useful purpose.

ADVISORY COMMITTEE ON URANIUM. *See* URANIUM COMMITTEE.

AEROSOL. A liquid or solid suspended in air. Aerosols are an important means of delivering toxic chemicals, biological pathogens, and radiological materials; hence, aerosols figure prominently in weapons involving these substances. For example, an effective method for delivery of many biological warfare agents is as an aerosol consisting of particles of a size (1–5 microns) that allows for penetration into the lung and transfer into the bloodstream via the alveoli sacks. The term was reportedly introduced by M. A. Trillat in 1938 as part of a concept for sterilizing air.

AGENT ORANGE. The U.S. code name for a mixture of the *n*-butyl ester of 2,4-dichlorophenoxyacetic acid (2,4-D) (50 percent) and the *n*-butyl ester of 2,4,5-trichlorophenoxyacetic acid (2,4,5-T) (50 percent). Agent Orange is a **defoliant** and was used extensively for these purposes by the U.S. military during the Vietnam War as part of Operation Ranch Hand. The use of Agent Orange was viewed by many as an example of chemical warfare, but the U.S. government took the view during the war that it was not. The use of defoliants as part of combat operations is now prohibited under the 1993 **Chemical Weapons Convention (CWC)**.

After the war, U.S. veterans and veteran support groups sued the U.S. government and manufacturers of defoliants for compensation for adverse health effects that many veterans believe are connected to the use of this and similar agents. There continue to be reports of adverse environmental and health effects from the use of defoliants in Vietnam. However, demonstrating a causal link has been problematic. 2,4-D and 2,4,5-T are only mildly toxic to humans, but some batches of Agent Orange were contaminated with chemicals known collectively as *dioxins*, which are extremely harmful. This dioxin contamination, coupled with the widespread use of Agent Orange, rather than the human toxicities of the chemicals 2,4-D and 2,4,5-T themselves, led to concerns over adverse long-term health effects. Such concerns caused use of Agent Orange and the related **herbicide** "Agent Purple" to be restricted by the U.S. military as of April 1970.

The code name derives from the orange stripe painted around the 55-gallon containers in which Agent Orange was shipped. Other defoliants used in the Vietnam War that contained 2,4-D or 2,4,5-T were Agent Green, Agent Orange II, Agent Pink, and Agent White. Agent Blue was also used, but contained **cacodylic acid** as its active ingredient. *See also* GULF WAR SYNDROME.

ALAMOGORDO BOMBING AND GUNNERY RANGE, NEW MEXICO. *See* TRINITY TEST SITE.

ALARM CLOCK. In 1946, U.S. physicist Edward Teller invented a single-stage design for a **thermonuclear** device. He dubbed the design the "alarm clock" because it would awaken the world to the possibility of a new generation of nuclear explosives. The **United States** never tested this particular design, although Teller's ideas for a thermonuclear device would eventually be realized. Some analysts concluded, though, that the Soviet Union used a single-stage design such as "alarm clock" for its first successfully detonated thermonuclear device, which the United States dubbed "**Joe** 4."

ALBANIA. Albania is a party to the **Chemical Weapons Convention (CWC)**. In 2003, in accordance with its CWC obligations, Albania reported that it had discovered a **chemical weapon (CW)** stockpile. According to the government, the stockpile consists of approximately 35,000 pounds (16 metric tons) of CW agents, with the primary agent being **sulfur mustard**; other agents include **adamsite**, **lewisite**, and mixtures of sulfur mustard and lewisite. The government went on to report that the agents are stored at a single location in an unused military bunker dating from the previous Communist regime. Albania will destroy the stockpile with assistance provided by the **United States** under the **Cooperative Threat Reduction (CTR) Program**.

The Albanian government reportedly has failed to uncover any paperwork regarding the origin of the stockpile and has been unable to locate any witnesses willing to discuss its origin. However, there have been periodic reports stating that many of the estimated 600 CW containers have **Chinese**-language labels that describe the contents. Efforts were under way in 2006–2007 to destroy the CW using portable high-temperature thermal treatment equipment.

ALIBEK, KENNETH. In 1987, Alibek was promoted to deputy head of **Biopreparat**, capping a career in the Soviet Union devoted primarily to biological warfare (BW) activities. Born in Kauchuk, Kazakhstan, and trained as a scientist and physician, Alibek was originally known as Kanatjan Baizakovich Alibek. While at Biopreparat, he served on a team from the USSR that traveled to the **United States** as part of the **trilateral process**. He resigned from Biopreparat in 1991 and moved to the United States in 1992, changing his name to Kenneth. In the United States, Alibek helped enhance understanding by the U.S. government of the BW research and production activities that had been under way in the USSR. In 1993, he released *Biohazard: The Chilling True Story of the Largest Covert Biological Weapons Program in the World—Told from Inside by the Man Who Ran It*. Written with Stephen Handleman, this book relates some of his experience in the Soviet BW program. *See also* 15TH DIRECTORATE.

AL-KAMAL, HUSSEIN. *See* KAMAL, HUSSEIN AL-.

ALPHA PARTICLE. An electrically charged particle of ionizing radiation emitted by **radioactive materials**. An alpha particle is identical to the nucleus of a helium-4 atom, consisting of two protons and two neutrons and acting as a single particle. When an alpha particle is emitted from an unstable radioactive nucleus of an atom, that atom is transmuted into a different element. For instance, **plutonium**-238 is a well-known alpha emitter; when an alpha particle escapes, plutonium-238 is transmuted into **uranium**-234. Alpha particles have a short range and cannot penetrate the outer, dead layer of human skin. Therefore, external sources of alpha particles pose little threat to human health. However, if radioactive materials emitting alpha particles are inhaled, ingested, or injected, then the alpha emissions can be very harmful to human health. *See also* AMERICIUM; BETA PARTICLE; GAMMA RADIATION; POLONIUM.

ALSOS MISSION. The **United States** led an effort during World War II to determine the nature and extent of **Germany**'s **nuclear weapon** program, and a special scientific intelligence field unit was established for this purpose. Given the code name "ALSOS," its activities included recovering documents and equipment and interviewing selected individuals as Allied forces advanced through western Europe. ALSOS carried out its mission from 16 November 1943 until 15 November 1945. As a scientific intelligence unit, ALSOS was administered by the U.S. Army chief of staff for intelligence (G-2) but cooperated closely with the civilian **Office of Scientific Research and Development (OSRD)**. The tasking for ALSOS was eventually expanded to include an evaluation of German activities in other areas, including the country's **biological weapon (BW)** and **chemical weapon (CW)** programs. In its final reporting, ALSOS assessed the BW program as solely defensive in nature rather than a combination of defensive and offensive.

Although the analysis dates from the 1940s, the final ALSOS mission report is still a useful case study today, in that it illustrates an analysis of whether a country's BW activities are "defensive" or "offensive." This is a crucial distinction, because if BW activities are assessed as defensive, the program is permitted under current international law as embodied in the **Biological and Toxin Weapons Convention (BTWC)**, but if the activities are assessed as offensive, the program is prohibited by the BTWC.

The word *alsos* is the plural form of the classical Greek word for "grove." This word was selected to honor **Leslie R. Groves**, the U.S. military official who headed the **Manhattan Project**. The symbol of the ALSOS Mission was the Greek letter alpha with a lightning bolt running through it. This symbol was affixed to ALSOS vehicles to help distinguish them as the unit traveled in concert with Allied combat troops. *See also* GOUDSMIT, SAMUEL ABRAHAM; KLIEWE, HEINRICH; PASH, BORIS T.

AMERICAN UNIVERSITY. The **United States** declared war on **Germany** on 6 April 1917. Later that month, the Board of Trustees of American University in Washington, D.C., offered the use of its buildings and grounds to President Woodrow Wilson for the war effort. The university, then 24 years old, had only two buildings but 92 acres of relatively open grounds in the northwest section of Washington. Within three months, the U.S. **Bureau of Mines** arranged to occupy one of the buildings as a research laboratory. By the end of World War I, the U.S. government had built more than 60 buildings on what came to be designated "Camp American University." The grounds were designated "Camp Leach" and used for testing and training in techniques of chemical warfare (CW), including the release of various CW agents. Eventually, the laboratories and grounds came under the control of the **Chemical Warfare Service (CWS)**, along with similar laboratories at the **Catholic University of America (CUA)**. By June 1918, the CWS had nearly 1,700 personnel working at American University, and many more military personnel passed through as part of their training.

When the war ended, the government returned the properties to American University for its use. However, insufficient attention was paid to cleanup and removal of toxic chemicals and munitions that had been abandoned in place at camps American University and Leach. In 1993, residents of Spring Valley, an exclusive neighborhood built on property that had been used by these camps, were surprised when workmen constructing new homes uncovered items eventually determined to be World War I–era **chemical weapons (CW)**. Further discoveries followed, including a cache of weapons and chemical-filled containers buried on the grounds where the Republic of Korea had one of its official residences. The U.S. Army responded promptly by undertaking a cleanup that has lasted over a decade. Cleanup work will continue for some years, partly because access to the area is at the discretion of the property owners, some of whom do not wish to grant access or who have stopped the U.S. army from continuing their cleanup work. This situation reflects concerns over the disruption caused by cleanup crews as well as the possibility that property values could fall if munitions are uncovered during exploratory excavations.

AMERICIUM. A man-made element, with atomic number 95 and symbol "Am." All known americium **isotopes** are **radioactive material**. Americium-243 is an **alpha particle** emitter and has been used in **gamma radiography**. Trace quantities of americium-241 are used commercially as ionization sources in smoke detectors and in neutron moisture gauges. The quantity of americium-241 used in a single smoke detector is minuscule, although occasional reports surface of threats to use smoke detectors as a radiation source for a **radiological dispersal device (RDD)**.

AMITON. During research on improved pesticides, scientists at the British firm Imperial Chemical Industries, Ltd. (ICI) discovered a class of organic compounds of phosphorus and sulfur having enhanced insecticidal properties. ICI gave the first of these compounds the trade name *Amiton* and shared news of its discovery with the scientific community in January 1955. Eventually, scientists recognized the exceptional human toxicity of Amiton, causing it to be withdrawn from many markets.

In 1953, prior to notifying the scientific community of its discovery, ICI had alerted the British government. Scientists at **Porton Down** gave Amiton-like substances the code name "C11 series" and began systematic studies in a search for improved nerve agents. The British shared news of these studies with the **United States**, which opened its own investigations and named the C11 series "V-type nerve agents." One result of these investigations was the selection of **VX** as a standard chemical warfare (CW) agent. The Soviet Union learned of the development of V-type nerve agents and initiated similar research, selecting a structural isomer of VX as its standard CW agent. *See also* ORGANOPHOSPHORUS NERVE AGENT.

AMMASH, HUDA SALIH MAHDI. Iraqi scientist. Ammash, sometimes dubbed "Mrs. **Anthrax**," was involved in **Iraq**'s **biological weapon (BW)** program during the regime of Saddam Hussein.

AMMONIUM THIOCYANATE. A colorless, deliquescent solid having the chemical formula CH_4N_2S. It is toxic, especially to plants, and is used as an **herbicide** and **defoliant**. Its herbicidal properties caused it to be proposed by the **United States** for use during World War II. In October 1944, the U.S. military proposed using ammonium thiocyanate as a

chemical means for destruction of Japanese gardens. . . . It was stated that the Japanese are adept at utilizing local resources to augment their food supply and in that way releasing shipping space for other military requirements. It was considered desirable to reduce their local sources of food supply to a minimum by destruction of the small gardens which they were cultivating. . . . It is believed that use of [ammonium thiocyanate] will assist and accelerate the mopping up of the many isolated groups of Japanese. . . . From the standpoint of ethics, it is not believed that this method of destroying food crops is any worse than the cutting off of food supplies by the sinking of supply ships. However, it is pointed out that this method involves the use of chemical sprays containing poisonous ingredients.

There is no evidence that this proposed use of ammonium thiocyanate was carried out.

AMOS. During World War II, engineers at the University of Michigan developed Proximity Measuring Radar (PMR) devices used in fuses by the U.S. military. Two of these PMR devices were dubbed "Amos" and "Andy," presumably after the characters in a popular American radio comedy. By 1945, both Amos and Andy were ready for testing. Amos was selected for use in the "**Little Boy**" bomb. Four Amos units were installed in the bomb and functioned as radar altimeters, using radar to determine the distance above ground. At a predetermined distance, the Amos device would send a signal closing a relay. As a safety precaution, the bomb needed at least two units to send such a signal before a firing signal was transmitted, setting in motion the electronics needed to detonate the **nuclear weapon**. Events of 6 August 1945 proved that the Amos units functioned properly. *See also* ARCHIE; X UNIT.

ANTHRAX. The name of both a biological pathogen and the disease it produces. The pathogen, *Bacillus anthracis*, has an extensive history of development for use as a **biological weapon (BW)**, but actual use has been more limited. *B. anthracis* is a large, **Gram-positive**, aerobic bacterium. Its ability to form spores contributes its ability to survive for extended periods in soils and on surfaces. This feature has been an important characteristic in its selection for use in BW. The disease afflicts quadrupeds, such as bison, cattle, goats, and sheep. For humans, the disease is often categorized according to the main point of entry into the body as cutaneous (skin), gastrointestinal (ingestion), or pulmonary (inhalation). If untreated, the disease often proves fatal, with pulmonary anthrax having the highest incidence of lethality. Effective treatments emerged with the advent of antibiotics in the mid-20th century, contributing to lessened lethality in the limited numbers of human cases that have been diagnosed.

During World War I, **German** agents used anthrax, as well as **glanders**, in attempts to infect animals in Argentina, France, Norway, Romania, and the **United States**. The idea appears to have been to hamper war-fighting efforts by eliminating animals that might be used for labor or food. The success of these attempts is uncertain.

During World War II, many nations pursued more ambitious efforts with anthrax. The **United Kingdom** conducted large-scale tests with anthrax spores, including one that left **Gruinard Island**, Scotland, contaminated for decades. Britain, as part of **Operation Aladdin**, produced 5,000,000 linseed cakes laden with anthrax spores. The plan was that these cakes, which **Porton Down** testing had shown would be eagerly consumed by cattle, were to be dropped on the north German countryside. Cattle would consume them, and subsequent infections in cattle and humans would reduce food supplies and damage the leather industry. The cattle cakes were never used, however, and most of the stockpile was destroyed immediately after the war. The United Kingdom briefly considered using homing pigeons as a means of disseminating anthrax spores or possibly other biological pathogens. Records of the British "Pigeon Policy" reveal that the head of the Air Ministry's pigeon section advocated such use, noting that each pigeon could carry a payload of 2 ounces while flying undetected by radar to targets some 100–200 miles away. In 1950, the United Kingdom formally discontinued funding for pigeon lofts held in reserve for such use.

The United States also adopted anthrax during World War II as a potential biological agent, designating the organism "Agent N" and, later, "Agent TR." The government set about producing *B. anthracis* first at Camp Detrick (**Fort Detrick**), Maryland, and later at the Vigo Plant in Indiana; the war ended before the Vigo Plant was fully operational, however. The United States continued to explore anthrax, concluding in the 1960s that the latency period (that is, the time between exposure and onset of the disease) varied considerably. This conclusion contributed to the government's decision to abandon anthrax as a strategic weapon.

Other notable anthrax programs included those of **Japan** and the Soviet Union. The Japanese program was centered at **Unit 731** in Japanese-occupied Manchuria and was most active during the period of 1937–1945. In 1938, the Japanese used anthrax against the USSR during the conflict in the Kholgin-Gol region of Mongolia. While the Soviet records from that period fail to indicate any harm to Red Army troops, the Japanese clearly were harmed when their forces unknowingly occupied areas previously contaminated by Unit 731 personnel. This episode illustrates one of the limitations to use of biological weapons: the difficulty in knowing which areas are contaminated.

The USSR noted the work done by Great Britain, the United States, and Japan and pursued its own ambitious anthrax program following World War II. A major production facility was constructed in Sverdlovsk (now Yekaterinburg, **Russia**), which was the site of an accidental release in 1979 that killed several dozen people. Soviet authorities attempted to cover up the accident, attributing the illnesses and deaths to naturally infected meat. Investigation by outside experts demonstrated that this explanation was bogus. In 1992, following the collapse of the Soviet Union, Russian president Boris Yeltsin acknowledged that the epidemic had been caused by military researchers rather than natural causes.

In fall 2001, anthrax was deliberately enclosed in certain letters sent through the U.S. mail. Their intended recipients included two members of the U.S. Senate and various media organizations, such as the *New York Post* and NBC News. The anthrax events also demonstrated the extent to which the spores could be released from supposedly taped and sealed envelopes, contributing to significant cross-contamination and leaving assorted postal facilities uninhabitable. These mailings, seen by many as an example of biological terrorism, resulted in five deaths, all from pulmonary anthrax; more than a dozen other persons were known to have contracted cutaneous or pulmonary anthrax as well. The mailings also caused substantial disruption, including the closing of portions of the congressional offices until they could be decontaminated. *See also* BOYLES, WILLIAM ALLEN; TRILATERAL PROCESS.

ANTIBALLISTIC MISSILE (ABM) TREATY. The Antiballistic Missile Treaty placed limits on ABM systems of the **United States**

and the Soviet Union and was considered to be an important arms control mechanism to limit the threat posed by an attack by **nuclear weapons**. The ABM Treaty was signed in Moscow on 26 May 1972 and entered into force on 3 October 1972. The original treaty provided that each state might have two ABM deployment areas and that each agreed to limit improvements in its ABM technology. The United States and USSR signed a protocol to the treaty that went into effect in 1976, reducing the number of deployment areas from two to one. This protocol provided that the single deployment area could be around either the state's national capital area or a single **intercontinental ballistic missile (ICBM)** deployment area. The Soviet Union elected to deploy an ABM system around its capital, Moscow, while the United States chose to use its ABM system to protect a Minuteman ICBM deployment area near Grand Forks, North Dakota, in lieu of a system around Washington, D.C. *See also* INTERMEDIATE-RANGE NUCLEAR FORCES (INF) TREATY.

ANTICONVULSANTS. One treatment for exposure to **organophosphorus nerve agents** is the administration of anticonvulsant drugs such as diazepam. Such drugs are administered to reduce brain damage caused by the prolonged seizure activity that is a possible symptom of nerve agent poisoning. *See also* CHOLINESTERASES.

ANTICROP AGENTS. Chemicals, biological pathogens, and insect pests that preferentially harm crops or other plants can be classified as anticrop agents. The term *antiplant agents* is also used; it encompasses uses such as **defoliation** where the intent is other than to deny an adversary access to plants needed as foodstuffs. Examples of chemical anticrop agents include **ammonium thiocyanate**, which the **United States** produced during World War II for potential use against **Japanese** rice crops. Also during the war, the United States and **United Kingdom** studied the use of the chemicals 2,4-dichlorophenoxyacetic acid (2,4-D) and 2,4,5-trichlorophenoxyacetic acid (2,4,5-T), which cause plants to lose their foliage. This defoliation can both reduce crop yield and expose enemy assets that might otherwise be hidden. The British used 2,4,5-T in what was then called Malaya immediately after the war and up into the 1950s. The United States made extensive use of both chemicals during the Vietnam War, with the various agents having designations such as Agent Blue, **Agent Orange**, and Agent Purple.

During World War II, the United States studied biological pathogens as anticrop agents for possible use against **Germany** and Japan. Such use never occurred, but from 1951 to 1969, the United States launched full-scale production of three anticrop biological agents: the fungal organisms responsible for wheat stem rust (*Puccinia graminis* f. sp. Tritici, "Agent TX"), rye stem rust (*Puccinia graminis* f. sp. Secalis, "Agent SX"), and rice blast (*Piricularia oryzae*, "Agent LX"). Various munitions were prepared for possible use, first during the Korean War and later as a matter of strategic defense. The M1115 500-pound bomb was type-classified for use with B-29 and B-36 aircraft and loaded with Agent TX. The U.S. military also experimented with the E77 bomb, which was to be transported by an unmanned free balloon and disseminate pathogenic anticrop agents carried on feathers. The bomb would automatically inactivate the agents if the balloon flight prematurely terminated. There is no evidence the United States ever used any anticrop biological agent. All stockpiles of agents and munitions were destroyed by February 1973.

Certain insect pests are natural anticrop agents, inspiring fears that adversaries might intentionally release such pests. The best-known example of this situation occurred during World War II. Both the British and the Germans feared the Colorado potato beetle (*Leptinotarsa decemlineata*) would be deliberately spread over their countryside, potentially devastating the potato crop and seriously reducing food supplies. By 1942, German fears of British or American attacks with this insect prompted the government to establish the Potato Beetle Defense Service, complete with a Potato Beetle Research Institute in Kruft. By fall 1944, German concerns had reached the point where **Gerhard Schrader**, discoverer of the first **organophosphorus nerve agent**, **tabun**, and inventor of a second, **sarin**, was pulled off nerve agent research and ordered to find an insecticide to save the potato crop.

No evidence exists to suggest the United States, Britain, or Germany made any effort to use the Colorado potato beetle as an offensive anticrop agent during World War II. The notion of this beetle as a weapon survived the war, however. In June 1950, Paul Mercker, minister of agriculture and forestry in the German Democratic Republic (East Germany), accused the United States of releasing the beetle from airplanes flying over East Germany. German youth were enlisted to scour the countryside for the pest, dubbed "Amikäfer" for American potato beetle. A similar concern emerged in the USSR and persisted for decades, with Young Pioneers periodically being enlisted to collect *koloradsky zhuk*, as the Colorado potato beetle was called.

ANTIPLAGUE SYSTEM. In the 1890s the government of tsarist Russia created a commission to develop and implement measures to fight **plague**, a disease endemic in large portions of **Russia**. By the time this commission was set up, plague was known to be a bacterial infection caused by *Yersinia pestis*. Additionally, it was recognized that certain animals were host to this bacterium and, thus, capable of spreading the disease and of being a natural reservoir for the bacterium. One such host was the marmot, a burrowing animal prevalent in the plains of Asian Russia. Measures adopted by the commission included developing plague vaccines and other treatments, taking and testing samples, and trapping and exterminating the animals that carried *Y. pestis*. A system of research institutes and field stations was established under the tsarist government and was commonly referred to as the "anti-plague system." The coverage of the system was vast and extended down to individual peasants, who were paid to trap marmots and other suspected plague hosts so that these animals might be tested. When test results were positive, these same peasants were dispatched to exterminate animals, commonly with the toxic chemical **chloropicrin**.

The system survived the fall of tsarist Russia and was embraced by the Soviet government, which ensured one or more antiplague institutes existed in each of the Soviet republics. The antiplague system also became a cover for Soviet defensive and offensive **biological weapon (BW)** work. A Russian scientist who pursued BW research from within the antiplague system estimated that when the Union of Soviet Socialist Republics (USSR) collapsed in 1991, the system employed approximately 10,000 people. The antiplague system is of continuing interest to those involved in implementing the **Cooperative Threat Reduction (CTR)** and similar programs, partly because elements of the system were used to support the Soviet BW program and might be diverted to such purposes again. *See also* DOMARAD-SKY, IGOR VALERYANOVICH; P.O. BOX A-1968.

ANTONOV, NIKOLAI SERAFIMOVICH. Antonov rose to the rank of major general in the Soviet and **Russian** armies. He was a professor and doctor of technical sciences. When World War II ended, Antonov commanded an antiaircraft battery. Following the war, he studied military chemistry, and in 1968–1970, he served as commander of the **Shikhany** military chemical establishment with the rank of colonel-engineer. In 1994 he published an account of the Soviet **chemical weapon (CW)** establishment. *See also* TOMKA.

A. Q. KHAN NETWORK. *See* KHAN, ABDUL QADEER.

ARCHIE. By 1944, the U.S. military was studying the use of radar warning devices for possible use in proximity fuses. One such device was the U.S. Army Air Corps APS-13. Dubbed "Archie," this device was designed to warn a pilot about another aircraft approaching the rear of his plane. These same devices were used on the "**Fat Man**" bomb as radar fuses. Four Archies were installed on this one bomb, in a design similar to that used for the "**Amos**" units installed in the "**Little Boy**" bomb. Archie had a higher altitude range, however, and was considered more reliable. Events of 9 August 1945, when Fat Man was dropped over Nagasaki, proved that Archie functioned as designed.

ARGENTINA. Argentina pursued a covert **nuclear weapons** program for many years. However, in December 1991, Argentina, **Brazil**, the **Brazilian-Argentine Agency for Accounting and Control of Nuclear Materials (ABACC)**, and the **International Atomic Energy Agency (IAEA)** concluded a safeguards agreement. It entered into force 4 March 1994. More importantly, it acceded to the **Nonproliferation Treaty (NPT)** in February 1995 as a non–nuclear weapon state. Evidence of the Argentinean nuclear weapons program includes its construction of a **gaseous diffusion** enrichment plant and nuclear fuel reprocessing facilities and its development of facilities for mining and milling **uranium** and for nuclear fuel fabrication. Finally, a missile development program was pursued, which would have given it capabilities of launching long-range strikes with nuclear weapons. Various nations supported Argentina's nuclear weapon ambitions. Switzerland supplied a **heavy water** plant. West Germany and Canada supplied nuclear reactors. Finally, the Soviet Union supplied assorted equipment that could be used in a nuclear weapons program. *See also* BRAZIL; BRAZILIAN-ARGENTINE AGENCY FOR ACCOUNTING AND CONTROL OF NUCLEAR MATERIALS (ABACC).

ARSINE. A colorless gas with a distinct, disagreeable garlicky odor. It has the chemical formula AsH_3. Exposure induces vomiting, and arsine can be classified as a **vomiting agent**. In a few cases, it has been adopted as a chemical warfare (CW) agent. For example, **France** adopted arsine as a CW agent during World War I, dubbing it "Mithrithe." Similarly, the **United States** adopted it prior to World War II as the CW agent "SA." During World War I, the **Germans** used arsine as a minor component in a CW land mine. Intriguing **binary chemical weapon** approaches to producing arsine were considered by the **United Kingdom** during World War I and by the United States and Germany during World War II. The British looked at two methods. One was dispersing solid calcium arsenide, Ca_3As_2, which would react with atmospheric moisture or rain to liberate arsine in situ. The second was to produce arsine in a projectile by breaking vessels containing calcium arsenide and hydrochloric acid and allowing their contents to mix. The Americans followed a process similar to the second method, substituting magnesium arsenide for calcium arsenide and a dilute solution of sulfuric acid for hydrochloric acid. The German method involved a mix of solid magnesium and aluminum arsenides, reacting with moisture to liberate arsine.

ARZAMAS-16. The code name given by the Soviet Union to a town now known by its historical name of Sarov, **Russia**. The town is located in the Nizhny Novgorod region northeast of Moscow. In 1946, the USSR selected this site for constructing the All-Russian Scientific Research Institute of Experimental Physics, which became the primary Soviet facility for designing **nuclear weapons**. Shortly after this selection, the town of Sarov disappeared from unclassified maps of the Soviet Union. The town remains "closed," and visitors from within and outside Russia require special permission for entry. *See also* KHARITON, YULI; KURCHATOV, IGOR VASILIEVICH.

ASHMARIN, IGOR PETROVICH (1925–). Russian biologist. Ashmarin is a State Prize Laureate, academician of the **Russian** Academy of Medical Sciences, doctor of biological sciences, and, as of 2004, major general of the Medical Service of the Russian Federation. He graduated from the S. M. Kirov Military-Medical Academy. From 1951 until 1954 he served at the **biological weapons (BW)** facility in Sverdlovsk that would receive international attention decades later as a result of an accidental release of **anthrax** spores. From 1976 until 1986 he was deputy head of the **15th Directorate** of the USSR Ministry of Defense. He later worked at the present-day Virology Center of the Ministry of Defense of the Russian Federation. He is credited with actively opposing the theory of Trofim Denisovich Lysenko on the inheritance of acquired traits. That theory was eventually discredited, but it hampered development of molecular biology and genetics in the USSR during a period when such knowledge was essential to proper understanding of biological disciplines such as virology and bacteriology.

ATOMIC ANNIE. The successful detonation of a nuclear device by the Soviet Union in August 1949 caused the U.S. Congress to rescind its prohibition on small nuclear warheads. This change ultimately led to development of the T-131 280-mm atomic cannon, dubbed "Atomic Annie." When fielded in the early 1950s, Atomic Annie was the world's first field artillery piece capable of firing a **nuclear weapon**. Each cannon weighed nearly 50 tons and was almost 40 feet long when emplaced. Twenty such cannon and transporters were made, and the U.S. Army formed a battalion of 280-mm atomic cannons. The fielding of a more mobile, smaller howitzer with its M422 eight-inch nuclear projectile made the atomic cannon obsolete. The last atomic cannon was retired from U.S. military service in 1963. *See also* MARK-9 AND MARK-19 280-MM PROJECTILES.

ATOMIC DEMOLITION MUNITION (ADM). A **nuclear weapon** intended for military use as a means of denying enemy forces the use of various routes and facilities during combat. U.S. military planning called for ADMs to be used by Army engineers to destroy airfields, bridges, strategic buildings, highways, and tunnels before these structures could be captured. Similar plans were probably developed by other nuclear-capable nations. The United States stockpiled ADMs in Europe as early as 1955. All such stockpiles were removed to the United States by 1985. *See also* MONTEBELLO DECISION; SEWER PIPE; SPECIAL ATOMIC DEMOLITION MUNITION (SADM).

ATOMIC ENERGY ACT OF 1946. On 20 December 1945, Sen. Brien McMahon (D-Conn.) introduced legislation to create a civilian authority to oversee the U.S. arsenal of **nuclear weapons** and to be responsible for research and development of nuclear energy. This legislation was intended to replace the **May-Johnson Bill**, which had stalled in Congress owing to opposition by scientists, among others. The legislation became known as the McMahon Bill and was approved by the Senate on 1 June 1946. The House of Representatives approved a slightly modified bill on 20 July. Differences between the Senate and House versions were resolved shortly thereafter, and the legislation was sent to President Harry S. Truman, who signed it into law on 1 August. The legislation was popularly known as the McMahon Act, although its official title is the Atomic Energy Act of 1946. The Act transferred responsibility for the U.S. stockpile of nuclear weapons from the army to the newly established **Atomic Energy Commission (AEC)** and effectively gave over to this commission control of all aspects of nuclear technology. The Act also called upon Congress to establish a Joint Committee on Atomic Energy.

ATOMIC ENERGY COMMISSION (AEC). Established by the **Atomic Energy Act of 1946**, the Atomic Energy Commission was an independent civilian agency responsible for the security of the U.S. arsenal of **nuclear weapons**, regulating the safety of atomic energy–related activities, and encouraging use of atomic energy. While all production facilities associated with nuclear materials and nuclear reactors were government-owned, all technical information and research results were under commission control. The Atomic Energy Act of 1954 expanded the scope of the AEC by enabling the development of commercial nuclear power plants. Some critics worried that the AEC was entrusted with functions that brought it into conflict internally, both promoting the use of nuclear energy and regulating the safety of nuclear facilities. Congress addressed this situation with the Energy Reorganization Act of 1974, establishing the Nuclear Regulatory Commission and giving it the regulatory functions previously assigned to the AEC. The 1974 Act placed the nuclear stockpile security and promotional activities of the AEC under the newly created Energy Research and Development Administration (ERDA), which would later become the U.S. Department of Energy (DOE). *See also* MANHATTAN PROJECT.

ATOMS FOR PEACE. In a 3 December 1953 speech to the **United Nations (UN)**, President Dwight D. Eisenhower proposed a plan to allocate **fissionable** materials to peaceful uses, promote production of power using nuclear fuel, and divert uranium stockpiles from the race to build **nuclear weapons**. This plan, labeled "Atoms for Peace," included a central repository or bank for nuclear materials. While well-received, the proposal failed to garner the backing of the Soviet Union needed for success. By June 1954, the U.S. government had decided to implement bilateral agreements on key points of the Atoms for Peace plan, barring a multinational agreement. In 1955, the United States established the first such agreement, providing for U.S. assistance in establishing nuclear reactors to be used solely for research. These agreements allowed the plan to achieve some success relative to the first and second goals. However, the plan failed to achieve Eisenhower's vision of curbing the nuclear arms race. There were unintended consequences of this plan as well. **India** would later develop its nuclear bomb using **plutonium** obtained from its domestic nuclear reactors that had been constructed with U.S. assistance under the Atoms for Peace plan.

ATROPINE. *See* CHOLINESTERASES.

AUM SHINRIKYO. In 1984, Chizuo Matsumoto set up a yoga training center in Shibuya, a busy district of Tokyo. He named the center Aum, Inc., using a variant of *om*, a Sanskrit syllable often chanted in yoga meditation or in prayers. Shortly thereafter, Matsumoto took the name Shoko Asahara ("Bright Light") and reorganized his yoga school as a sort of religious group or cult named Aum Shinrikyo ("Aum Divine Truth"). Asahara, as he preferred to be called, set about fulfilling his vision of saving Japan. That vision required that his group take control of the Diet, Japan's national parliament, using violence where necessary. Aum Shinrikyo was organized along quasi-governmental lines in that it had a "shadow cabinet" or government-in-waiting structure.

The group is known to have carried out three incidents with **organophosphorus nerve agents**, all of which resulted in human fatalities, and to have attempted other attacks, including one or more with **anthrax**. Its first known **chemical weapon (CW)** attack took place in June 1994 when Aum Shinrikyo members used a specially modified van to disperse **sarin** in Matsumoto, Japan. This attack took place at night and targeted the homes of three judges involved in a legal action involving Aum Shinrikyo. These three and their families were the intended victims. Although seven people died and approximately 300 were injured in the incident, it was not immediately recognized as a deliberate use of a CW agent. The police investigation was indecisive and poorly coordinated.

A second incident followed on 12 December 1994. A 28-year-old former member of Aum Shinrikyo, Tadahiro Hamaguichi, was attacked by two men on a street in Osaka. The two assailants sprinkled **VX** on the victim's neck. After chasing his assailants briefly, the victim collapsed, and then lapsed into a coma. He died 10 days later, becoming the "only victim of VX [poisoning] ever documented in the world." An organophosphorus nerve agent was suspected at the time, but the source was imagined to be a commercial pesticide. The link between this death and Aum Shinrikyo failed to emerge until some cult members had been arrested for other crimes.

The third and most infamous incident occurred on 20 March 1995, when Aum Shinrikyo members succeeded in releasing sarin in the Tokyo subway. The results were sensational and unmistakable. A deliberate release of a CW agent had taken place, resulting in the deaths of at least 12 people. Some 5,500 people sought medical help, with about 500 of these requiring medical attention or hospitalization. The means of attack and the identity of the perpetrators were quickly determined. Japanese law enforcement personnel carried out mass arrests and widespread searches of properties owned by Aum Shinrikyo.

At the time of the Tokyo subway incident, the group had assets worth an estimated $1 billion. Several members had advanced degrees in the natural sciences, including chemistry. Yet despite this wealth and academic training, Aum Shinrikyo largely failed in its efforts to create toxic chemicals and biological pathogens. The sarin it produced was impure and rapidly degraded to substances having little toxicity. The safety precautions used by Aum Shinrikyo during its testing and production efforts were poor, and several group members were poisoned as a result.

In February 2004, Asahara received the death sentence for his role in various crimes. As of 2006, his legal counsel was appealing the conviction, citing evidence of mental illness on the part of Asahara. Criminal proceedings against other cult members were continuing. Despite this record of violence, the group survives. Its name has been changed to Aleph, and it remains under formal Japanese police surveillance until at least 2009.

AUSTRALIA. Australian troops were exposed to **chemical weapons (CW)** during fighting in Europe in World War I. However, the Australian development of a national CW capability was limited partly because the **United Kingdom** retained, at least in practice, certain prerogatives over its former colony, mainly in the fields of foreign relations and defense matters. The United Kingdom was in a dominant position in the area of CW because it had developed certain technical expertise as well as the necessary related infrastructure, such as its research establishment at **Porton Down**, during World War I. A major policy question confronting the Australian government in the late 1930s and the during the first years of World War II was whether and to what extent the country should develop its own CW-related production capabilities, as opposed to relying on British colonial territories or the United Kingdom itself for these materials and the actual weapons. Australian defense policy was largely planned and coordinated at this time by a Defence Committee, while more specialized CW-related matters were handled by the Chemical Defence Committee. **Japan**'s military successes at the start of the war had the effect of convincing Australia of the need to quickly import raw materials and CW from Britain, to which the British agreed. Australian-British wartime cooperation on CW was also facilitated by the fact that the countries dispatched chemical liaison officers to each other.

Australia, Canada, the United Kingdom, and the United States cooperated closely on CW-related research, including carrying out field tests in Australia. Much of the work involved field trials during World War II in which Australian and New Zealand troops were exposed to CW agents, mostly **sulfur mustard**. A goal of these trials was to determine the extent to which a soldier's ability to fight would be degraded following exposure to a CW agent. Australia and New Zealand volunteered for these trials because they were aware of reports that Japan had used CW in China and they knew that there was great uncertainty over the characteristics of CW agents in tropical jungle environments.

During the war, the Allies stockpiled CW in all major theaters of operation, including Australia. Among the CW imported were **phosgene** and sulfur mustard. Australia apparently carried out little or no indigenous CW production during the war beyond laboratory-scale efforts, with the United Kingdom and the United States being the principal and, perhaps, only suppliers of CW stocks to Australia. Australian policy during the war was one of no first use of CW, which would be used for retaliatory purposes only. When the war ended, the Australian military and the U.S. Army reportedly dumped some 14,634 tons of CW off the country's coast.

Australia is a state party to the 1993 **Chemical Weapons Convention (CWC)** and played a key role during its negotiation. In 2003 Australia declared to the **Organization for the Prohibition of Chemical Weapons (OPCW)** that it had uncovered a limited number of **old chemical weapons (OCW)** dating from World War II, which were subsequently verifiably destroyed. There is continuing concern that the sea-dumped CW may pose a future human and environmental hazard in the region.

AUSTRALIA GROUP (AG). An informal export control arrangement established to prevent the misuse of technology, equipment, and materials for **chemical** and **biological weapon (CBW)** purposes. It was established in 1985 in response to the use of chemical weapons during the 1980–1988 **Iran-Iraq War**. The arrangement takes its name from the custom of AG participants meeting at the Australian embassy in Paris.

AVIAKHIM. AviaKhim is an acronym from the **Russian** for Volunteer's Society of the Friends of Aviation and the Chemical Industry

(*Obshchestvo Druzei Aviatsionnoi i Khimicheskoi Promyshlennosti*). The Cyrillic acronym is АвиаХим. It was a volunteer patriotic military organization that existed in the Union of Soviet Socialist Republics (USSR) from 1925 to 1927. AviaKhim was created 23 May 1925 by merging **DobroKhim** and OVF ("The Society of Friends of Aviation"). It encouraged the development of the aviation and chemical industries and promoted defense against air and chemical attacks among the general population. In January 1927, AviaKhim united with the USSR Society of [Military] Defensive Systems to become **OsoAviaKhim**.

AVIAN FLU. Avian flu, also called "bird flu," refers to viral influenza primarily affecting birds. Some human deaths have been attributed to exposure to avian flu virus. These deaths appear to have occurred mainly in cases where individuals have lived or worked in proximity to poultry. Its spread in recent years has led to concern that a highly infectious strain, such as the H5N1 strain, could combine with the common cold virus and result in a human pandemic. One reason for the small number of human deaths is the apparent fact that most strains of avian flu virus are unable to penetrate beyond the upper respiratory tract of humans. The spread of avian flu has highlighted the vulnerability of humans to disease outbreaks, whether from natural causes or deliberate releases. *See also* SMALLPOX.

AYRTON FAN. Initiation of chemical warfare in April 1915 brought with it many suggestions for means of combating its effects. British physicist Hertha Marks Ayrton (1854–1923) made one such suggestion, which came to be dubbed the "Ayrton fan." It was a handheld, broom-like device made of wood and canvas. Soldiers were issued these fans with instructions to use them to sweep away the poisonous gases that would otherwise drift into their trenches. The Ayrton fans proved a failure, as winds would force the vapors back into the trenches, and using them to sweep proved nearly impossible to do while under attack. Ayrton's prominence in British science, however, forced the government to adopt them, and at least 25,000 were produced and issued, primarily to British Expeditionary Force personnel. Ayrton was the first woman to read a paper before the British

Royal Society, the author of a well-received text (*The Electric Arc*), and recipient of the Hughes Medal honoring her research.

– B –

BACKGROUND RADIATION. Radiation that is emitted from **naturally occurring radioactive materials (NORM)** in the earth and to the radiation received from cosmic rays that bombard the Earth from outer space.

BAGHWAN SHREE RAJNEESH. *See* DALLES SALAD BAR INCIDENT, THE.

BALLOON DOPE. The name commonly used during World War I by the British (and possibly by others) for *iso*-amyl acetate, a colorless liquid with a persistent odor. Its use during the war was principally as a doping agent to cement fabric onto aircraft wings and balloons. It later came to be used by the British as an ingredient in **stinks**, a chemical mixture intended to cause an adversary to believe a **chemical weapon (CW)** had been released. The notion was that the adversary would don protective masks and garments when they were otherwise unneeded, which would degrade the adversary's combat effectiveness, thus contributing to the general wearing-down associated with chemical warfare. Common names for *iso*-amyl acetate include banana oil and pear oil, because to some individuals its odor resembles those fruits. *See also* CAMOUFLAGE GAS.

BANANA OIL. *See* BALLOON DOPE.

BARI INCIDENT. In December 1943 the **German** Luftwaffe bombed the Italian harbor of Bari. Among the ships sunk was the USS *John Harvey*, which was carrying approximately 100 tons of 100-pound bombs filled with the chemical warfare (CW) agent **sulfur mustard**. Allied service personnel who jumped into Bari harbor, either to escape the sinking ships or to render aid to victims, unwittingly exposed themselves to this agent, which combined with floating gasoline and oil on the water's surface. Up to 700 service personnel were exposed, and at least 81 of these died. Those affected did not receive proper medical assistance because the identity of the *Harvey*'s cargo had been classified. Those who were aware of the cargo were either unable or unwilling to relay the relevant information to those providing assistance. Some of the survivors contaminated the crew of another Allied ship, the *Bisteria*, after being rescued. Most of the crew of the *Bisteria* was temporarily blinded, and it was only with great difficulty that the ship was able to dock at its next port of call. The incident was kept secret by Allied authorities, perhaps to avoid provoking the initiation of CW by Germany. In an effort at preventing possible German misunderstanding of Allied intentions, the Allied forces had reportedly provided informal assurances to Germany through back channels that they did not intend to initiate CW. The Bari incident may have stimulated interest by the **United States** after the war in developing a **binary chemical weapon (CW)** that could be more safely transported and stored aboard ship and elsewhere.

BARUCH PLAN. On 14 June 1946, American financier and statesman Bernard Baruch (1870–1965) spoke to the newly created **United Nations**. His speech unveiled the U.S. government's proposal to establish an international nuclear development authority that would control all activities dangerous to global security. The authority would also license and inspect all other nuclear projects. Once the authority was established, no more **nuclear weapons** would be built, and existing bombs would be destroyed. His proposal became known popularly as the Baruch Plan. Drawn along lines presented in the Acheson-Lillenthal report of March 1946, the Baruch Plan went further by setting specific penalties for violations, such as illegally possessing nuclear weapons. Baruch proposed that the United Nations (UN) should disallow member nations from using their veto on matters involving penalties for atomic energy or nuclear weapon violations; instead, simple majority rule should prevail. Baruch, who had been advising U.S. presidents since World War I, labeled his plan "the last, best hope of earth." The Baruch Plan was debated in the UN, with the proposal to surrender veto powers being a contentious issue, especially for the Soviet Union. By 1947, the plan had become a dead issue, although token debate would continue into 1948. The Baruch Plan was never adopted.

BECQUEREL. The fundamental unit of measurement for radioactivity in the International System for Measurement (SI). One becquerel, abbreviated "Bq," equals one **disintegration** per second. The unit honors French physicist Antoine-Henri Becquerel (1852–1908), who shared the 1903 Nobel Prize in Physics with Marie and Pierre Curie for fundamental discoveries related to radioactivity. *See also* CURIE; RUTHERFORD.

BELLWETHER STUDIES. Investigations initiated in the late 1950s by the U.S. Department of Defense into the biting behavior of mosquitoes. These studies were aimed at enhancing understanding of the role mosquitoes might play as a **vector** for biological warfare (BW) purposes. Bellwether 1, for example, was a study conducted from 1 September to 9 October 1959 in which uninfected, virgin female *Aedes aegeypti* mosquitoes were released in 52 separate field trials using humans and guinea pigs as subjects. Following release, the number of bites on humans and guinea pigs were tabulated. The studies conducted into the early 1960s.

BENT SPEAR. The U.S. Department of Defense uses BENT SPEAR as a code name for identifying and reporting an incident involving a nuclear weapon, nuclear warhead, or other nuclear component. *See also* BROKEN ARROW; DULL SWORD; EMPTY QUIVER; FADED GIANT; SPAIN HYDROGEN BOMB INCIDENT.

BERSOL. In the aftermath of World War I and the Russian Revolution, both **Germany** and the Union of Soviet Socialist Republics (USSR) sought technical assistance on matters related to **chemical weapons (CW)**. The **Treaty of Versailles** prohibited Germany from seeking such assistance, but the 1922 Treaty of Rapallo that ended the conflict between Germany and **Russia** had no such prohibition. Both countries exploited this situation. Bersol was one outgrowth of that assistance.

In May 1923, the USSR and Germany established a joint venture called the Russo-German Factory "Bersol." *Bersol* is a trivial Russian term for potassium chlorate, $KClO_3$, which can be used in manufacturing explosives. The Bersol factory was to produce **phosgene**, **sulfur mustard**, and other toxic chemicals. Germany assisted in its design and construction, but the factory itself was constructed in Ivashchenkovo, along the Volga River in the Samara region southeast of Moscow where a chlorine plant stood in World War I. The construction and operation were overseen by **Hugo Stoltzenberg**.

The venture proved a failure and was canceled by a Soviet Politburo resolution on 13 February 1927. In 1927, Ivashchenkovo was renamed Troitsk or Trotsk to honor Communist leader Lev Trotsky. This name lasted only briefly, however, as Trotsky was purged from the Soviet leadership around this time. Thereafter, the town was renamed Chapayevsk to honor V. I. Chapayev, a hero of the Russian Revolution.

Although the joint venture CW production facility was a failure, some CW production did take place there. In the 1980s, the USSR constructed a CW destruction facility on the site. That facility never operated, however, owing to intense opposition by local residents to incineration as a method of CW destruction and opposition to allowing CW to be transported from other areas of the country to be destroyed locally. The facility has nevertheless been used to train Russian technicians on the operation of CW destruction facilities and to instruct some **Organization for the Prohibition of Chemical Weapons (OPCW)** inspector trainees. *See also* TOMKA.

BETA PARTICLE. An electron or positron emitted by the nucleus of an atom during **radioactive decay**. A negatively charged beta particle is an electron; a positively charged beta particle is a positron. *Beta ray* and *beta radiation* are synonyms for *beta particle*. Beta decay— emission of a beta particle by an atom—transmutes the atom into a new element having a different atomic number. Beta decay can occur in two ways. First, a proton can emit an antineutrino and a negatively charged beta particle. An example is the (negative) beta decay of **uranium**-239 to neptunium-239, which undergoes further beta decay to **plutonium**-239. Second, a neutron can emit a neutrino and a positively charged beta particle. An example is the (positive) beta decay of phosphorus-30 to silicon-30. *See also* ALPHA PARTICLE; GAMMA RADIATION.

BHABHA, HOMI JEHANGIR (1909–1966). Indian nuclear physicist credited as the founder of the nuclear sciences program in **India**. In

1948, Bhabha established the Atomic Energy Commission of India. He served as the president of the **United Nations** Conference on Peaceful Uses of Atomic Energy. His efforts to develop nuclear reactors in India coincided with the interest of the **United States** in promoting "**Atoms for Peace**." The capabilities India acquired for peaceful use of nuclear energy, however, supported its national efforts to develop **nuclear weapons**. Bhabha's role in such developments is unclear. *See also* PEACEFUL NUCLEAR EXPLOSIONS (PNE) TREATY; SMILING BUDDHA.

BHANGMETER. An optical sensor placed into satellites that is intended to detect the flash accompanying detonation of a **nuclear weapon**. *See also* VELA INCIDENT.

BIG BROTHER. While attending the Potsdam Conference in July 1945, U.S. president Harry S. Truman received a top-secret message signaling the successful test conducted at the **Trinity Test Site** on 16 July. The coded message read in part: "Doctor was just returned most enthusiastic and confident that the little boy is as husky as his big brother." Truman knew that *little boy* referred to "**Little Boy**," the bomb that was to be dropped on Japan. He correctly deduced that *big brother* referred to "**Gadget**," the device used in the Trinity test.

BIGEYE. In the 1970s and 1980s, the U.S. Department of Defense developed a **binary chemical weapon** known as the BIGEYE. Officially designated the BLU-80/B bomb, the BIGEYE was a 500-pound air-droppable munition compatible with U.S. Air Force, Marine Corps, and Navy fixed-wing aircraft. It contained two separate canisters, each containing relatively nontoxic compounds, meaning that the BIGEYE was nontoxic in storage and shipment, greatly enhancing its safety. When the BIGEYE was dropped over its intended target, however, the two canisters would rupture and their contents would mix. One canister contained a polymeric sulfur mixture, which was given the code name "NE." The other contained the organophosphorus chemical O-ethyl O´-(2-diisopropylaminoethyl) methyl phosphonite, which was given the code name "QL." On mixing, NE and QL formed **VX**. To denote the binary nature of the VX formed, it was given the designation "VX2." The BIGEYE was never approved for use and did not enter into large-scale production. *See also* M687 155-MM ARTILLERY PROJECTILE.

BILATERAL DESTRUCTION AGREEMENT (BDA). On 1 June 1990, the **United States** and the Union of Soviet Socialist Republics (USSR) signed the Bilateral Destruction Agreement. The BDA was negotiated in parallel to **Chemical Weapons Convention (CWC)** negotiations by the Conference on Disarmament in Geneva. The full name of the BDA is the Agreement between the United States of America and the Union of Soviet Socialist Republics on the Destruction and Nonproduction of Chemical Weapons and on Measures to Facilitate the Multilateral Convention on Banning Chemical Weapons. Some of the text in the BDA and the CWC overlaps or is similar. However, the CWC makes allowances for **chemical weapon (CW)** destruction and verification provisions to be reduced or dispensed with if the provisions of other agreements are "complementary."

Unlike the CWC, the BDA has never entered into force. **Russia**, which has succeeded to the USSR on this matter following the dissolution of the Soviet Union, takes the position that the BDA has been superseded by the CWC. The Preparatory Commission (Prep-Com) of the **Organization for the Prohibition of Chemical Weapons (OPCW)** assumed for planning purposes that the BDA would be in effect when the CWC entered into force. As this situation failed to materialize, the OPCW has experienced increased costs for its verification activities. The United States has maintained the position that the BDA is desirable, despite the entry into force of the CWC. This position is thought to reflect in part a preference by some U.S. officials for bilateral agreements, as opposed to multilateral agreements open to universal membership. Another contributing factor might be the fact that the members of inspection teams visiting Russia in support of the BDA would report directly to the U.S. government rather than to the OPCW, as is the case for the CWC. The BDA also reaffirms the commitment by the two parties to provide information specified under a 1989 memorandum of understanding. In particular, the U.S. government has indicated that it would like Russia to provide information regarding its **novichok** agents.

BINARY CHEMICAL WEAPON. Two distinct, but opposing, meanings are associated with the term *binary chemical weapon*. In one meaning, the term refers to a munition in which two relatively harmless substances combine to form a more harmful substance. Prime examples were the U.S. binary processes for forming **sarin** and **VX** in munitions such as the **M687 155-mm artillery projectile** and the BLU-80/B (**BIGEYE**) 500-pound bomb. A second meaning is a munition having a mix of two toxic substances. Examples include the mix of **chlorine** and sulfur chloride that the British designated "Blue Star" and used during World War I, and the mix of **sulfur mustard** and **lewisite** that the **United States** designated "HL" and stockpiled but never used in combat. Both Blue Star and HL had physical properties more favorable to combat use than did the unitary chemicals used in each mix. For instance, lewisite acts as a **freezing-point depressant** for sulfur mustard, greatly extending the useful temperature range over which the mix would be a liquid rather than a solid when dispersed.

The first meaning of binary chemical weapon—a mix of two relatively harmless substances combining to produce a harmful substance—is the one more commonly intended currently, perhaps because of the international attention given to U.S. government efforts in the 1970s and 1980s to develop the M687 and BIGEYE. *See also* BARI INCIDENT.

BIOINDUSTRY INITIATIVE (BII). A U.S. program begun in 2002 intended to ensure that the **biological weapon (BW)** infrastructure and related technology and expertise in the nations of the former Soviet Union (FSU) are used for peaceful purposes. BII assists through funding collaborative civilian research projects that involve scientists from the FSU whose expertise was in BW or **chemical weapons (CW)**.

BIOLOGICAL AND TOXIN WEAPONS CONVENTION (BTWC). An arms control and disarmament agreement that entered into force on 26 March 1975. Its full name is the Convention on the Prohibition of the Development, Production and Stockpiling of Bacteriological (Biological) and Toxin Weapons. Unlike the 1993 Chemical Weapons Convention (CWC), no international secretariat exists to oversee implementation of the BTWC. Treaty implementation matters, including questions regarding compliance, are considered by Review Conferences of the States Parties, generally held every five years.

Following the December 1991 dissolution of the Union of Soviet Socialist Republics (USSR), **Russia** became its legal successor state to the BTWC. In 1992, Russia admitted that there had been a delay in its implementation of the BTWC. This admission was taken as acknowledgment that the USSR had violated the BTWC.

Since entry into force, there have been concerns over the relevance of the BTWC in view of continuing scientific and technological developments and specific compliance concerns. From January 1995 to August 2001, an ad hoc group of BTWC parties met periodically to negotiate a protocol to strengthen treaty compliance. Negotiations were suspended during the Fifth Review Conference of BTWC parties, held in 2001 and 2002. Expert and political meetings took place among BTWC states parties annually from 2003 to 2005 to discuss and exchange information on selected BTWC implementation topics, including on national mechanisms regarding codes of conduct for scientists as well as security and oversight of pathogenic microorganisms and **toxins**.

The Sixth Review Conference of the BTWC met at the end of 2006 and agreed to a series of annual meetings to be held in 2007–2010. The meetings will, among other things, consider measures to promote effective implementation of the treaty, to improve **biosafety** and biosecurity at biological facilities, and to improve national capabilities for disease surveillance, detection, and diagnosis. These goals will be achieved partly through the establishment of a temporary treaty implementation support unit.

BIOLOGICAL WARFARE COMMITTEE (BWC). A U.S. body headed by **George W. Merck** that operated during World War II and was responsible for developing and coordinating U.S. policy on biological warfare (BW). The BWC was disbanded in October 1945 when its responsibilities were transferred to the War Department (the British equivalent during the war was the Inter-Service Sub-Committee on Biological Warfare).

BIOLOGICAL WEAPON (BW). A weapon that spreads disease or other infection among humans, animals, or plants. The 1972 **Biological and**

Toxin Weapons Convention (BTWC) includes infectious microorganisms and **toxins** in its definition of a biological weapon. Infectious, noncontagious (or essentially noncontagious) agents are generally preferable in the context of a traditional military conflict between states in that such agents are usually more predictable in their effects. This is because they will not cause uncontrolled secondary infections.

BIOPREPARAT. The All-Union Science Production Association "Biopreparat" was created under the Main Administration of the Microbiological Industry (Glavmikrobioprom) of the Union of Soviet Socialist Republics (USSR) in 1973. Biopreparat was also the general name given to the civilian (but military directed) component of the post-1973 Soviet **biological weapon (BW)** program. Biopreparat initially consisted of at least six scientific production organizations (NPOs): Biomash, Biosyntez, Enzym, FarmPribor, Progress, and **Vektor**. Following the collapse of the USSR, Biopreparat was privatized, with military officers occupying a number of key leadership positions. *See also* AL-IBEK, KENNETH; PASECHNIK, VLADIMIR ARTEMOVICH.

BIOSAFETY (BIOSECURITY). Much of the current international focus on attempting to prevent biological warfare (BW), including bioterrorism, is focused on implementing measures to promote "biosafety" and "biosecurity" (in many languages the same word can be translated with either meaning). The World Health Organization (WHO) defines *laboratory biosafety* as "the containment principles, technologies and practices that are implemented to prevent the unintentional exposure of pathogens and **toxins**, or their accidental release." Similarly, WHO defines *laboratory biosecurity* as "the protection, control and accountability for valuable biological materials . . . within laboratories, in order to prevent their unauthorized access, loss, theft, misuse, diversion or intentional release."

These terms are used as an umbrella under which a variety of disparate activities and expectations fall. The two main communities involved in these discussions are public health officials and the arms control and security communities. Some are primarily concerned with improving physical security at facilities where work with dangerous pathogens is carried out and with ensuring that proper material accountancy and control measures are effectively implemented.

Other groups are primarily interested in improving disease surveillance and response, promoting pharmaceutical research and development, developing codes of conduct of scientists, or promoting good laboratory practice (GLP) and good manufacturing practice (GMP) at biological facilities. One of the difficulties of assessing the effectiveness of biosecurity and biosafety measures is the uncertainty associated with BW threat and risk assessments. This is especially true in cases where there is little or no historical record to serve as a guide. It is often said that the risk of an attack with BW is low, but that the consequences of such an attack would be high or even catastrophic—either in terms of casualties and deaths or in economic damage.

A principal mechanism for making predictions is to examine past experiences. However, past experience with BW is limited and may be an inaccurate or poor predictor. Even quantitative risk assessments have a qualitative element that is produced during, for example, the process of selecting risk factors. There are also sensitivities surrounding the sharing of law enforcement and intelligence information, particularly at the international level. Furthermore, there is philosophical and political disagreement over the division of responsibility among international and national organizations. For example, some states prefer to work within ad hoc coalitions of like-minded states on some areas of concern (e.g., to try to clarify the status of a given state's **nuclear, biological,** or **chemical (NBC) weapon** program), while other states tend to try to address such issues within multilateral **United Nations (UN)** frameworks open to universal membership, such as the **International Atomic Energy Agency (IAEA)**. In other words, efforts to prohibit a given weapon type can become overshadowed by the various political and technical challenges connected with each organization or framework that is involved. Various "threat reduction" programs have also been developed in recent years in order to prevent the misuse of technologies, equipment, and human expertise to support BW programs, as well as those involving missiles, nuclear weapons, and chemical weapons. *See also* COOPERATIVE THREAT REDUCTION (CTR) PROGRAM; PROJECT BIOSHIELD.

BIOSECURITY. *See* BIOSAFETY.

BLAUKREUZKAMPFSTOFFE. *See* BLUE CROSS AGENT.

BLIND (BLINDS). A **chemical weapon (CW)** that fails to function properly, thus leaving its contents available for analysis. The Americans and British used this term (often with the plural *blinds* used as a singular noun) during World War I when referring to enemy munitions.

BLISTER AGENT. *See* VESICANT.

BLITZABLEITER COMMITTEE (BLITZARBEITER COMMITTEE). **Germany** established the Blitzableiter Committee (also referred to as the Blitzarbeiter Committee) following its capture in 1940 of four French laboratories, located outside Paris at the Poudrerie Nationale du Bouchet, that had been engaged in **biological weapon (BW)**–related work. The French had abandoned culture specimens and photographs of bacterial cultures containing metal fragments. The bacterial cultures were found to be *Bacillus anthracis*, the causative agent for **anthrax**. Germany also recovered paperwork that had been taken away and hidden. The discoveries were important, in that previously Germany had given BW developments a low priority. The committee was charged with, among other things, determining the nature of the work carried out by the French and to evaluate BW threats generally. **Heinrich Kliewe**, a specialist in **aerosol** sciences and disinfection, served as chairman.

BLOME, KURT. Blome was a physician, medical researcher, and military officer who served in the Stürm Abteilung (SA) during the Nazi regime, eventually rising to the rank of major general. During World War II, Blome was the biological warfare (BW) representative on the Reich Research Council. He was taken into custody by U.S. Army Counterintelligence Corps personnel detailed to work for the **ALSOS Mission**. One of Blome's principal responsibilities during the Nazi regime had been to report on the political reliability of **German** scientists and technicians; therefore, his knowledge was valuable to ALSOS in helping the **United Kingdom** and **United States** to identify German weapon experts who might work for them. His activities resulted in his being charged with war crimes. As a defendant at the Nuremberg Doctors' Trial, Blome was accused of human experimentation with **biological weapon (BW)** materials on concentration camp prisoners, but he was acquitted. Blome reportedly signed a contract in 1951 to work for the U.S. Army **Chemical Corps (CmlC)** on BW-related research. *See also* ACONITINE; HIMMLER, HEINRICH.

BLOOD AGENT. A substance that disrupts oxygen transport through the blood to tissues. Examples include hydrogen cyanide and other cyanide-containing chemicals. The term was applied to toxic chemicals during World War I. Subsequent research has shown that the blood carries many toxic chemicals, including **organophosphorus nerve agents** and **vesicants**. Therefore, *blood agent* is an obsolete term. A better term for cyanide-containing chemicals is, simply, *cyanides*. A broader term currently in use is *metabolic agents*. Prior to the development of organophosphorus nerve agents, blood agents were sometimes referred to as *nerve agents*. *See also* CHOKING AGENT; LACHRYMATOR.

BLUE CROSS AGENT. In July 1917, the **German** military introduced use of the sternutator (sneezing agent) diphenylchloroarsine (Clark I). In keeping with its practice of designating separate types of **chemical weapons (CW)** with distinctive markings, Germany marked Clark I–filled CW with a blue cross and referred to this substance as a "blue cross agent" (*Blaukreuzkampfstoffe*). Use of Clark I was followed by that of other blue cross agents: diphenylcyanoarsine (Clark II, May 1918) and ethylcarbazole (July 1918). The agents proved a colossal failure, although the Germans failed to appreciate it at the time. The Germans selected the blue cross agents because they would break through the protective masks being worn by the Allies on the Western Front. The agent would rapidly penetrate the gas mask's filter, causing the wearer to start sneezing and vomiting. These effects would prompt the wearer to discard his mask or would break the seal between the mask and the wearer's face, thus exposing him to this agent and any others that might have been used.

The concept of a "mask breaker" is sound, but the German design for its weapon failed to disseminate the agent into the air. Instead, most of the solid diphenylchloroarsine merely fell to the ground harmlessly in the area surrounding the explosion of its shell. In the rush to get blue cross agent shells into use, the German military failed to test the shells adequately and were unaware of the limited extent to which the blue cross agents were being dispersed into the air. The British military, however, was aware of both the potential of the blue cross agents and the flaw in the German design. British scientists developed a means of dispersing Clark I and related substances as a particulate suspended in **smoke**. This suspension was effected by means of a candle-type device called a thermogenerator (**M Device**). The device was developed too late for use in World War I, but it did see use by the British in the conflict against the **Russian** forces in northern European Russia in 1919. *See also* GREEN CROSS AGENT; VARICOLORED CROSS; WHITE CROSS AGENT; YELLOW CROSS AGENT.

BOCK'S CAR. On 9 August 1945, the United States exploded the "**Fat Man**" bomb over Nagasaki, **Japan**. The B-29 aircraft that departed from Tinian Island and carried this bomb was named *Bock's Car* (also rendered *Bockscar*) in honor of Captain Frederick C. Bock, the Army Air Corps officer who usually commanded the plane. However, he was not in command that day; instead, *Bock's Car* was piloted by Maj. Charles W. Sweeney. The primary target designated for the 9 August mission was Kokura, but visibility over that target was deemed insufficient, causing *Bock's Car* to divert to its secondary target, Nagasaki, and sparing Kokura the destruction visited on Nagasaki and Hiroshima. *See also* ENOLA GAY; 509TH COMPOSITE GROUP; SHEIGEYOSHI MORIMOTO.

BOHR, NIELS (1885–1962). Danish physicist who made fundamental contributions to the growth of nuclear physics. Bohr's work was recognized by receipt of the 1922 Nobel Prize in Physics, which noted his work on the structure of atoms. Bohr spent most of his career in Denmark at the University of Copenhagen. After the Nazi occupation of Denmark, however, his situation became difficult. In 1943, he was targeted for arrest but succeeded in fleeing to Sweden. From there, Bohr traveled to England and the **United States**, where he joined the **Manhattan Project** at Los Alamos, using the pseudonym "Nicholas Baker" to hide his identity. Bohr felt the Manhattan Project should be shared with the Soviets. He met with President Franklin Roosevelt to advocate this position, and Roosevelt encouraged Bohr to meet with

British prime minister Winston Churchill to get his backing. Bohr then traveled to the **United Kingdom** and met with Churchill, who rejected the idea. *See also* BOHR-HEISENBERG CONVERSATION.

BOHR-HEISENBERG CONVERSATION. German physicist **Werner Heisenberg** studied under **Niels Bohr** at the University of Copenhagen. In September 1941, after Heisenberg had taken a senior position with the **German** effort to build a nuclear reactor, the two met secretly in Copenhagen. What transpired at this meeting is not clear because there is no contemporary record, but the meeting has become a matter of intense speculation and controversy. Heisenberg would later claim he stressed to Bohr that Germany intended to develop a nuclear reactor solely for use as an energy source, but this explanation is unsatisfactory in view of Bohr's immediate and adverse reaction to their conversation. An alternative explanation regarding this important conversation appears to be that Heisenberg told Bohr, first, that a German victory in World War II would be preferable for Europe to a victory by the Soviet Union and, second, that Bohr should use his influence to prevent Allied scientists, who were trailing the Germans in nuclear research, from building a **nuclear weapon** that could be used against Germany. Bohr apparently wrote an account of their September 1941 conversation, but these papers remain sealed until 2012.

BONE OIL. Bone oil is a dark-colored oil produced by destructive distillation of animal bones and has a particularly foul and fetid odor. It was one of the chemicals used by the British during World War I in **stinks**.

BOTHE, WALTHER (1891–1957). German physicist. Bothe helped to lay the foundation for nuclear spectroscopy, for which he received the 1954 Nobel Prize in Physics. He contributed to **Germany**'s **nuclear weapon** program during the Nazi regime, and some observers point to his 1941 error regarding graphite as contributing to the failure of that program. Bothe conducted experiments with graphite in which he tested whether it might work as a *moderator*—a substance that acts to slow neutrons. A nuclear reactor requires such "slow neutrons," which are more likely to be captured by a nucleus than are **"fast neutrons,"** to achieve a sustained nuclear reaction. Bothe concluded from his experiments that graphite would be unacceptable as a moderator. However, his conclusion appears to be in error. Bothe failed to account for the presence of impurities (notably boron and cadmium) in the samples of graphite used. These impurities markedly reduced the effectiveness of the graphite. In any event, Bothe's conclusions caused the Germans to abandon use of graphite and, instead, to commit to using **heavy water** as a moderator. That decision made the **Norsk Hydro plant** of tremendous importance to Germany's nuclear program.

BOTULINUM TOXIN (BTX). A **neurotoxin** produced naturally by the bacterium *Clostridium botulinum*, a spore-forming, anaerobic organism found worldwide in soil. It is reportedly the most toxic substance known to science. BTX poisoning causes botulism and is seen in humans who consume improperly preserved foods, such as smoked meats, blood sausages and puddings, and canned vegetables. The Latin *botulis* means "sausage" or "blood pudding," which reflects a tendency for ancient Romans who ate improperly smoked or cured blood sausages and puddings to develop botulism. Botulism is also seen in infants and is tied to the ongoing colonization of the intestines during the first years of life by the usually benign *C. botulinum* organism. For reasons that are incompletely understood, the flora of newborns, their intestinal environment, or both are such that the bacteria grow and produce **toxins**. Nitrates and nitrites (which can be introduced in the preservation process for meats) inhibit the growth of *C. botulinum* bacteria.

The action of BTX is opposite to that of the **organophosphorus nerve agents**. While nerve agents cause a potentially fatal accumulation of the neurotransmitter acetylcholine, BTX *blocks* release of this neurotransmitter. To date, seven distinct serotypes of BTX have been isolated, designated types A through G. Only types A, B, E, and F have been clearly identified with multiple human poisoning episodes. Type A is believed to be the most toxic to humans and is the active ingredient in the pharmaceutical Botox, used clinically to treat various muscular disorders and cosmetically for the "surgery-free," temporary reduction of both wrinkles and excessive perspiration.

The extreme toxicity of BTX gave rise to research into its potential as a warfare agent. During World War II, the **United States** prepared a stockpile for use as an assassination weapon. Multiple sources report that BTX toxin contributed to the June 1942 death of Reinhardt Heydrich, the Nazi "protector" (governor) of Bohemia and Moravia. According to these reports, the Czech patriots responsible for assassinating Heydrich used one or more grenades containing BTX. The grenade supposedly originated with the British **biological weapons (BW)** program at **Porton Down**. No evidence to support these reports has surfaced at Porton Down, however, and the story is likely legend rather than fact.

BOYLES, WILLIAM ALLEN (1905–1951). U.S. microbiologist. In November 1951, Boyles was working in the U.S. Army's **biological weapons (BW)** laboratories at **Fort Detrick**, Maryland. A laboratory accident resulted in his exposure to spores of the Vollum strain of the biological pathogen *Bacillus anthracis*, the causative agent of **anthrax**. Shortly following his exposure, he developed pulmonary (inhalational) anthrax. Despite extraordinary efforts to keep him alive, Boyles died of the effects of anthrax on 25 November. Reportedly, his internal organs were harvested in order to isolate anthrax from them. Unlike the Vollum strain, which had been isolated from a cow in England prior to World War II, this strain of anthrax had passed once through a human and, thus, had been potentiated toward humans. The strain was dubbed "V1B," for "Vollum passed once through a human (Boyle)." The V1B strain was subsequently used by the **United States** throughout its further development of an offensive anthrax-laden BW.

BRAVO. The **United States** successfully tested its first deliverable **thermonuclear** weapon at Bikini Atoll on 1 March 1954. Given the code name "Bravo," the device had an estimated yield of nearly 15 megatons, triple the expected yield of five megatons. *See also* GEORGE; JOE; MIKE.

BRAZIL. Brazil pursued a covert **nuclear weapons** program for many years. In 1978, during a time of military rule, Brazil launched "Solimoes," its covert program to acquire nuclear weapons. Civilian rule was restored in 1985, but military nuclear developments continued. However, Brazil now appears to have abandoned its nuclear weapon ambitions. On 13 July 1998, Brazilian president Fernando Henrique Cardoso signed and ratified both the **Nonproliferation Treaty (NPT)** and the **Comprehensive Test Ban Treaty (CTBT)**. These actions came following other steps taken by Brazil to push for nuclear disarmament.

Brazil maintains a civilian nuclear program under **International Atomic Energy Agency (IAEA) safeguards**, managed by the state-owned Brazilian Nuclear Corporation (Nuclebras). Throughout the 1980s, the country attempted to develop indigenous **gas centrifuge** technology, and it announced in 1987 that it had succeeded in constructing a pilot facility at the Institute of Energy and Nuclear Research (Instituto de Pesquisas Energéticas e Nucleares, IPEN), located on the campus of São Paulo University. This experimental facility first produced slightly enriched **uranium** in September 1982 and opened a cascade of nine machines in 1984. The Brazilian Navy operates a much larger plant at the Aramar Research Center near Ipero in the state of São Paulo. It was inaugurated in 1988 and now operates under the name Isotopic Enrichment Facility. Brazil apparently possesses the capability of enriching uranium to **weapons-grade** levels but it is not known to have done so. Enrichments up to at least 10 percent have been announced, but most uranium is enriched to just 3 percent. The Brazilian Army disclosed in September 1991 that it was designing a natural uranium graphite reactor, evidently for **plutonium** production, although this reactor probably will not be built in view of the 1998 developments. *See also* BRAZILIAN-ARGENTINE AGENCY FOR ACCOUNTING AND CONTROL OF NUCLEAR MATERIALS (ABACC).

BRAZILIAN-ARGENTINE AGENCY FOR ACCOUNTING AND CONTROL OF NUCLEAR MATERIALS (ABACC). The Brazilian-Argentine Agency for Accounting and Control of Nuclear Materials (ABACC in Spanish and Portuguese) was established in 1991 to verify that all nuclear materials in all nuclear activities in **Argentina** and **Brazil**, or under their jurisdiction or control, are used exclusively for peaceful purposes. In 1998 ABACC concluded a cooperation agreement with the **International Atomic Energy Agency (IAEA)**, the body that implements the 1968 **Nonproliferation Treaty (NPT)**. ABACC was established partly in order to serve as a **confidence-building measure (CBM)** between the two countries to ensure that their respective **nuclear weapon**–related activities have been ended. *See also* NUCLEAR FUEL CYCLE.

BREEDER REACTOR. A nuclear reactor that produces **plutonium-239** for use in other research or power reactors or for **nuclear weapons**. Such reactors are considered to represent a nuclear proliferation risk and therefore are subject to special controls. *See also* INTERNATIONAL ATOMIC ENERGY AGENCY (IAEA); NUCLEAR FUEL CYCLE.

BROAD SPECTRUM. The basic idea of a broad-spectrum treatment is to develop antibiotics and/or vaccines that are effective against a range of potential biological warfare agents. Interest in such work has been heightened in recent years due to concerns that the Soviets may have developed **biological weapon (BW)** agents that have been modified to evade standard detection methods and treatments or that display symptoms not normally associated the agent. There is also concern that technological and scientific developments will make such threat scenarios increasingly possible.

BROKEN ARROW. The U.S. Department of Defense uses BROKEN ARROW as a code name for identifying and reporting an accident involving a **nuclear weapon**, nuclear warhead, or other nuclear component. *See also* BENT SPEAR; DULL SWORD; EMPTY QUIVER; FADED GIANT; NUCLEAR EMERGENCY SEARCH TEAM (NEST); SPAIN HYDROGEN BOMB INCIDENT.

BROWN DERBY EXERCISE. From 7 to 20 November 1953, the U.S. Army **Chemical Corps** and U.S. Air Force conducted the Brown Derby Exercise as a means of assessing their ability to produce and transport **biological weapons (BW)** overseas. A **simulant** BW agent was manufactured at Pine Bluff Arsenal, Arkansas, filled into cluster bombs, and shipped to Eglin AFB, Florida, via Shreveport, Louisiana. The exercise showed that an attack using BW could be launched within several days.

\LLOSIS. A disease of large animals, especially camels, cat-\s, sheep, and swine. The disease can also appear in humans, although such instances are rarer than are animal infections. Brucellosis is caused by small, nonmotile, nonsporulating, aerobic, **Gram-negative** coccobacilli of the genus *Brucella*. Assorted species of *Brucella* have been isolated, with several of them being pathogenic toward humans. In animals, brucellosis causes abortion, fetal death, and genital infection. Human infections occur from ingesting infected animal food products, by directly contacting infected animals, and through improper handling of the organisms in the laboratory.

Brucella bacteria are highly infectious by the airborne route, which may account for the interest shown by various nations in studying *Brucella* for use in **biological weapons (BW)**. Human infections lead to various debilitating symptoms such as fever and muscle pain but are seldom fatal. During World War II, the **United States** prepared BW containing *Brucella suis* (designated "Agent AB" as well as "Agent NX"), the species typically associated with swine. The M114 four-pound antipersonnel bomb became the first U.S. BW to be standardized. It was tested in 1944–1945 at **Dugway Proving Ground (DPG)**, Utah, in open-air releases against animal targets. These studies validated U.S. concerns that *Brucella* pathogens would prove effective if used against troops. None of these weapons were used in combat, and all remaining stockpiles of *Brucella* weapons were destroyed when the United States unilaterally renounced use of BW in 1969. The status of *Brucella* weapon development in other countries is uncertain, although it seems likely such development was considered, given the ease of airborne transmission and the high rate of infectivity by inhalation.

BUREAU OF MINES. During World War I, the Bureau of Mines of the U.S. Department of Interior played an important role in the research and development of chemical warfare (CW) agents and respirators. Since its establishment in 1910, the bureau had carried out research into the nature of poisonous and explosive gases encountered in mines, and it had developed measures to protect against toxic and harmful gases. When the **United States** entered the war, the expertise of the bureau was thought to be applicable to problems facing the military with regard to CW. The bureau initiated the research activities undertaken at **American University**, although responsibil these activities was given over to the **Chemical Warfare Service (CWS)** when that organization was established.

BURGASOV, PYOTR N. Burgasov was the deputy minister of health and chief medical officer of health of the Soviet Union at the time of a 1979 **anthrax** outbreak in humans around Sverdlovsk (present-day Yekaterinburg), in the Ural Mountains east of Moscow. Burgasov traveled to the city as part of a secret high-level delegation to investigate the outbreak. Subsequently, he was prominently involved in promoting the view that the outbreak had been the result of the accidental ingestion of contaminated meat. However, most authorities agree that the incident can be traced to an accidental release from a Sverdlovsk military facility involved in exploiting anthrax for use in **biological weapons (BW)**. *See also* TRILATERAL PROCESS.

BURNET, SIR FRANK MACFARLANE (1899–1985). Australian physician and scientist. Burnet made fundamental discoveries in microbiology, virology, and bacteriology. He was recognized for his work with the award of the 1960 Nobel Prize in Physiology or Medicine. His work elucidating the nature of the causative agent of **Q fever** led to his name being given to that agent, *Coxiella burnetii*. During and immediately after World War II, he consulted for the Australian government on matters related to **chemical** and **biological weapons (CBW)**. For instance, in 1946, Burnet advised the government that the most effective counteroffensive to a threatened invasion of **Australia** by overpopulated Asiatic countries would be directed toward the destruction by biological or chemical means of tropical food crops and the dissemination of infectious disease capable of spreading in tropical, but not typical Australian, conditions. He was knighted in 1951.

BUSH, VANNEVAR (1890–1974). Bush made important contributions as an educator, engineer, and science administrator. He was the first chairman of the **National Defense Research Committee (NDRC)** and later of the **Office of Scientific Research and Development (OSRD)**. He received B.S. and M.S. degrees from Tufts University in 1913, and in 1916 he received a degree in engineering simultaneously from the Massachusetts Institute of Technology (MIT) and

Harvard. Bush spent World War I working on submarine detection technology and then held various positions at MIT from 1919 to 1938: teaching in 1919, professor of electrical engineering in 1923, vice president and dean of engineering in 1932. In 1939 he was appointed president of the Carnegie Institute of Washington, where he advocated enhanced cooperation between civilian scientists and the military as the **United States** prepared for entry into World War II. In June 1940, Bush presented his ideas to President Franklin Delano Roosevelt, who quickly approved the establishment of the NDRC. The NDRC was subsumed by the OSRD in 1941, and Bush became its chairman. From this position, he was in effect responsible for all wartime scientific research, including the **Manhattan Project**.

Bush wrote *Modern Arms and Free Men*, in which he predicted the Soviet Union would require at least 10 years before succeeding in its efforts to build a **nuclear weapon**. However, the USSR achieved its first successful nuclear detonation in August 1949, as Bush's book was going to press. Bush was able to halt the printing and have the now-inaccurate prediction deleted.

BZ. A military code name that has come into common use as a shortened name for the hydrochloride salt of 3-quinuclidinyl benzilate. It was discovered in the early 1950s during pharmaceutical research and was adopted by the U.S. military in the early 1960s for use in **chemical weapons (CW)** as an **incapacitant**. **South Africa** selected a chemical analogue of BZ for its CW program, although the precise chemical nature of this analogue is uncertain. Yugoslavia is reported to have produced BZ munitions prior to the early 1990s breakup of that nation. BZ depresses the central nervous system, and exposure to it can cause drowsiness, inability to concentrate, confusion, and near-term memory loss. The **United States** rushed BZ into production following the Berlin Wall crisis, amid concerns over civil disturbances in **Germany**. Testing later suggested BZ munitions would have limited, if any, functionality. By 1990, the United States had destroyed all BZ stockpiles.

– C –

CACODYL. The common name for tetramethyldiarasine ($C_4H_{12}As_2$), an oily liquid having an almost intolerable garlicky odor. Cacodyl was proposed for military use during the 19th century, prior to the modern era of chemical warfare. Its actual use in **chemical weapons (CW)** is unproven. One report describes a proposal by a U.S. Army captain, E. C. Boynton, to use cacodyl during the Civil War (1861–1865). Boynton pointed out that cacodyl is spontaneously flammable (in dry air), giving off deadly fumes. Prior to the U.S. entry into World War II, the U.S. Navy tested chemical munitions containing cacodyl mixed with another toxic chemical. There is no evidence any cacodyl-filled CW were adopted for military use.

CACODYL CYANIDE. The common name for cyanodimethylarsine oxide (C_3H_6AsNO). During the Crimean War (1853–1856), the **Russian** Artillery Committee undertook field trials of **chemical weapons (CW)** containing cacodyl cyanide. The weapons were 196-mm artillery shells, each weighing approximately 35 pounds. The Russian military apparently feared cacodyl cyanide might be used against one or more of its fortified cities involved in the war. This fear likely was spurred by word of the proposals to this effect made by **Lyon Playfair** to the British Admiralty. The trials were held at Volkovo Pole, an artillery proving range near St. Petersburg, Russia. Shells loaded with cacodyl cyanide were placed inside a roofless log house. Cats were secured in cages, and these were also placed in the log house. The shells were fired by remote control. After waiting 24 hours for the cacodyl cyanide to dissipate, Russian observers entered the test site. They found the cats alive, although weeping profusely from the **lachrymatory** effects of the cacodyl cyanide. The Russians regarded these results as showing such shells would prove ineffective during field use and thus posed no threat to Russian defenses.

CACODYLIC ACID. The common name for dimethylarsinic oxide ($C_2H_7AsO_3$), a solid that is harmful to animals and plants. The **United States** used cacodylic acid as a **defoliant** during the Vietnam War as the active ingredient in Agent Blue. Its use in **chemical weapons (CW)** may have been considered much earlier, however, in one of the 1855 proposals from **Lyon Playfair** to the British Admiralty.

CALUTRON. One objective of the **Manhattan Project** was the production of sufficient **uranium**-235 for use in testing and, especially, constructing one or more **nuclear weapons**. Producing this **isotope**

proved technically challenging and relied almost exclusively on specialized electromagnetic separation equipment known as "calutrons." The name is a contraction of "California University cyclotron." In the design used for the Manhattan Project, there were two stages of calutrons, designated simply "alpha" and "beta." The alpha stage produced **low-enriched uranium (LEU)** having about 15 percent uranium-235. The product of the alpha stage was fed into the beta stage, which produced **weapons-grade material**. Each alpha stage used 96 calutrons in an oval, racetrack-like arrangement, while each beta stage had 72 calutrons in a square arrangement. The uranium-235 production took place at the Y-12 plant, Oak Ridge, Tennessee. At its peak, the plant operated 1,152 calutrons in nine alpha and four beta stages. Although the plant calutron array has been dismantled, a few calutrons remain in operation to produce isotopes for research purposes. In the 1990s, the **United States** reclassified some technical information on calutrons following the discovery that **Iraq** had used such information in its enrichment program.

CAMOUFLAGE GAS. A substance that either masks the presence of a toxic chemical warfare agent or simulates the presence of such an agent. Camouflage gases were the subject of considerable research during World War I, and some might have been used in combat. For instance, 2-ethoxynaphthalene was considered by the **United States** for use to mask or disguise the presence of a toxic agent. **Balloon dope**, n-butyl mercaptan, and dimethyl trithiocarbonate are examples of chemicals that either were used or were studied for use to simulate the presence of a toxic agent. *See also* STINKS.

CANVASS TRENCH FAN. *See* AYRTON FAN.

CARBON DISULFIDE. Carbon disulfide (CS_2) is a toxic, flammable, volatile liquid with a strong disagreeable odor. Its use as a chemical warfare (CW) agent was proposed indirectly by 19th-century British naval officer **Thomas Cochrane**, 10th Earl of Dundonald (1775–1860). At various times, Lord Dundonald suggested military use of a toxic **smoke** created by passing sulfur vapor over red-hot coke. Such a process would create carbon disulfide. The British government failed to adopt this suggestion. Its use was also proposed to the British Admiralty by **Lyon Playfair** in 1855.

After **German** use of **chlorine** in April 1915, the Allies used assorted chemicals that were both easy to get (thus could be used promptly) and toxic. Carbon disulfide was one of these. Its use as a CW agent during this period of Allied retaliation for the chlorine attack was insufficiently promising to warrant continued use, however. While carbon disulfide was used by the **Russians** and as an ingredient in some British munitions, it failed to become a standard CW agent.

CARRIER. A substance added to a chemical warfare agent to increase the airborne dose one might receive, thus enhancing the military effectiveness of the agent. A carrier might be added either to enhance the evaporation of an otherwise low-volatility agent or to retard the evaporation of an otherwise high-volatility agent. Examples of the former are carbon tetrachloride and chlorobenzene, which were added to certain mixes of **sulfur mustard**. An example of a carrier used to retard evaporation is diatomaceous earth. Highly volatile hydrogen cyanide was adsorbed into diatomaceous earth in the commercial formulation known as **Zyklon B**. This resultant material provided a slower-releasing form of hydrogen cyanide, thereby increasing the chances that an exposed person would receive a lethal dose before the full quantity of hydrogen cyanide would fully dissipate through natural evaporation. Similarly, **Germany** used pumice, a highly porous igneous rock, as a carrier for **phosgene**. This development occurred late in World War I, when Germany perfected a design comparable to the **Livens Projector**. The pumice adsorbed the liquid phosgene, allowing it to be released more slowly, thereby prolonging the contamination on any targeted area.

CATHOLIC UNIVERSITY OF AMERICA (CUA). Catholic University is located in the northeastern section of Washington, D.C. During World War I, CUA housed a branch laboratory of the **Bureau of Mines** that engaged in research, development, and production of potential chemical warfare agents. Eventually, this laboratory was designated Organic Unit No. 3 of the U.S. Army **Chemical Warfare**

Service (CWS). This unit had a staff of 75, including Capt. Winfred Lee Lewis, who oversaw development **lewisite** at CUA. Additionally, the **toxins ricin** and **juglone** were produced here as part of a poison-bullet development program that was reportedly initiated because of intelligence information that indicated the **Germans** were carrying out such work. *See also* AMERICAN UNIVERSITY.

CENTRE D'ÉTUDES DU BOUCHET. Located outside Paris, the Centre d'Études du Bouchet is the primary establishment in **France** for research into defensive measures against **chemical** and **biological weapons (CBW).** *See also* BLITZABLEITER COMMITTEE.

CG. *See* PHOSGENE.

CHAIN REACTION. In the context of nuclear materials, *chain reaction* refers to a series of reactions occurring in **fissionable** materials. During these reactions, neutrons produced by **fission** reactions induce other fission reactions. A fission chain reaction becomes self-sustaining when one new fission is produced by each previous fission. *See also* NUCLEAR PILE.

CHAPAYEVSK. *See* BERSOL.

CHEMICAL AGENT IDENTIFICATION SET (CAIS). A handheld kit containing small quantities of toxic chemicals associated with **chemical weapons (CW)** that is used by the U.S. military to train personnel in the identification, handling, and decontamination of CW agents. The CAIS was used by the U.S. Army from 1928 to 1969. The **United States** produced two standard configurations of CAIS. One configuration had glass ampoules and vials containing pure cyanogen chloride, pure **phosgene,** 5 percent **lewisite** in chloroform, 5 percent **sulfur mustard** in chloroform, 10 percent **nitrogen mustard** in chloroform, 50 percent **chloropicrin** in chloroform, and a **simulant** for **tabun.** The second configuration contained glass bottles filled with solid **chloroacetophenone,** pure sulfur mustard, solid **adamsite,** solid triphosgene, lewisite adsorbed on a charcoal base, chloropicrin adsorbed on a charcoal base, sulfur mustard adsorbed on a charcoal base, and nitrogen mustard adsorbed on a charcoal base. CAIS kits were widely distributed to U.S. military units throughout the United States and overseas, including to National Guard units. Although withdrawn from the inventory after 1969, CAIS kits occasionally are discovered at military facilities. Such discoveries are reported, and the kits recovered for destruction.

CHEMICAL ALI. A nickname widely used for Ali Hasan al-Majid al-Tikriti, an **Iraqi** general and cousin to Saddam Hussein. "Chemical Ali" is believed to have been responsible for the use of **chemical weapons (CW)** against Iraq's Kurdish population at **Halabja** in 1988, which resulted in several thousand deaths. Chemical Ali was number five on the list of the 55 Iraqi officials most wanted by the coalition forces that invaded Iraq in 2003. He was captured in August 2003. As of 2006, he was standing trial for, among other things, involvement in Iraqi use of CW.

CHEMICAL CORPS (CmlC). A branch of the U.S. Army established 6 September 1946 out of the War Department's **Chemical Warfare Service (CWS)**. According to the U.S. Army Chemical School, Fort Leonard Wood, Missouri, the mission of the CmlC is to

Protect the force and allow the Army to fight and win against a nuclear, biological or chemical (NBC) weapon threat.

Develop doctrine, equipment and training for NBC defense which serve as a deterrent to ANY [sic] adversary possessing weapons of mass destruction (WMD).

Provide the Army with the combat multipliers of smoke, obscurant, and flame capabilities.

CHEMICAL WARFARE SERVICE (CWS). A technical service branch of the U.S. Army that existed from 1918 to 1946. General Order 62 of the U.S. War Department established the CWS on 28 June 1918, with Maj. Gen. William L. Siebert as its first commander. Assorted government functions related to offensive and defensive chemical warfare (CW) were consolidated by their transfer to the CWS when it was established, including the following:

- War Gas Investigations, Department of Interior
- Chemical Service Section, National Army, War Department

- Gas Defense Division, Surgeon General's Office, War Department
- Gas Offense Production Division, Office of the Chief of Ordnance, War Department

An Act of Congress signed into law on 2 August 1946 changed its name to the **Chemical Corps (CmlC)**, effective 6 September 1946. *See also* FIRST GAS REGIMENT; FRIES, AMOS A.; GILCHRIST, HARRY LORENZO; HANLON, JOSEPH T.; WAITT, ALDEN HARRY.

CHEMICAL WEAPON (CW). The internationally accepted definition of a CW is that contained in the 1993 **Chemical Weapons Convention (CWC)**, which states that such weapons consist of one or more of three elements:

1. toxic chemicals and their precursors (the chemicals used in the synthesis of the toxic chemicals) where intended for use as a method of warfare
2. munitions and devices specifically designed to cause harm or death through the use of such toxic chemicals
3. any equipment specifically designed to be used directly in connection with such chemicals, munitions, and devices

According to the CWC definition, the presence of a chemical in a munition does not automatically make the munition or the chemical into a chemical weapon. Thus, weapons containing napalm or white phosphorus, for example, are not chemical weapons because the primary effect of such weapons depends on the **incendiary** properties of these chemicals rather than on their toxicity.

The CWC contains a "general purpose criterion" (GPC) that bans the production and use of all toxic chemicals except where they are to be used for peaceful purposes, such as would be the case for a commercial pesticide. The GPC is the principal mechanism by which technological and scientific developments can be taken into account by the **Organization for the Prohibition of Chemical Weapons (OPCW)**, the organization that implements the CWC. The definition in the CWC is phrased to ensure that bulk CW storage containers and **binary chemical weapon** or other multicomponent systems are covered by the convention. *See also* BIOLOGICAL

AND TOXIN WEAPONS CONVENTION (BTWC); CLASSES OF CHEMICAL WEAPONS; TOXIN.

CHEMICAL WEAPON PRODUCTION FACILITY (CWPF). The **Chemical Weapons Convention (CWC)** defines a CWPF as any facility that has produced **chemical weapons (CW)** at any time since 1 January 1946.

CHEMICAL WEAPONS CONVENTION (CWC). The Convention on the Prohibition of the Development, Stockpiling, and Use of Chemical Weapons and on Their Destruction, commonly called the Chemical Weapons Convention, was opened for signature on 13 January 1993 and entered into force on 29 April 1997. The treaty is implemented by the **Organization for the Prohibition of Chemical Weapons (OPCW)** in The Hague, Netherlands. As of November 2006, the OPCW had 181 members. The declared **chemical weapon (CW)** possessors are **Albania, India, Libya, Russia**, the **United States**, and a state that declines to be officially designated as a CW possessor but is widely understood to be the Republic of Korea (South Korea). As of the same date, of the approximately 71,000 metric tons of declared CW agents and 8,700,000 declared items, about 15,000 metric tons of agents and 2,600,000 munitions and containers had been verifiably destroyed. Twelve states (Bosnia-Herzegovina, **China, France,** India, **Iran, Japan,** Libya, Russia, Serbia and Montenegro, South Korea, the **United Kingdom,** and the United States) had declared 65 **chemical weapon production facilities (CWPF),** of which 57 had been certified by the OPCW as being destroyed or converted for purposes not prohibited under the CWC. The CWC also has provisions that allow for informal consultation, clarification, and fact-finding that have been successfully used to clarify many (but not all) concerns that some of the parties have had regarding the completeness of declarations to the OPCW on past CW programs and current activities being carried out by other parties' national defense establishments as part of CWC-permitted protective programs. *See also* COMPLETENESS OF DESTRUCTION.

CHICAGO PILE. *See* STAGG FIELD.

CHICKEN FARM. The popular name used for a site in **Iraq** that was inspected by the **United Nations Special Commission on Iraq (UNSCOM)**. In August 1995, the inspectors were shown paperwork and material related to Iraq's **biological weapon (BW)** program at this site. Iraqi authorities claimed that one of the sons-in-law of Saddam Hussein, **Hussein al-Kamal**, had secretly pursued a covert BW program that was neither authorized by nor known to them. These claims were given little credence at the time, and subsequent information revealed by, among others, the **Iraq Survey Group (ISG)** suggests that the program was in fact authorized by the government.

CHINA. As of 2006, the People's Republic of China (PRC) was estimated to possess 145 operational strategic nuclear weapons. China is thought to possess operational *tactical* nuclear weapons as well, although no unclassified information is available regarding numbers and types of such weapons. The PRC is a party to the **Chemical Weapons Convention (CWC)** and has declared that it possesses **chemical weapons (CW)** abandoned on its territory by **Japan** during World War II. It is estimated that at least 700,000 **abandoned chemical weapons (ACW)** are located in the PRC, mainly in the northeastern provinces. The nature and scope of a Chinese **biological weapons (BW)** program, if one exists or did exist, are unknown.

CHINA SYNDROME. A term referring to a catastrophic accident in which a nuclear reactor core melts through the containment of a nuclear power plant and metaphorically burns its way downward through the Earth from the United States to China. American physicist Roger S. Boyd claimed to have coined the phrase in the early 1960s while he was working for the U.S. **Atomic Energy Commission (AEC)**. *See also* MELTDOWN; NUCLEAR PILE.

CHLORINE. A toxic chemical widely used in the chemical industry that became the first **chemical weapon (CW)** employed successfully in combat. On 22 April 1915, **Germany** released chlorine near **Ypres**, Belgium, catching French and Canadian forces by surprise and opening a large gap. Its use was overseen by the eminent chemist **Fritz Haber**, who later won the Nobel Prize in Chemistry. However, Germany was unable to exploit the gap because the German High

Command had failed to station sufficient reserves in the sector. *See also* JAEGER, AUGUST.

CHLOROACETOPHENONE. Chloroacetophenone (2-chloro-1-phenylethanone, C_8H_7ClO) is a crystalline solid whose vapors are intensely irritating. Its irritating or **lachrymatory** effects were known during World War I, but its use in combat was rejected owing to its low volatility. Shortly after the entry of the **United States** into the war, the U.S. Army **Chemical Warfare Service (CWS)** evaluated chloroacetophenone, and testing showed it to be superior to other lachrymators. On this basis, the United States adopted it for use in **chemical weapons (CW)**, giving it the code name "CN." This adoption occurred too late for chloroacetophenone to be used in the war, but it did see extensive use for decades afterward by the military and law enforcement for crowd control and humanitarian purposes. Eventually, chloroacetophenone was replaced by **CS**.

CHLOROPICRIN. Chloropicrin (CCl_3NO_2) is a liquid that is colorless to slightly yellow and has an intensely irritating odor. Exposure to chloropicrin causes various effects. It is a **lachrymator** and a **choking agent**, and exposure irritates the lungs, producing nausea and vomiting as seen with a **vomiting agent**. It was used extensively as a **chemical weapon (CW)** during World War I by **France, Germany, Russia**, and the **United Kingdom**. Russian use came about in large measure because it had been used for decades as a fumigant and rodenticide in the Soviet **antiplague system**.

After World War I, interest in chloropicrin shifted from its toxic effects to its harassing effects, causing it to see use in training by the **United States**, the Soviet Union, and others. The United States used chloropicrin with **chloroacetophenone** and chloroform in a military formulation designated "CNS." This mixture was declared obsolete in 1957. From 1955 to 1960, the USSR loaded chloropicrin into 250-kilogram bombs, which were stockpiled. These bombs were not declared by Russia following the entry into force of the **Chemical Weapons Convention (CWC)**, suggesting that either the stockpile had been destroyed or the bombs were retained for noncombat uses permitted by the CWC, such as domestic law enforcement purposes.

CHOKING AGENT. A substance that causes fluids to be released and accumulate in the air spaces and tissues of the lungs. The immediate sensation is that of choking. The accumulation of fluids in the lungs, known as *pulmonary edema*, makes breathing difficult. If it persists, air exchange—a principal function of the lungs—can cease, and death ensues. Examples of choking agents include **chlorine** and **phosgene**. *See also* DRY-LAND DROWNING.

CHOLINESTERASES. Enzymes that catalyze the breakdown of choline-containing compounds. **Organophosphorus nerve agents** inhibit these enzymes and thus are called anticholinesterases. Various cholinesterases can be found in humans; among the most important ones are acetylcholinesterase (AChE), found in the nervous system; red cell or erythrocyte cholinesterase, found in red blood cells; and plasma or serum cholinesterase, found in the blood plasma.

While all three types of cholinesterases are inhibited by organophosphorus nerve agents, the effects of AChE inhibition are the most readily experienced and noticed. Acetylcholine is a neurotransmitter; that is, it is a chemical that carries a nerve signal across the *synapse*, the tiny gap between two nerve cells. Once it has done its job, acetylcholine is broken down into acetic acid and choline, a process brought about by AChE. When AChE is inhibited, excess acetylcholine overstimulates the nervous system. This overstimulation causes involuntary motion in the skeletal muscles; excess secretions from glands in the nose, mouth, armpits, and elsewhere; and constriction of the gastrointestinal (GI) tract. The involuntary skeletal muscle motions include jerking, twitching, and ultimately convulsions. The eye muscles constrict, causing *miosis*, often one of the more noticeable early signs of nerve agent exposure. Excess secretions include a runny nose, salivation, and sweating. GI tract constriction causes cramps, nausea, vomiting, and diarrhea. If the hyperactivity persists, then the systems being stimulated will become fatigued and eventually will cease functioning. If enough systems shut down, death ensues.

Treatment for cholinesterase inhibition includes injecting atropine or various oximes. Atropine acts in a manner opposite acetylcholine; therefore, it affords symptomatic relief but does not reverse the cholinesterase inhibition caused by the organophosphorus nerve agent. Furthermore, overmedication with atropine can cause harm. Oximes, such as the chemicals 2-PAM-chloride and pralidoxime mesylate, are used to restore the normal activity of AChE. This treatment is effective, however, only if the person has received a "pretreatment" (for example, with pyridostigmine bromide) that inhibits a certain percentage of the AChE. This pretreated AChE can then be reactivated by the oxime following exposure to an organophosphorus nerve agent.

CIRCULAR ERROR PROBABLE (CEP). A standard estimate of the accuracy for munition delivery systems. It is defined as the radius of a circle in which one-half of the missile warheads, tube-launched projectiles (such as artillery shells and mortar rounds), or air-droppable munitions would land. CEP can be applied to calculate the number of **nuclear**, **biological**, or **chemical weapons (NBC)** needed for a particular effect.

CLASSES OF CHEMICAL WEAPONS. Various schemes have been used to classify **chemical weapons (CW)**. One involves using the physiological effects produced by the toxic chemicals in the CW. Categories within this type of classification scheme include **blood agents**, **choking agents**, **incapacitants**, **lachrymators**, **organophosphorus nerve agents**, **neurotoxins**, **vesicants**, and **vomiting agents**. A drawback to this scheme is that many toxic chemicals cause more than one type of physiological effect, making assignment to a single category problematic or impossible. Another disadvantage is that the categories might carry limited or no meaning to the military personnel responsible for selecting CW for use in combat.

This latter drawback might have inspired the second major system, which involves classifying the toxic chemicals according to their expected persistency when used in combat. This results in fewer categories (originally just two; later, three), making classification simpler, though not necessarily straightforward. In this scheme, the toxic chemicals were originally categorized as *persistent* ("stays around for a long time") or *nonpersistent* ("stays around briefly or not at all"). Later, some authorities inserted a third category, *semipersistent*, intermediate between the other two. The problem with using persistency for classification of CW is that persistency depends not only on intrinsic factors associated with the toxic chemical itself but also on the meteorological conditions associated with use of any chemical at the time it is used and on terrain. Under most battlefield conditions, **sulfur mustard** and **VX** would be expected to persist, while **phosgene** would remain effective briefly or not at all. But for many other chemicals, persistency will be heavily influenced by the weather and the terrain. Therefore, precise classification as persistent, nonpersistent, or semipersistent becomes difficult.

An alternative to classifying by physiological effects or persistency is to use an intrinsic property of the toxic chemical that will not vary, but is relative to the use of that chemical on that battlefield or by terrorists. The prime example of such a property is volatility—the tendency of a solid or liquid to pass into the gaseous state. In this scheme, a chemical might be classified as "high volatility" (such as phosgene), "intermediate volatility" (such as **sarin**, **soman**, and **tabun**), and "low volatility" (such as sulfur mustard, VX, and most **toxins**).

CLINTON PILE. *See* X PILE.

CLOUD CHAMBER EFFECT. The "cloud chamber effect" refers to a mist of tiny water droplets or condensation cloud that is temporarily formed around the fireball generated by a **nuclear weapon** explosion. This effect is produced by the expansion of air in the negative-pressure phase of the blast wave (a nuclear detonation produces a negative-pressure phase, followed by a positive-pressure phase, which is experienced as the shock wave). The drop in pressure brings about an equivalent drop in temperature, and as a consequence, any water vapor present condenses. *See also* BHANGMETER.

CLOUD-TOP HEIGHT. The maximum altitude reached by a mushroom cloud generated by a **nuclear weapon** explosion.

CN. *See* CHLOROACETOPHENONE.

COBALT BOMB. *See* DIRTY BOMB.

COCHRANE, THOMAS, LORD DUNDONALD. Cochrane, the 10th Earl of Dundonald, was a 19th-century British naval officer who advocated the use of **Greek Fire**–like compounds and, later, of **cacodylic acid** and sulfur against **Russian** forces during the Crimean War. His proposals were rejected, partly because the British government viewed the use of **chemical weapons (CW)** as unethical.

COCOM. *See* COORDINATING COMMITTEE FOR MULTILATERAL EXPORT CONTROLS (COCOM).

COMPLETENESS OF DESTRUCTION. The term used by the **Organization for the Prohibition of Chemical Weapons (OPCW)** to describe the extent to which any chemical warfare (CW) agent must be destroyed in order to satisfy **Chemical Weapons Convention (CWC)** requirements for destruction of such agents. There is consensus within the OPCW that any CW agent must be subjected to some process such that at least 99.99 percent of the original agent can be confirmed as having been destroyed. This level of completeness of destruction is referred to as "four nines." Some of the parties believe that completeness of destruction should entail destruction to "six nines," meaning that 99.9999 percent of the original CW agent can be confirmed as destroyed.

COMPREHENSIVE NUCLEAR TEST BAN TREATY (CTBT). On 6 September 1996, the **United Nations** General Assembly (UNGA) adopted the CTBT, banning all nuclear test explosions whether for weapons-related or peaceful purposes. The CTBT has been signed by more than 175 nations and ratified by more than 125 of them, but it has not entered into force. Entry into force requires ratification by 44 nations identified in Annex 2 to the CTBT. To date, of these 44, **North Korea**, **India**, and **Pakistan** have neither signed nor ratified the treaty, and another eight nations (**China**, Colombia, Congo, Egypt, Indonesia, **Iran**, **Israel**, and the **United States**) have signed the CTBT but not ratified it. The United States is currently declining to ratify it citing concerns over its verifiability. As of 2006, a Preparatory Commission (PrepCom) was continuing to develop the infrastructure and procedures to ensure that the Secretariat of the CTBT will be able to implement the treaty upon its entry into force, including carrying out on-site inspections. An International Monitoring System (IMS) to detect nuclear explosions has also been put in place to prepare for entry into force of the CTBT. The organization shares some seismic data from its IMS system with tsunami-monitoring stations in near real-time.

CONANT, JAMES BRYANT (1893–1978). U.S.-born chemist. Conant had a distinguished career as a scientist, educator, and government official. After obtaining his doctorate from Harvard University in 1916, he served in the U.S. Army **Chemical Warfare Service (CWS)**, commanding a Willoughby, Ohio, facility engaged in the then-secret task of making the novel chemical warfare agent **lewisite**. After a brief career in private industry, Conant returned to Harvard, serving on the chemistry faculty until 1933, when he was named president of the university. He served in this position until 1953. During World War II, Conant took on the additional roles of serving as a science advisor to the president of the **United States** and chairing the **National Defense Research Committee (NDRC)** of the **Office of Scientific Research and Development (OSRD)**. The NDRC directed U.S. scientific and technical efforts to meet the combat needs of World War II, including the **Manhattan Project** and similar projects on **chemical** and **biological weapons (CBW)**. In 1953, Conant was appointed U.S. high commissioner for the western zone of occupied **Germany**, becoming the first U.S. ambassador to West Germany in 1955. He served until 1957, and thereafter he pursued ways to improve secondary education, especially with regard to science and mathematics. *See also* BUSH, VANNEVAR.

CONDENSATION CLOUD. *See* CLOUD CHAMBER EFFECT.

CONFIDENCE-BUILDING MEASURE (CBM). Confidence-building measures are those taken to reduce concern over whether international security commitments are being observed. Such measures may include officer training exchange programs, the carrying out of on-site inspections, and overflights of one another's territory with aircraft equipped with approved photographic and other equipment.

CONVENTIONAL COMMITTEE. Russian Federation president Boris N. Yeltsin issued Presidential Decree No. 160, dated 19 February 1992, establishing the Presidential Committee on Problems of

Chemical and Biological Weapon Conventions, colloquially known as the Conventional Committee. It was established in part to address the concerns of the **United Kingdom** and the **United States** that elements of the Soviet offensive **biological weapons (BW)** program were continuing. The committee was, among other things, to "establish that development and implementation of biological programs in violation" of the **Biological and Toxin Weapons Convention (BTWC)** is "not permitted on the territory" of Russia. The committee was also charged with providing the Russian president, within one month, with "proposals for amplifying measures of openness and trust and expanding international cooperation within the framework" of the BTWC. The report was prepared by **Anatoly D. Kuntsevich**, the first chairman of the committee. It reportedly confirmed that the Soviet offensive BW program had not been fully dismantled. Kuntsevich was dismissed from the committee in early 1995 amid allegations that he had been involved in providing sensitive, proscribed chemicals to Syria, and Pavel Siutkin was named to replace him as chairman. The committee was disbanded in the late 1990s and replaced by the Munitions Agency. In 2004 the Munitions Agency was folded into the Federal Agency on Industry, which is subordinate to the Ministry of Industry and Energy of the Russian Federation. *See also* TRILATERAL PROCESS.

COOPERATIVE THREAT REDUCTION (CTR) PROGRAM. The Nunn-Lugar Cooperative Threat Reduction Program was established at the instigation of U.S. senators Richard Lugar and Sam Nunn in 1991. It is intended to fund nonproliferation and threat reduction assistance programs in the former Soviet Union. CTR activities include efforts to assist with the dismantlement of nuclear warheads, enhancements to the security afforded to biological pathogens to limit diversion of these materials into use in **biological weapons (BW)**, and the destruction of the Soviet stockpile of **chemical weapons (CW)**. The CTR program has spent more than $17 billion since its inception.

COORDINATING COMMITTEE FOR MULTILATERAL EXPORT CONTROLS (COCOM). The principal international organization responsible for coordinating restrictions on dual-use exports, from its founding in 1949 until 1994 when the organization was replaced by the **Wassenaar Arrangement**. *See also* NUCLEAR SUPPLIERS GROUP (NSG).

COUNTERPROLIFERATION. Actions taken to address the threat or use of **weapons of mass destruction (WMD)**. These measures include coercive (e.g., military) measures undertaken by a single state or limited number of states. Counterproliferation policies are often viewed as being at odds with multilateral arms control and disarmament regimes that are structured to operate, where possible, cooperatively on the principle of consensus.

CRITICAL MASS. The least mass of **fissionable** material that will allow a self-sustaining nuclear **chain reaction**. Any **nuclear weapon** must have a critical mass in order for the nuclear fuel to act as an explosive. *See also* DRAGON EXPERIMENT; PREINITIATION.

CRYOFRACTURE. In the context of the destruction of **chemical weapons (CW)**, cryofracture is a process involving freezing a CW into a solid (typically with liquid nitrogen) and then chopping it into pieces for further treatment, such as incineration. The process was envisioned as one that would minimize the danger that a munition would undergo unintended detonation during disassembly. It was tested on a pilot scale in the 1990s with limited success.

CS. An intensely irritating solid that causes profuse weeping and other effects typical of a **lachrymator**. It has been used widely as a **riot-control agent (RCA)**. The chemical name for CS is 2-chlorobenzilidene malononitrile ($C_{10}H_5ClN_2$), but it is widely known by the designation "CS," which honors two U.S. chemists, R. B. Corson and R. W. Stoughton. These Middlebury College, Vermont, scientists reported its synthesis and irritating properties in 1928.

CUBAN MISSILE CRISIS. The 1962 confrontation between the Soviet Union and the **United States** over the Soviet deployment of nuclear-tipped missiles in Cuba. On 16 October 1962, U.S. president John F. Kennedy convened a meeting at the White House to review photographic intelligence of the missile sites under construction. Kennedy then informed Soviet leader Nikita Khrushchev that the United States would not allow the sites to be completed and ordered a naval blockade of Cuba to prevent all Soviet ships, including some carrying what were believed to be nuclear warheads. The Soviet ships turned away from Cuba at the last moment several days later and, on 28 October, Khrushchev publicly announced that the USSR would dismantle the Cuban missile installations. The United States secretly agreed to remove its Jupiter missiles from Turkey.

Subsequent information from the Soviet side revealed a strong desire among some in the Soviet military to run the blockade and fire on U.S. warships. The Cuban Missile Crisis strengthened the Soviet leadership's view that it must achieve **nuclear weapon** parity with the United States in terms of number of weapons and the ability to deliver them against targets in the United States. It is also led to a conviction that the USSR must never again back down in such a situation. The crisis also contributed to Khrushchev's retirement and contributed momentum for concluding the 1963 **Limited Test Ban Treaty (LTBT)**. *See also* ABLE ARCHER '83.

CURIE. A common unit of measurement for radioactivity. One curie is equal to 37 billion **disintegrations** per second or 37,000,000,000 **becquerel**, the metric unit for measuring radioactivity. The unit, abbreviated "Ci," honors the Polish-French scientist Marie Curie (1867–1934), who is credited with coining the term *radioactive*. Curie and her husband Pierre (1859–1906) received the 1903 Nobel Prize in Physics in recognition of their investigations of radioactivity, sharing the award with Henri Becquerel. Marie Curie was also recognized with a second Nobel Prize, the 1911 award in Chemistry, for her discoveries of the elements radium and **polonium**.

CURVEBALL. A code name given to an otherwise anonymous **Iraqi** source. "Curveball" is credited as one of the principal sources for U.S. intelligence on the alleged existence of mobile **biological weapon (BW)** production facilities in Iraq. Any such BW facility (mobile or fixed) would have violated **United Nations (UN)** prohibitions regarding **weapons of mass destruction (WMD)**. Despite suspicion by intelligence officials such as Germany's Federal Intelligence Service (*Bundesnachrichtendienst*, BND) regarding the credibility of Curveball's information, U.S. officials used this information to support the case for attacking Iraq in 2003. Subsequent investigations in Iraq failed to validate the allegations of such a mobile BW facility. *See also* IRAQ SURVEY GROUP (ISG).

CYCLOSARIN. The discovery of **sarin** spurred the synthesis and testing of other **organophosphorus nerve agents** having a chemical structure nearly the same as that of sarin. Two such analogues were discovered and selected for use in **chemical weapons (CW)**: **soman** and O-cyclohexyl methyl phosphonofluoridate ($C_7H_{14}FO_2P$). This latter compound came to be known as cyclohexyl-sarin and, eventually, cyclosarin. The U.S. military gave it the military code name "GF." It was produced by **Iraq** during the regime of Saddam Hussein and used in a **binary chemical weapon** mixture with sarin in 122-mm rockets, 400-pound aerial bombs, and al-Hussein missile warheads. It is uncertain, however, whether any such chemical weapons were used in combat during the **Iran-Iraq War**.

– D –

DAGHLIAN, HARRY KRIKOR, JR. (1921–1945). U.S. physicist. On 15 September 1945, Daghlian died of acute radiation sickness, 24 days after an accident during an unauthorized "**Dragon Experiment**." His death is credited as the first peacetime nuclear **fission**-related fatality.

Daghlian was working in the Critical Assembly Group under **Otto Frisch** at Los Alamos, New Mexico. As part of its work, the group had determined that precisely arranging five layers of tungsten carbide bricks around a sphere of **plutonium**-239 reflected the neutrons being given off, thereby enabling the plutonium to achieve a critical reaction. Late on the evening of 21 August, Daghlian decided to conduct further experiments with the sphere and the bricks. He was working alone, in violation of policy mandating a two-person rule for any such work. After building four layers of the bricks, he dropped a brick near the sphere. The dropped brick reflected sufficient neutrons to allow the plutonium-239 to reach critical reaction. Recognizing the danger, Daghlian swept bricks away from the sphere, but not before an intense burst of radiation had escaped. Events proved that Daghlian had received a lethal dose of this radiation. U.S. Army private Robert J. Hemmerly (1916–1978), assigned to guard the plutonium and other sensitive materials, was seated nearby but was shielded from most of the radiation and survived. Contemporary news reports of Daghlian's death incorrectly attributed his death to chemical burns rather than acute radiation sickness. On 20 May 2000 during Armed Forces Day commemorations, a flagpole in Daghlian's hometown of New London, Connecticut, was dedicated to his memory. The marker at the base of the flagpole proclaims, "During an experiment gone awry, [Daghlian] became the first American casualty of the atomic age."

This claim may be in error. For instance, in September 1944 two **Manhattan Project** chemists, Peter N. Bragg Jr. and Douglas Paul Meigs, while working at the Philadelphia Navy Yard on a process to make **low-enriched uranium**, died from acid burns received when a uranium hexafluoride cylinder exploded, mixed with steam, and produced a cloud of hydrofluoric acid. In addition, various Americans were being held in Hiroshima as prisoners of war when it was bombed on 6 August 1945 and died either immediately from the bomb or shortly thereafter from the effects of the bomb, although the exact number of such victims remains uncertain. *See also* NATIONAL PEACE MEMORIAL HALL FOR ATOMIC BOMB VICTIMS; SLOTIN, LOUIS.

DALLES SALAD BAR INCIDENT, THE. *See* THE DALLES SALAD BAR INCIDENT.

DASHIELL, THOMAS RONALD (1928–1998). U.S. biologist and chemical engineer. Dashiell began work as a microbiologist at **Fort Detrick**, Maryland, in 1950 and continued to work there for 20 years. Following the 1969 decision by President Richard M. Nixon to end the U.S. **biological weapons (BW)** program, Dashiell was given overall responsibility for the project to destroy the U.S. inventory of BW at Fort Detrick. He then joined the Office of the Secretary of Defense in 1970 as a staff specialist in chemical technology and in 1984 became director of defense research and engineering for the Department of Defense.

DECOUPLING. A process in which a nuclear explosion is conducted in an underground, energy-absorbing cavity specifically designed to alter (mostly by muffling) the seismic signature characteristic of such explosions. As such, decoupling would be a means of subverting or frustrating seismic monitoring for **nuclear weapons** tests. This process has been considered by those specialists aiding in the development and implementation of nuclear arms control and disarmament agreements. The technical feasibility of decoupling is uncertain. *See also* COMPREHENSIVE NUCLEAR TEST BAN TREATY (CTBT).

DEFOLIANT. A substance used to destroy foliage. Defoliants include chemicals that overstimulate plant growth as well as those that desiccate the plant. They have been linked to chemical warfare (CW), although defoliants, because they cause direct harm to plants and only indirect or no harm to humans and animals, fall outside the coverage afforded by the **Chemical Weapons Convention (CWC)**. *See also* AGENT ORANGE; AMMONIUM THIOCYNATE.

DEOXYNIVALENOL. *See* TRICHOTHECENE MYCOTOXINS; YELLOW RAIN.

DEPLETED URANIUM (DU). Uranium that is depleted of the specific **isotope** uranium-235. DU has a smaller percentage of uranium-235 than is found in naturally occurring uranium. It is used for military purposes because it is very dense, can be machined at relatively low cost, and is available as a by-product of producing nuclear fuel and **nuclear weapons**. However, because it is low in uranium-235, it cannot be used as a fuel source for a nuclear weapon and has little or no radioactivity, making it unusable as a source in a **radiological dispersal device (RDD)**.

DEUTERIUM. The **isotope** of hydrogen having an atomic mass of two. Ordinary hydrogen has one electron, one proton, and a mass of one, whereas deuterium has one electron, one proton, and one neutron. Deuterium is a stable isotope, meaning that it does not undergo decay and is not radioactive. *See also* HEAVY WATER; TRITIUM.

DEW OF DEATH. A popular term for **lewisite**. **Amos Fries** of the U.S. Army **Chemical Warfare Service (CWS)** claimed to have originated the term.

DF. *See* M687 155-MM ARTILLERY PROJECTILE.

DIACETOXYSCIRPENOL. *See* TRICHOTHECENE MYCOTOXINS; YELLOW RAIN.

DIRECTORATE OF TUBE ALLOYS. In fall 1941, the British Department of Scientific and Industrial Research established a new division under the direction of W. A. Akers charged with overseeing the development of a **nuclear weapon**. For security reasons, the division was designated the Directorate of Tube Alloys. The British efforts on the nuclear bomb project came to be referred to by the Americans, British, and Canadians as "Tube Alloys" or "T.A." projects. *See also* ROTBLAT, SIR JOSEPH.

DIRTY BOMB. Designers of **nuclear weapons** recognized that incorporating certain metals into the bomb could enhance the fallout and residual radiation hazards following detonation. In particular, using stable (that is, nonradioactive) **isotopes** of cobalt as part of the bomb casing was found to be effective, because the intense radiation from the nuclear detonation converted some of the cobalt to radioactive isotopes. Certain cobalt radioisotopes remain radioactive for a long time, thereby adding to the health hazards for those exposed to the fallout as well as for those who might later enter areas affected by the blast. Such a weapon design was referred to as a "dirty bomb."

More recently, this term has changed its meaning from a nuclear weapon containing a stable isotope that might become radioactive during detonation to any conventional explosive device containing **radioactive material**. Consequently, "dirty bomb" has become synonymous with **radiological dispersal device (RDD)**, and the original meaning is often overlooked. *See also* SALTED WEAPON.

DISINTEGRATION. In a nuclear context, *disintegration* refers to the breaking up of an unstable atom, with the concomitant emission of radiation. This process is measured in disintegrations per unit time (most commonly, per second). The SI (metric) unit for disintegration is the **becquerel**. Other units used for this purpose include the **curie** and the **rutherford**.

DOBROKHIM. DobroKhim is an acronym from the Russian for Volunteer's Society of the Friends of Chemical Defense and Chemical Industry (*Dobrovol'noe obshchestvo pomoshchi druzey razviti khimii i oborony i promyshlennosti*), a volunteer patriotic organization that existed in the Union of Soviet Socialist Republics (USSR) from 1924 to 1925. The Cyrillic acronym is ДоброХим. It was established 19 May 1924 to encourage activities of the chemical industry and to foster knowledge of defense against chemical warfare (CW) among the youth of the Soviet Union. Russian chemist **Vladimir N. Ipatiev** is credited with suggesting its creation in a February 1924 note he sent to the Presidium of the USSR. On 23 May 1925, DobroKhim was merged with the Society of Friends of Aviation, forming **AviaKhim**.

DOMARADSKY, IGOR VALERYANOVICH (1925–). Russian microbiologist. Domaradsky is prominent for his research on *Yersinia pestis*, the causative agent for **plague**. In the 1960s, he worked in the Soviet **antiplague system** and, in the 1970s and 1980s, for the Soviet **biological weapon (BW)** program. He is a member of the **Russian** Academy of Medical Sciences and, as of 2003, was the chief research fellow at the Moscow Gabrichevsky G. N. Institute of Epidemiology and Microbiology. In 1995 he published his memoirs privately in Russia. These memoirs became the basis for *Biowarrier*, coauthored with Wendy Orent and released in the United States in 2003.

DRAGON EXPERIMENT. Designing **nuclear weapons** required precise knowledge of the quantity of **fissionable** materials needed for a **critical mass**. In 1944, Austrian-born physicist **Robert Otto Frisch**, by then a British citizen assigned to the **Manhattan Project** in the **United States**, suggested an experiment to determine this mass by getting as near as possible to a nuclear explosion without actually having one occur. Frisch's suggestion involved a configuration of **uranium**-235 having a hole in its center. A plug, also made of uranium-235 and having the exact dimension of this hole, would then be dropped through the hole. The plan was that the plug would travel through the larger configuration, reaching a critical reaction as it traveled through the mass. Then after the plug passed through the larger configuration, the reaction would abate. Because this experiment would come close to achieving a nuclear explosion, American physicist Richard Feynman (1918–1988) likened it to tickling the tail of a sleeping dragon. His observation led to the experiment being dubbed the "Dragon Experiment." Despite the danger, it was approved. On 18 January 1945, Frisch carried out his experiment and became the first person to determine the critical mass of uranium-235 experimentally. He repeated the experiment on 12 April 1945, this time using **plutonium**-239 to determine its critical mass. *See also* DAGHLIAN, HARRY KRIKOR, JR.; SLOTIN, LOUIS.

DRY-LAND DROWNING. Choking agents cause the lungs to fill with fluid, much like what happens during drowning. But unlike drowning, where the fluid comes from outside the body, choking agents cause the body to release the fluids internally. The effect is sometimes called "dry-land drowning."

DUBROVKA THEATER INCIDENT. *See* MOSCOW THEATER INCIDENT.

DUGWAY PROVING GROUND (DPG). U.S. entry into World War II prompted efforts to test **chemical weapons (CW)** and **biological weapons (BW)** for both offensive and defensive purposes. To best simulate combat environments, such testing needed to be done in the open atmosphere ("open-air testing"), requiring an extensive and sparsely populated area. A suitable site was found in west-central Utah, southwest of the Great Salt Lake and nearly 100 miles from Salt Lake City. The site was activated on 1 March 1942 as the U.S. Army Dugway Proving Ground. Today, the site continues to be operated as a military reservation, covering an area of nearly 1,000 square miles. Open-air testing of CW and BW was discontinued in the late 1960s, following an accidental release of **VX** that killed several thousand sheep in nearby **Skull Valley**. The **United States** abandoned offensive use of BW in 1969, and any BW stored at DPG were destroyed shortly thereafter. All CW were removed from DPG in the late 1970s.

DULL SWORD. The Department of Defense uses DULL SWORD as a code name for identifying and reporting a **nuclear weapon** safety deficiency. *See also* BENT SPEAR; BROKEN ARROW; EMPTY QUIVER; FADED GIANT; NUCLEAR EMERGENCY SEARCH TEAM (NEST); SPAIN HYDROGEN BOMB INCIDENT.

DUNNAGE. Chemical weapon (CW) destruction processes generally involve a separation of the weapon components into different types of materials, which are then treated and disposed of through specialized processes. The three main types of materials are agent fill, explosive components, and *dunnage*, which refers to metal parts and miscellaneous other solid materials such as packing materials.

DUSTY AGENT. The term to describe **chemical weapons (CW)** in which a toxic chemical has been absorbed onto particulate matter, such as a silicate or diatomaceous earth. Two perceived benefits to a dusty agent are cited. The first is that it slows the release of an otherwise highly volatile substance, thereby increasing the persistence of that toxic substance. This benefit was derived by **Germany** during World War I when it introduced the use of **phosgene** absorbed onto pumice, a highly porous igneous material. That experience may have inspired Ferdinand Flury, a key participant in Germany's World War I–era CW program, to develop **Zyklon B**, in which highly volatile hydrogen cyanide is absorbed on kieselguhr (a diatomaceous earth). The second perceived benefit is that a dusty agent places the toxic substance in a form more likely to foul the filter of a protective mask or to be carried through protective clothing by a bellows effect. Concern over dusty agents reemerged in the 1990s with speculation that **Iraq** was developing such agents.

DWARF DUD. A **nuclear weapon** that does not provide the specified yield when used under normal operating parameters. *See also* ABSOLUTE DUD; PREINITIATION.

– E –

EDGEWOOD ARSENAL. U.S. entry into World War I carried with it a need to prepare for chemical warfare (CW). One outgrowth of this need was the establishment of Edgewood Arsenal in Maryland. A presidential proclamation issued in October 1917 allowed the government to take possession of Gunpowder Neck, a parcel of land along the west bank of the Chesapeake Bay some 20 miles north of Baltimore. Shortly thereafter, the first U.S. **chemical weapon (CW)** filling plant was built there, and the army designated the site Gunpowder Reservation, Maryland. In early 1918, the name was changed to Edgewood Arsenal. By 1920, Edgewood Arsenal housed all U.S. CW activities, including the **Chemical Warfare Service (CWS)** schools, a research division for selecting and testing new chemical weapons, and a gas mask production plant. Eventually, the site became the Edgewood Area of the Aberdeen Proving Ground, with two locations being separated by the Bush River. Edgewood Arsenal has been redesignated many times. Its most recent name is the Edgewood Chemical Biological Center, although many continue to refer to it as Edgewood Arsenal.

EIGHT-BALL. A one-million-liter metal sphere located at **Fort Detrick**, Maryland is commonly referred to as the "Eight-Ball." The 40-foot-high, gastight sphere was constructed during the period when the **United States** had an active offensive biological warfare (BW) program, and it provided a novel means of testing BW munitions and agents, such as *Coxiella burnetii* (the causative agent of **Q fever**) and *Francisella tularensis* (the causative agent of **tularemia**). The Eight-Ball has not been used since 1969, when the United States renounced its offensive BW program. The surrounding building was destroyed by a fire in 1974, but the sphere survived. Its uniqueness as an aerobiology test chamber was recognized some years later when it was placed on the U.S. National Registry of Historic Places.

EINSTEIN, ALBERT (1879–1955). German-born physicist. Einstein is generally regarded as one of the greatest scientists ever. He is well known for originating a general theory of relativity of space and time and for demonstrating the equivalence between energy and mass, as simply expressed in the famed equation E=mc^2. Einstein played an important role in the development of **nuclear weapons**.

In 1933, Einstein departed his native **Germany** owing to his opposition to the Nazi regime and settled in the **United States**, eventually gaining U.S. citizenship. At the urging of Leo Szilard, he wrote a letter on 2 August 1939 to President Franklin Delano Roosevelt in which he described how **uranium**, through a **fission chain reaction**, could be used as a powerful source of energy and that the power of such reactions could be harnessed, making possible "extremely powerful bombs." In the letter, Einstein stated his belief that the German government was actively supporting research along such lines and urged that the U.S. government do likewise.

Roosevelt did not respond immediately to the letter, and it took two months before decisions were made. In particular, the letter prompted Roosevelt to establish what came to be known as the **Uranium Committee**, thereby setting in motion events that would culminate in the establishment of the **Manhattan Project** and the successful development of nuclear weapons. Einstein also expressed deep concern about the moral implications of the development and use of nuclear weapons. *See also* ALSOS MISSION; EINSTEIN-RUSSELL MANIFESTO; GROVES, LESLIE RICHARD.

EINSTEIN-RUSSELL MANIFESTO. On 9 July 1955, a manifesto was issued in London in the names of philosopher and mathematician Bertrand Russell (1872–1970) and physicist **Albert Einstein**, who had died three months earlier. It described the dangers posed by **nuclear weapons** to the future survival of mankind and urged that scientists "should assemble in conference to appraise the perils that have arisen as a result of the development of **weapons of mass destruction (WMD)**." This helped lead to the establishment of the **Pugwash Conference on Science and World Affairs**.

ELECTROMAGNETIC PULSE (EMP). The explosion of a **nuclear weapon** creates a strong pulse of electromagnetic radiation, referred to as an electromagnetic pulse. It is capable of damaging electrical or electronic systems, including command-and-control systems such as surveillance and communications equipment. Efforts have therefore been undertaken to shield or "harden" such systems against EMP.

EMPTY QUIVER. The Department of Defense uses EMPTY QUIVER as a code name for identifying and reporting the loss, seizure, or theft of a **nuclear weapon** or nuclear component. *See also* BENT SPEAR; BROKEN ARROW; DULL SWORD; FADED GI- ANT; NUCLEAR EMERGENCY SEARCH TEAM (NEST); SPAIN HYDROGEN BOMB INCIDENT.

ENDO SEI-ICHI. Endo headed the **chemical** and **biological weapon (CBW)** program of **Aum Shinrikyo**. He had trained as a microbiol- ogist, but failed to complete his doctoral work. Despite his lack of ex- tensive training in chemistry, he was placed in charge of manufactur- ing the **sarin** used in the March 1995 attack in the Tokyo metro. In 2002, a Japanese court sentenced Endo to death.

ENEWETAK ATOLL. An isolated Pacific Ocean island group in the northwest corner of the Marshall Islands. The atoll consists of a col- lection of 40 low, sandy islets surrounding a lagoon. Following World War II, the Marshall Islands became part of the Trust Territory of the Pacific, with administration given to the **United States**. In 1947, the United States selected Enewetak as a site for testing **nuclear weapons**. The U.S. government forced inhabitants to move to Uje- lang, another atoll within the Marshall Islands group. The United States conducted 43 nuclear weapon tests at Enewetak prior to ceas- ing use of this site. The tests left Enewetak contaminated by radia- tion, but the United States conducted removal and cleanup of the ra- diation to a safe level, and in 1980, inhabitants were permitted to return and resettle the atoll.

ENOLA GAY. On 6 August 1945, the **United States** became the first nation to use a **nuclear weapon** in combat when the "**Little Boy**" bomb was dropped over Hiroshima, Japan. U.S. Army Air Corps colonel Paul W. Tibbets commanded and flew the B-29 aircraft that carried this bomb. As was typical in the Army Air Corps, the aircraft commander had the privilege of naming the aircraft, and Tibbets named his plane *Enola Gay* in honor of his mother. The call sign for the *Enola Gay* during the mission was "Dimples Eight Two." *See also BOCK'S CAR*; 509TH COMPOSITE GROUP.

ETHIOPIA. Italy invaded Ethiopia on 3 October 1935. The invasion and subsequent fighting would have important but unfortunate consequences for the **League of Nations** and the **Geneva Protocol of 1925**. Early in the conflict, charges emerged that Italy was using **chemical weapons (CW)**. Initially denying these charges, the Italian government soon implicitly confirmed them by maintaining that the Geneva Protocol failed to prohibit CW use in reprisal against other illegal acts of war. Ethiopian emperor Haile Selassie addressed the Assembly of the League of Nations on 30 June 1936, providing details of the Italian use of CW but offering no concrete proof. In 1937, Italy withdrew from the League of Nations, in part over the Ethiopian conflict.

Although contemporary accounts regarding CW in Ethiopia lacked clarity regarding the types and amounts of agents used, more recent research has unearthed documents substantiating use of **sulfur mustard**, including extensive use of aerial bombs and spray tanks containing this agent. Use of other, less toxic agents also seems likely, but documentation is weak. Some Italian archival information is available, as well as information derived from European military observers attached to Ethiopian and Italian armies.

– F –

FADED GIANT. The Department of Defense uses FADED GIANT as a code name for identifying and reporting accidents or incidents involving nuclear reactors or other radiological events. *See also* BENT SPEAR; BROKEN ARROW; DULL SWORD; EMPTY QUIVER; NUCLEAR EMERGENCY SEARCH TEAM (NEST).

FALLOUT. Radioactive materials that are created by a nuclear explosion and that fall to earth following this explosion. Some of these materials are residual radioactive materials from the nuclear explosive itself, though most are likely to be created by the explosion.

FARM HALL. As World War II was drawing to an end in Europe, the governments of Canada, the **United Kingdom**, and the **United States** attempted to seize the data, equipment, and scientists from **Germany**'s **nuclear weapons** program. This material was important both to learn the actual state of that program and to deny the fruits of it to the Soviet Union. The attempt largely succeeded. For example, a small nuclear reactor near Haigerloch in Germany's Black Forest region was located, and all its **heavy water** and **uranium** ore were captured and sent to the United States. Scientists and engineers from this program were detained, and a select group of 10 was sent to England, where they were housed at the Farm Hall estate, near Cambridge. From 3 July 1945 until 3 January 1946, the conversations among Erich Rudolf Bagge, Kurt Diebner, Walther Gerlach, **Otto Hahn**, Paul Harteck, **Werner Heisenberg**, Horst Korsching, Max von Laue, Carl-Friederich von Weizsäcker, and Karl Wirtz were recorded surreptitiously, translated, and analyzed by American, British, and Canadian experts. In February 1992, the British government confirmed the existence of the Farm Hall transcripts and made them available to the public. *See also* ALSOS MISSION.

FAST NEUTRON. A neutron traveling at a high velocity or having a high state of energy. Fast neutrons are important in the context of nuclear reactors and **nuclear weapons**. For example, fast neutrons produced during **fission** have energies in the range of 1 million to 14 million electron-volts (eV). By contrast, a **thermal neutron** has an energy of around 0.025 eV—which means a fast neutron has approximately 10 billion times the energy of a thermal neutron.

FAT MAN. The second **nuclear weapon** used in warfare was dropped by the **United States** on 9 August 1945 over Nagasaki, **Japan**. The bomb, nicknamed "Fat Man," used **plutonium** in an **implosion**-type **fission** bomb. This design called for an ordinary explosive charge to crush a hollow sphere of plutonium into a beryllium-**polonium** core. Although the mass did not change as a result of the initial explosion, the volume of the core decreased, creating conditions needed for a **supercritical** process. A fission reaction followed, resulting in an explosion of several thousand tons of **TNT-equivalent**.

The original design of the Fat Man bomb was officially designated "model 1561." While this design proved successful, it suffered from various defects, as did its successor, the Mk-III Fat Man bomb. Both were aerodynamically unstable at high speeds, causing the bomb to wobble during its drop when it reached terminal velocity approaching the speed of sound. To minimize the wobble, drag plates, which would slow down the bomb during its drop, were installed in the tail box, but these drag plates proved unreliable. For instance, a modified Mk-III bomb missed its target (a battleship) by more than 1,000 feet during the **Operation Crossroads** Able nuclear test. This miss was attributed to wobble, perhaps resulting from a collapsed or missing drag plate. The design for the Mk-III Fat Man required that each bomb be assembled by hand. This assembly took an average of two days for a 39-person team of specialists at Los Alamos, New Mexico. Once assembled, the bomb could remain combat-ready for only 48 hours, after which it had to be partially disassembled to recharge or replace batteries that powered the bomb's fuses.

To address these deficiencies and others with the Mk-III, development of an improved bomb—the Mk-IV—began in 1947. When deployed in 1949, the Mk-IV Fat Man had improved aerodynamic properties that eliminated the wobble problem. Moreover, the new design permitted the nuclear explosive core to be inserted during flight, enhancing in-flight safety and adding considerably to the service life of each bomb. The Mk-IV remained in the U.S. nuclear weapon stockpile until 1953. By the time the last of the Fat Man series of bombs was removed from service in 1953, about 250 of them had been produced.

The Fat Man series also holds the distinction of being the first U.S. nuclear weapons to be dropped accidentally—on 13 February 1950, when a U.S. B-36 aircraft had to jettison a Mk-III bomb casing and dummy core (that is, a core containing no functional nuclear explosive) after three of the aircraft's six engines failed. The casing exploded on impact with the ocean. Two months later, on 11 April 1950, a U.S. B-29 aircraft carrying a Mk-IV bomb casing and nuclear explosive core crashed three minutes after taking off from Kirkland AFB, New Mexico.

Three more incidents involving U.S. bombers carrying Mk-IV bombs happened that same year: crashes on 13 July and 5 August, and an in-flight emergency on 10 November when a Mk-IV bomb casing was jettisoned. In all cases, the nuclear explosive core had not been inserted into the Mk-IV bomb casing, and none of the accidents resulted in a nuclear detonation. *See also* AMOS; ARCHIE; GADGET; LITTLE BOY; THIN MAN.

FERTILE ISOTOPE. A fertile **isotope** or fertile material is a substance that is not itself **fissionable** by **thermal neutrons** but can be converted into **fissile material**. This conversion is typically carried out by irradiation in a nuclear reactor. There are two basic fertile isotopes: thorium-232 and **uranium**-238. When these fertile materials capture neutrons, they are converted into the fissile isotopes uranium-233 and **plutonium**-239, respectively.

15TH DIRECTORATE. The 15th Directorate of the Soviet Ministry of Defense (MOD) was established in accordance with a 25 June 1973 decision of the Soviet Communist Party Central Committee (No. 444–138) and an 11 January 1973 MOD decree (No. 99). The directorate was responsible for implementing the offensive Soviet **biological weapon (BW)** program in violation of the **Biological and Toxin Weapons Convention (BTWC)**.

FIFTH WASHINGTON CONFERENCE ON THEORETICAL PHYSICS. Many of the world's leading physicists gathered in Washington, D.C., in late January 1939. Among those attending were Hans Bethe, **Niels Bohr**, Enrico Fermi, Edward Teller, and Isidor Rabi. Bohr arrived from Denmark, carrying with him a note from **Robert Otto Frisch** that gave news of the conclusions that Frisch and his aunt, **Lise Meitner**, had reached regarding certain experiments conducted by **Otto Hahn** and Fritz Strassmann in **Germany**. The experiments were described in the 6 January 1939 issue of the German scientific journal *Naturwissenschaften* and thus were known to many of the conference attendees. But the work of Meitner and Frisch would not be published for another two weeks, in the 11 February 1939 issue of the British scientific journal *Nature*. Their work correctly interpreted the Hahn-Strassmann experiments as evidence of nuclear **fission**.

When Bohr announced this news of proof of nuclear fission at the conference, the attendees recognized the seriousness of this announcement. The work proved **Albert Einstein**'s Special Theory of Relativity (as embraced by his famed equation, $E=mc^2$), meaning that enormous quantities of energy could be released by splitting the atom. Moreover, the work showed that Germany was ahead in this critical area of nuclear physics and caused concern for many conference attendees that Germany might be developing a fission-type weapon.

FIRST GAS REGIMENT. When the **United States** entered World War I in April 1917, the military recognized a need to prepare for offensive and defensive operations involving **chemical weapons (CW)**. Accordingly, on 15 August 1917, the War Department issued General Order No. 108, establishing the 30th Engineer Regiment ("Gas and Flame") to provide capabilities similar to those of the British **Special Brigade**: troops capable of waging chemical warfare and training other troops in how to survive in a chemically contaminated environment. On 28 June 1918, the regiment was redesignated the First Gas Regiment. Regimental personnel began arriving in **France** in January 1918, and by that March, the entire regiment was committed to frontline duties. The First Gas Regiment became known as the "Hell Fire Regiment" in reference to the chemical, **smoke**, and **incendiary** rounds it used, and the troops came to be called "gassers" and "hell fire boys." In March 1919, as part of U.S. demobilization following the war, the First Gas Regiment was disestablished. Its functions were eventually assumed by the army's **Chemical Warfare Service (CWS)**.

FISHMAN, YAKOV MOISEEVICH (1887–1962). Soviet chemist and army officer. Fishman directed the Military Chemical Directorate of the Red Army from its creation in 1925 until 1937, when he was purged. He was an important figure in the development of the Soviet **chemical weapons (CW)** program during the period between the world wars.

Born in Odessa, Fishman was educated in Italy, receiving a doctorate in chemistry around 1912. He fought in the Russian Revolution and joined what became the Red Army, where he published several texts on CW and advanced rapidly. In 1928, he was named to head both the Military-Industrial Department of the Red Army and the Institute of Chemical Defense. Fishman was instrumental in implementing joint **German**-Soviet CW cooperation under the terms of the 1922 Treaty of Rapallo. He traveled periodically to Germany to discuss technical cooperation measures in his capacity as a deputy military attaché and traveled to other countries, including Italy in 1934, to exchange views and information on CW. Such international travel and, especially, his dealings with Germany contributed to his being purged in 1937.

In 1937, he was arrested, tried, convicted, stripped of all honors and military rank, and imprisoned for sabotage. During a portion of his imprisonment, he continued to contribute to the Soviet CW program by working in a Moscow **sharashka** that supported an organization now known as **GosNIIOKhT**. He was released in August 1954, rehabilitated in January 1956, and ultimately restored to his rank of major general. *See also* BERSOL.

FISSILE MATERIAL. A fissile **isotope** is one that readily undergoes **fission** after absorbing a neutron. There are four basic fissile materials: **plutonium**-239, plutonium-241, **uranium**-233, and uranium-235. Uranium-235 is the only naturally occurring fissile material. *See also* FERTILE ISOTOPE.

FISSION. Fission is the process of splitting of the nucleus of an atom into two or more lighter nuclei. Man-made fission occurred first in the laboratory of Italian physicist Enrico Fermi at some point in 1934, although Fermi and others were uncertain whether fission had taken place. In December 1938, German radiochemists **Otto Hahn** and Fritz Strassmann, working in their Berlin laboratory, bombarded **uranium** with neutrons. They observed results that they correctly interpreted as breaking up of the uranium nucleus into two roughly equal pieces. Furthermore, they deduced that the total products of their experiment had less mass than that of the original uranium nucleus. This deduction confirmed the prediction of **Albert Einstein's** famed equation $E=mc^2$—that the experimentally observed loss of mass resulted from the conversion of mass into energy. These results were known to Hahn's former colleague **Lise Meitner** and her nephew, **Otto Frisch**. Meitner and Frisch calculated the energy released and concluded that a previously undiscovered kind of process was at work when the uranium nucleus was split in this manner. Frisch borrowed a term used by biologists for cell division ("binary fission") and labeled the process of splitting an atom "fission." *See also* FIFTH WASHINGTON CONFERENCE ON THEORETICAL PHYSICS.

FISSION-FUSION-FISSION WEAPON DESIGN. One design concept for achieving a **thermonuclear** explosion calls for using three stages, in which a **fission** event initiates a **fusion** process that, in turn, feeds a fission event. This concept was used successfully with the "**Mike**" device, in which the first stage involved fission of **plutonium**-239 that in turn caused a liquid **deuterium** secondary stage to undergo nuclear fusion. High-energy neutrons produced by this fusion caused fission of **uranium**-235 in the third and final stage.

509TH COMPOSITE GROUP. The safe and precise delivery of **nuclear weapons** on **Japanese** targets during World War II presented severe technical aviation challenges. Each aircraft would have to drop a single bomb weighing about five tons, then execute a sharp turn while climbing to reduce its vulnerability to blast and flash effects when the bomb detonated. To address such challenges, the U.S. Army Air Force designated the 509th Composite Group to develop and practice the necessary tactics. Initially formed in Fairmont, Nebraska, as part of the 20th Air Force, the 509th Composite Group was activated on 17 December 1944 at Wendover Army Air Field, along the Utah-Nevada border. Dummy munitions, modeled after the design of the "**Fat Man**" bomb and dubbed "pumpkins" because of their size, shape, and mustard color, were loaded onto modified B-29 Superfortress aircraft. The crews would drop a single 5,500-pound pumpkin to test their skills at hitting a target from high altitude and adjusting to the effects of dropping such a large weight all at once, then execute a sharp turn and climb. The 509th Composite Group was the world's first nuclear bomber command, and its aircraft flew the successful missions against Hiroshima (**Enola Gay**) and Nagasaki (**Bock's Car**).

FIZZLE. *See* PREINITIATION.

FLYING COW; FLYING LAVATORY. The "flying cow" and "flying lavatory" were **chemical weapons (CW)** that could disseminate their contents without explosives. The former was designed for dispersing **thickened sulfur mustard**; the latter, for unthickened or regular sulfur mustard. Both designs apparently originated in the **United Kingdom** with **Porton Down** scientists and engineers, although the U.S. Navy received a patent in 1969 for the flying cow. The advantage to both weapons was that they overcame limitations of explosively disseminated CW, especially the flashing and burning of the toxic chemicals that occurs frequently when the weapon detonates. The design also facilitated broader distribution of the toxic chemical filling in the weapon than that typically seen for an explosively disseminated weapon. Another CW design that came out of Porton Down was the "squirt," a high-pressure device that projected two gallons of liquid hydrogen cyanide in a stream to a range of 25 yards.

FOOT-AND-MOUTH DISEASE (FMD). A contagious, febrile viral disease affecting cloven-hoofed animals such as cattle, goats, sheep, and swine. The effects of FMD are debilitating and can be fatal, especially if secondary infections occur or if the animal cannot feed. During World War II, Germany carried out research on FMD in a facility on the island of Rheims. This facility was later dismantled by occupying forces from the Soviet Union but it was eventually reestablished by East German authorities. U.S. intelligence inferred Soviet interest in FMD virus as a possible biological warfare agent partially based on this reestablishment. In the **United States**, FMD virus is deemed exotic, meaning it has been eradicated domestically, except on **Plum Island**, where the United States conducts research with the FMD virus and maintains the North American FMD vaccine repository.

FORT DETRICK. The **United States** selected Fort Detrick, located in Frederick, Maryland, as the site for its **biological weapon (BW)**

laboratories during World War II. At the time of the selection, the facility was known as Camp Detrick; previously, it had been designated the Detrick Airfield and belonged to the Maryland National Guard. Presently, Fort Detrick is home to the U.S. Army Medical Research Institute of Infectious Diseases (USAMRIID), as well as other laboratories engaged in biological research. *See also* ANTHRAX; BOYLES, WILLIAM ALLEN; EIGHT-BALL.

49 METAL. Personnel assigned to the **Manhattan Project** referred to **plutonium**-239 as "49 Metal." This designation was derived by combining the last digit of the atomic number for plutonium (94), the last digit of the **isotope** (239), and the fact that plutonium is a metal.

FOULKES, CHARLES HOWARD (1875–1969). Career British Army officer who served chiefly with the Royal Engineers. Following the initial use of **chemical weapons (CW)** by **Germany** in April 1915, Foulkes was tasked with establishing a unit that would specialize in offensive chemical warfare operations. Originally called the Special Companies, this unit expanded into the **Special Brigade** with nearly 260 officers and 5,900 enlisted personnel. Foulkes eventually rose to the rank of major general, retiring prior to World War II.

FRANCE. As of 2006, France was believed to have approximately 350 nuclear warheads. France is a party to the **Chemical Weapons Convention (CWC)** and is continuing to destroy **old chemical weapons (OCW)** dating from World War I. France is believed to have had offensive programs for **biological weapons (BW)** and **chemical weapons (CW)** through at least the 1960s. When **Germany** invaded France in World War II, the Germans uncovered documents and materials regarding its BW program following its 1940 capture of four French laboratories located outside Paris at the Poudrerie Nationale du Bouchet. The scope of this BW program raised concerns in Germany over its relative lack of preparedness for BW attacks and inspired the creation of the **Blitzableiter Committee**.

FREEZING-POINT DEPRESSANT. In the context of **chemical weapons (CW)**, a freezing-point depressant is an **adjuvant** that can be added to lower the freezing point of the final mixture, thereby extending the range over which the CW will be a liquid rather than a solid. The use of freezing-point depressants became common in the period following World War I. The need for such depressants was especially keen with regard to **sulfur mustard**. Pure sulfur mustard solidifies around 57°F (14°C), and in its solid form, its combat effectiveness is often less than that of the liquid. Additionally, the ballistic characteristics are less predictable for a CW filled with sulfur mustard if it has partially or wholly solidified. Various freezing-point depressants for sulfur mustard were tried, and some of the more effective ones were substances that were themselves CW agents, such as **lewisite**. The Americans gave the combination of sulfur mustard and lewisite the military code name "HL."

FRIES, AMOS A. (1873–1963). U.S. Army officer. Fries was instrumental in organizing the U.S. military for chemical warfare (CW) operations during World War I and in promoting the need for strong CW capabilities in the decades following that war. A West Point graduate and commissioned officer in the U.S. Army Corps of Engineers, Fries arrived in France with the American Expeditionary Forces (AEF) in June 1917. In mid-August, AEF commanding general John J. Pershing appointed Lt. Col. Fries "engineer in charge of gas." A month later, the Gas Service, AEF, was established, with Fries as its chief, promoted to colonel. When the **Chemical Warfare Service (CWS)** was established in spring 1918, Fries was appointed to command its Overseas Division and promoted to brigadier general.

In the aftermath of the war, the chief of staff of the U.S. Army advocated dissolving the CWS, testifying to this effect before Congress. Other important military figures, including General Pershing, expressed similar sentiments. Fries felt otherwise, testifying before Congress on the need for maintaining strong offensive and defensive CW capabilities. He used his official position with the CWS to encourage CWS veterans, chemists, and industrialists to lobby Congress on maintaining the CWS. Fries's view of CW is captured in a line from a lecture he gave to the U.S. Army General Staff College on 11 May 1921: "We believe that all opposition to chemical warfare today can be divided into two classes—those who do not understand it and those who are afraid of it—ignorance and cowardice." His lobbying efforts, while unconventional in a serving officer, succeeded. In 1920, Congress approved making the CWS a permanent part of the army, and Fries was appointed its first peacetime chief. He remained in this position until 1929, when he retired at the rank of major general. Fries is buried in Arlington National Cemetery, Virginia.

FRISCH, ROBERT OTTO (1904–1979). Austrian-born physicist. Frisch made several fundamental contributions to nuclear physics, especially to the development of **nuclear weapons**. In 1939, Frisch and his aunt, **Lise Meitner**, provided the first mathematical explanation for the results of **Otto Hahn** and Fritz Strassmann and correctly identified that these results confirmed the process of nuclear **fission**, a term chosen by Frisch himself.

Later that same year, Frisch visited England, remaining there when World War II broke out. British authorities recognized his genius for nuclear physics and permitted him to continue his research in England despite his **German** citizenship. In 1943, he was granted British citizenship and became a member of the team of British scientists who traveled to the **United States** to join the **Manhattan Project**. Project personnel were generally known by their first names only, their surnames being omitted as a security precaution, and Frisch found that many others assigned to this project were also named Robert. Therefore, he took to being called by his middle name, Otto, to avoid confusion and would continue to be known in American circles more often by that name.

Assigned to **Site Y** (which would later be designated the Los Alamos National Laboratory), Frisch conducted the **Dragon Experiment**, determining the critical mass of **uranium**-235, and later of **plutonium**-239. Both results were essential to developing the nuclear weapons that were used successfully against **Japan** in August 1945.

Following the war, Frisch returned to England and briefly headed the nuclear physics division of the Atomic Energy Research Establishment, Harwell. In 1947, he accepted a position as the Jacksonian Professor of Natural Philosophy, Cambridge University, where he remained until retiring in 1972.

FUCHS, KLAUS EMIL JULIUS (1911–1988). German-born physicist. Fuchs was a member of the **German** Communist Party studying at the University of Kiel when the Nazis came to power in 1933. He departed for the **United Kingdom**, where he continued his studies. Interned as a German national after the outbreak of World War II, Fuchs was released to do nuclear research. He became a British citizen in 1942 and then was sent to the **United States** to work on the **Manhattan Project**, the American-led effort to develop a **nuclear weapon**. He arrived at **Site Y** (Los Alamos) in 1944 and was part of the team that developed "**Little Boy**" and "**Fat Man**." After the war, he returned to the United Kingdom, becoming head of the physics department of the Atomic Energy Research Establishment, Harwell. Eventually, he came under suspicion as a spy for the Soviet Union. On 23 January 1950, Fuchs confessed that he had been passing classified information about nuclear weapons to the Soviets since 1943. Shortly thereafter, he was sentenced to 14 years' imprisonment. Released in 1959, he went to the German Democratic Republic (East Germany), where he was granted citizenship and appointed deputy director of the Central Institute for Nuclear Research, Rossendorf.

FUSION. In the context of **nuclear weapons** and nuclear reactors, fusion refers to the process of combining of two light-nuclei atoms into a single heavier nucleus. This process is accompanied by the release of a substantial amount of energy. The light-nuclei atoms typically used in this process are **deuterium** and **tritium**. *See also* GEORGE; HYDROGEN BOMB.

– G –

G8 GLOBAL PARTNERSHIP. The Group of Eight (G8) Global Partnership against the Spread of Weapons and Materials of Mass Destruction, commonly shortened to "Global Partnership," was established in June 2002. It is a mechanism similar to the **Cooperative Threat Reduction (CTR) Program**, in that it funds projects on disarmament, nonproliferation, **counterproliferation**, counterterrorism, and nuclear safety. It is scheduled to run through 2012. The G8 members and the European Commission are to allocate $20 billion, half of which is to be provided by the **United States**. Much of the focus is on securing or destroying **nuclear**, **biological**, and **chemical (NBC) weapons** in the former Soviet Union and ensuring that expertise in such weapons is not misused.

GA. *See* TABUN.

GADGET. The first successful detonation of a nuclear device took place at 5:29:45 a.m. Mountain War Time, 16 July 1945, at the **Trinity Test Site**, New Mexico. The spherically shaped device, about six feet in diameter, weighed five tons but exploded with a blast of about 20,000 tons **TNT-equivalent** (20 kilotons). Scientists working on the **Manhattan Project** had named the device "Gadget." It was an **implosion device**, with **plutonium** as the nuclear explosive. One similar in design, nicknamed "**Fat Man**," would be dropped over Nagasaki, **Japan**, on 9 August 1945. *See also* BIG BROTHER; LITTLE BOY.

GAMMA RADIATION. A form of electromagnetic radiation produced by **radioactive decay** or other nuclear or subatomic events. Gamma radiation, also known as "gamma rays," can have energies of between a few thousand and 10 million electron-volts. Gamma radiation is a form of ionizing radiation, as are **alpha particles** and **beta particles**, but gamma radiation is more penetrating and less ionizing. It is distinguished from **x-rays** by the source of the radiation. By convention among scientists, the term *gamma radiation* is applied to high-energy electromagnetic radiation produced by nuclear transitions, while the term *x-ray* is applied to similar radiation produced by energy transitions due to accelerating electrons. Some overlap in energy transitions is possible, however, between the low-energy region of gamma rays and the high-energy region of x-rays.

GAS CENTRIFUGE. Only certain **isotopes** of **uranium** are useful in producing **nuclear weapons** or for generating electricity. Typically, the desired isotope is uranium-235, which must be separated from uranium-238, the predominate form of uranium in its ores. One method of separation involves the use of a centrifuge, a machine that uses spinning cylinders and the accompanying centrifugal force to effect separation. In the case of uranium enrichment, uranium is converted to uranium hexafluoride (UF_6), which is a gas. Fluorine is selected for this purpose because it exists in nature as a single isotope. Gaseous UF_6 is fed into a centrifuge (called a gas centrifuge, because the substance being worked with in the rotating cylinders is a gas). The UF_6 containing the slightly heavier uranium-238 isotope concentrates at the walls of the centrifuge, while that containing the uranium-235 concentrates at the center.

China, **Japan**, **Pakistan**, **Russia**, and the **United Kingdom** are among the nations that use this uranium enrichment process. The prospects for diversion of gas centrifuge technology can be illustrated by **Iraq**, which used this process as part of its covert nuclear weapons program. Iraq initiated a gas centrifuge program in 1987. After laboratory trials and various designs, it launched mass production of gas centrifuges in 1989 at Al-Furat. Centrifuges were installed at Al-Rashdiya Engineering and Design Center, which also housed the UF_6 production facilities. *See also* GASEOUS DIFFUSION; IRAQ SURVEY GROUP (ISG).

GASEOUS DIFFUSION. Atoms and molecules that have the same momentum will have different velocities, proportional to the inverse of their atomic or molecular masses. Therefore, lower-mass atoms and molecules will travel at higher velocities than the higher-mass atoms and molecules. This property is used to practical effect as a means of separating **isotopes** through gaseous diffusion. As with separation using a **gas centrifuge**, gaseous diffusion separation is used to enrich **uranium** using gaseous uranium hexafluoride (UF_6). UF_6 is injected into a diffusion cell, with many such cells being connected in a cascade arrangement. Cells are connected by tiny pores through which diffusion takes place. The lighter uranium-235 UF_6 travels faster than does the heavier uranium-238 UF_6, which is the predominant species. If the diffusion were permitted to continue uninterrupted, no enrichment would take place. Instead, the diffusion between two cells is allowed to continue only until half the total gas has diffused, when the first half is pumped to the next stage and the remaining half is returned to the previous stage.

Successful enrichment by gaseous diffusion requires substantial electric power and thousands of diffusion cells. As part of the **Manhattan Project**, the **United States** designed and built a gaseous diffusion plant at **Site X** (Oak Ridge, Tennessee). That plant had approximately 4,000 diffusion stages. A similar approach to uranium enrichment has been used in **China, France,** and **Russia. Iraq**'s covert **nuclear weapon** program during the regime of Saddam Hussein initiated a gaseous diffusion enrichment effort in 1982. Facilities were constructed at the Al-Tuwaitha Nuclear Research Center and the Al-Rashdiya Engineering and Design Center. *See also* CALUTRON.

GB. *See* SARIN.

GB2. *See* M687 155-MM ARTILLERY PROJECTILE.

GD. *See* SOMAN.

GELBKREUZKAMPFSTOFFE. *See* YELLOW CROSS AGENT.

GENEVA PROTOCOL OF 1925. Prior to 1997 and 1975, respectively, the Geneva Protocol of 1925 was the principal international legal instrument dealing with **chemical weapons (CW)** and **biological weapons (BW)**. The Geneva Protocol did not, however, prevent the stockpiling of CW, and many of the major powers attached conditions to their instruments of ratification. For example, some parties asserted that a state would not consider itself bound by the obligations of the protocol if first attacked by CW or BW or if involved in a military conflict with states or coalitions not party to the protocol. BW agents have not generally been stockpiled in large quantities partly because of the limited shelf life of many agents and the fact that large quantities may be quickly grown using small initial quantities of agent. Later large-scale BW programs relied on putting into place standby production and filling capacities. The full name of the Protocol is the Protocol for the Prohibition of the Use in War of Asphyxiating, Poisonous, or Other Gases, and of Bacteriological Methods of Warfare. The **Chemical Weapons Convention (CWC)** and **Biological and Toxin Weapons Convention (BTWC)** both reaffirm the principles and objectives of the Geneva Protocol. *See also* ETHIOPIA; HAGUE CONFERENCES OF 1899 AND 1907.

GEORGE. The **United States** conducted the world's first successful detonation of a **thermonuclear** device when a device code-named

"George" exploded at **Enewetak Atoll** on 9 May 1951. George was estimated to have a yield of slightly more than 200 kilotons **TNT-equivalent**. The detonation validated the **Teller-Ulam concept**. *See also* BRAVO; JOE; MIKE.

GERMANY. *Biological Weapons Program.* Germany developed and used **biological weapons (BW)** during World War I. This use appears to have been restricted to small-scale releases targeting livestock rather than humans and may have lacked backing at higher levels of the German government. **Anthrax, glanders**, and perhaps other pathogens were used, sometimes by injecting animals with the pathogens, expecting the disease-causing microbes to contaminate others. Available documentation verifies attempted use or actual use at sites in Argentina, Norway, and the **United States** (all of which were officially neutral in the war at the time of the use). Less well-verified episodes involved attempts to infect animals with anthrax and glanders along the French front and in Romania; to infect mules with glanders during the British campaign in Mesopotamia; and to spread **plague** in St. Petersburg, **Russia**. The record of World War I fails to suggest that any BW use by Germany proved to be significant militarily.

BW development in Germany appears to have ceased at the end of the war, although certain German scientists (most notably **Hugo Stoltzenberg**, his wife, and his sister-in-law) prominently promoted using BW. Research into BW was restarted during World War II following the capture in 1940 of four French laboratories, located outside Paris at the Poudrerie Nationale du Bouchet, that had been engaged in BW-related work. Materials and documents seized at these laboratories spurred Germany to establish the **Blitzableiter Committee**. A comprehensive BW program was initiated, but it was intended most likely as a defensive measure in the event the Allies used such agents. The **ALSOS Mission** uncovered no evidence to suggest that Nazi-era Germany engaged in a serious offensive BW program.

No evidence has emerged suggesting either that the Federal Republic of Germany (West Germany) or the Democratic Republic of Germany (East Germany) had a significant BW program. Germany is a party to the **Biological and Toxins Weapons Convention (BTWC)**. *See also* BLOME, KURT; FOOT-AND-MOUTH DISEASE (FMD); HIMMLER, HEINRICH; KLIEWE, HEINRICH.

Chemical Weapons Program. Germany developed and used **chemical weapons (CW)** on a large-scale during World War I. Germany's interest in the offensive use of CW took root early in the war, with a view toward using them to overcome the debilitating losses and stalemate of trench warfare. Various CW developments were attempted, including the **Ni-Shell** and the **T-Shell**; neither proved successful. On 22 April 1915, this situation changed dramatically with the release of **chlorine** against French and Canadian positions around **Ypres**, Belgium. Thereafter, **Fritz Haber**, the architect of the chlorine attack, effectively took control of Germany's CW program and oversaw the development of other types of CW, including the first use of **phosgene** (1915), the arsenical **blue cross agents** (1917), and **sulfur mustard** (1917). The contribution of CW to the outcome of World War I continues to be debated, but undoubtedly the use of such weapons by all sides in that war was inspired by its first large-scale use by Germany.

Germany continued its CW program following World War I, in contravention of the **Treaty of Versailles**, initially by covert means involving joint cooperation with Russia. By the start of World War II in 1939, Germany was actively testing novel chemicals for potential use in combat. This led to the development of CW using the newly discovered **nitrogen mustards** and, more importantly, **organophosphorus nerve agents**. While the Allies were also aware of the nitrogen mustards, they failed to uncover the nature of the organophosphorus nerve agents until the end of the war.

Although Germany stockpiled CW for use in World War II, it does not appear to have employed CW as part of military operations. In the aftermath of the war, the stocks were either destroyed or transported to other nations. There is no evidence that Germany pursued a CW program after 1945, although West Germany permitted the United States to stockpile such weapons on its soil. In 1990, these U.S. stocks were transported to the Pacific Ocean island of Johnston Atoll as part of **Operation Steel Box**. Germany is a party to the **Chemical Weapons Convention (CWC)**. *See also* ACONITINE; BERSOL; JAEGER, AUGUST; PIONEER REGIMENTS 35 AND 36; SCHRADER, GERHARD; STOLTZENBERG, HUGO; TOMKA; ZYKLON.

Nuclear Weapons Program. At the outbreak of World War II in 1939, many scientists perceived Germany as having a head start toward developing a **nuclear weapon**. This perception was shaped by several factors. First, many outstanding physicists, including Nobel Prize–winning physicists Philipp Lenard, Max von Laue, Johannes Stark, **Otto Hahn**, Fritz Strassmann, and, especially, **Werner Heisenberg** were present in the country. Second, nuclear **fission** was discovered in 1938 by Hahn and Strassmann.

Concerns about a German lead in developing a nuclear weapon were well founded. In 1939, the German government had started a nuclear physics office, commonly called the **Uranium Club**. Also in 1939, Heisenberg was conscripted into this office, and physicist Paul Harteck wrote the War Office to recommend investigating nuclear explosives. Later, Harteck wrote Adolf Hitler directly to ask for a meeting, which was granted. During that meeting, Harteck emphasized the military possibilities of nuclear fission. Finally, Germany possessed a supply of **uranium** ore owing to its March 1939 occupation of Czechoslovakia, which allowed ready German access to the mines in St. Joachimsthal. When Germany occupied Norway in May 1940, the Allied powers grew even more concerned because Germany now had control over the world's only **heavy water** plant, **Norsk Hydro**.

By the end of the war, however, Germany had made only limited progress toward building a weapon and even failed to produce a sustaining **chain reaction**. Germany's nuclear weapon program had poor leadership. Its totalitarian regime also engendered regimentation at all levels in government and academia and therefore discouraged the creativity and free exchange of ideas necessary to advance understanding of nuclear physics and overcome the engineering obstacles inherent in building a nuclear weapon. This regimentation differed sharply from the more cooperative and informal attitudes that characterized work on the **Manhattan Project**. In addition, Heisenberg, who had become de facto director of the program by 1942, was ill-suited for this role. Despite his brilliance, he was a theoretician, rather than an experimentalist, and he was unable to cope with the severe organizational and technical challenges involved in coordinating the development of a nuclear weapon in wartime Germany. Furthermore, the Nazi-inspired rejection of relativity as **"Jewish physics"** constituted a significant barrier to scientists working on the program, where adherence to the Nazi political agenda was of paramount importance.

Germany was unwilling to make the necessary investment in its nuclear program. A massive investment of money, material, and manpower would have been required to build a nuclear weapon, as demonstrated by the U.S. experience with its Manhattan Project, and Germany never came close to making a comparable investment. The German government either failed to understand the magnitude of the effort required or lacked sufficient will to make such an investment, preferring instead to invest in other wartime projects such as rockets and jet aircraft.

The physicists in the program also committed a number of important technical errors, placing the German program on a more difficult developmental path while incorrectly rejecting others that would have proved more fruitful. Germany was never able to achieve a self-sustaining chain reaction and fell far short of producing the necessary amount of **fissile material** required to manufacture a nuclear weapon. *See also* BOTHE, WALTHER; FARM HALL.

GF. *See* CYCLOSARIN.

GILCHRIST, HARRY LORENZO (1870–1943). U.S. Army officer. During World War I, Gilchrist served as medical director of the **Chemical Warfare Service (CWS)** in the American Expeditionary Forces (AEF). After serving as the commander of the American **Typhus** Expedition to Poland in 1919, he returned to the **United States**, where he served in the CWS as chief of medical research at **Edgewood Arsenal**. He was appointed to succeed Maj. Gen. **Amos Fries** as chief of the CWS, serving in this capacity from 28 March 1929 until 16 May 1933.

Gilchrist was an ardent supporter of **chemical weapons (CW)** in the 1920s and 1930s. He advocated a view that use of CW in combat was a more humane method of warfare than was use of conventional weapons, citing statistics he diverted from studies of World War I casualties. These statistics, however, are questionable, because precise identification of combat casualties is problematic. Gilchrist also gained prominence in the 1920s for promoting the use of **chlorine** to treat or prevent colds, pneumonia, tuberculosis, and other respiratory illnesses. This notion inspired a short-lived chlorine-parlor fad in the United States.

GLANDERS. Glanders is a highly contagious disease caused by the bacterium *Burkholderia mallei*. The disease occurs principally in horses, mules, donkeys, and other solipeds and is found occasionally in other quadrupeds and, rarely, in humans. Glanders spreads through direct contact with infected animals and through contact with nasal discharges from these animals. Therefore, animals foraging and watering from the same sources as infected animals can themselves become infected. Human infections are now rare and are seen primarily in laboratory personnel working with the organism or in persons working with infected animals. Historically, the primary means of controlling glanders was to destroy infected animals, to discard possibly contaminated feed and water, and to disinfect affected premises. As a result, glanders can have important economic consequences. When donkeys, mules, and horses were important sources of transport for militaries, an outbreak of glanders could hamper military operations. This situation may have spurred interest in using glanders as a **biological weapon (BW)**.

During World War I, Germany is believed to have used glanders, as well as **anthrax**, on several occasions, including operations undertaken in the **United States** during 1914–1915 when the United States was officially neutral in the war. The military significance of such use during that war in the United States and elsewhere seems limited, although the record is unclear.

The extremely contagiousness and the lack of effective treatments other than slaughtering affected animals made glanders of concern to most militaries, causing it to be studied extensively. For example, **Japan** experimented extensively with glanders through its **Unit 731** beginning in the mid-1930s. These experiments included open-air trials in which the causative agent, *B. mallei*, was released. But it is uncertain whether Japan released glanders as a BW prior to the end of World War II.

GOSNIIOKHT. GosNIIOKhT is an acronym from the **Russian** for the State Scientific Research Institute for Organic Chemistry and Technology, the most recent name for a Moscow-based institute. The Cyrillic acronym is ГосНИИОХТ. From its founding in 1924, GosNIIOKhT has served as a key research and development institute for **chemical weapons (CW)** and CW destruction. For example, it developed a two-stage neutralization-based destruction technology that has been adopted by the Russian government to be used to destroy its stockpile of **organophosphorus nerve agents**. *See also* SHIKHANY.

GOUDSMIT, SAMUEL ABRAHAM (1902–1978). Dutch-born Jewish physicist and amateur Egyptologist who immigrated to the **United States**. Goudsmit served as the chief scientific officer of the World War II–era **ALSOS Mission**. In that capacity, he oversaw the technical evaluation of the **nuclear**, **biological**, and **chemical (NBC) weapon** programs in **Germany**. In recognition of his work, he was awarded the U.S. Medal of Freedom, the Order of the British Empire, the Max Planck Medal of the German Physical Society, and the American Institute of Physics's Karl T. Compton Award for Distinguished Statesmanship in Science. *See also* PASH, BORIS T.

GRAM-NEGATIVE; GRAM-POSITIVE. Danish bacteriologist H. C. J. Gram (1853–1938) developed a method for staining bacteria for light-based, microscopic analysis—a highly useful technique given the fact that bacterial cytoplasm is essentially colorless. After being dried and heated on a glass slide, a bacterial sample is stained with crystal violet, washed in a special iodine solution called "Gram's iodine," washed with an ethanol-based decolorizer, and finally flooded with safrinine, a red dye. After undergoing these steps, *Gram-negative* bacteria become red in color, while *Gram-positive* bacteria remain blue (from the crystal violet stain). In addition to preparing samples for microscopic viewing, the Gram-stain technique also allows one to make general distinctions (i.e., whether the microorganism is Gram-positive or Gram-negative) between types of microorganisms according to their function.

GRAY. The International System of Measurement (SI) unit for absorbed dose of ionizing radiation, abbreviated "Gy." One gray equals the energy in joules absorbed by one kilogram of irradiated material. Although gray is the preferred unit for reporting doses of ionizing radiation in the technical literature, many users prefer the more familiar units **rad**, **rem**, and **roentgen**. The unit honors Louis Harold Gray (1905–1965), an English physicist whose research into the effects of radiation on living organisms was fundamental to establishing the field of radiobiology.

GREEK FIRE. An **incendiary** mixture reportedly invented about 670 by the Syrian Callinicus for the Byzantine emperor Constantine Pogonatus. The invention was a development for military use against wooden ships. The composition of Greek fire is unknown. However, it is believed to have been partly composed of sulfur, resin, pitch, and some sort of oil. It may also have contained calcium phosphide or calcium carbide, either of which will ignite on contact with water. Greek fire was successfully used in naval engagements for several centuries before its composition was lost to history. It is often cited as an early example of a **chemical weapon (CW)**, although it might be more properly considered an incendiary.

GREEN CROSS AGENT. As its use of **chemical weapons (CW)** increased in World War I, **Germany** decided it needed an improved means of marking shells to make it easier for artillerymen to know they were using the proper CW. The military hit upon the scheme of colored crosses that would both differentiate chemical shells from conventional high explosives and distinguish among the various possible chemical fills. The first such designation was "green cross agent" (*Grünkreuzkampfstoffe*), used for asphyxiating or **choking agents** such as **chlorine**, **chloropicrin**, and **phosgene**. Other designations were **blue cross agent**, for arsenic-containing sternutators such as diphenylchloroarinse; **yellow cross agent**, for blister agents such as **mustard gas**; and **white cross agent**, for **lachrymators** such as bromoacetone and **chloroacetophenone**. *See also* VARICOLORED CROSS.

GREEN SALT. Some processes for enriching **uranium** involve an intermediate step in which uranium dioxide is converted to uranium tetrafluoride (UF_4), a green crystalline compound commonly called "green salt." This compound is then converted to uranium hexafluoride (UF_6), a volatile gas used in **isotopic** separation processes to yield uranium-235. *See also* GAS CENTRIFUGE; GASEOUS DIFFUSION; THERMAL DIFFUSION.

GROSSE ÎLE. Grosse Île is a small island in the St. Lawrence River, downstream from Quebec City, Canada. During World War II, Grosse Île became an important site for collaborative **biological weapon (BW)** work conducted by Canada and the **United States**. **Anthrax**

and **tularemia** were produced and loaded into munitions on this island. Grosse Île was also the site of a facility for the testing and production of a vaccine against the virus responsible for rinderpest, a highly contagious disease of livestock. The facility was later transferred to the Canadian Department of Agriculture.

GROUND ZERO. *See* ZERO POINT.

GROVES, LESLIE RICHARD (1896–1970). Career officer in the U.S. Army Corps of Engineers. As head of the **Manhattan Project**, Groves played a key role in the successful U.S. effort to develop a **nuclear weapon**. Groves was instrumental in establishing the **ALSOS Mission**. After World War II, he was named commanding general of the Armed Forces Special Weapons Project, the joint nuclear energy and nuclear weapons organization for the army and navy. Groves was promoted to the temporary rank of lieutenant general, retiring one month later to work in the private sector. In 1962, he released *Now It Can Be Told: The Story of the Manhattan Project*. He is buried in Arlington National Cemetery, Virginia.

GROWTH REGULATOR. A substance capable of accelerating or retarding the growth of plants by either increasing or decreasing the rate of cell division, respectively. Examples include hormones. Such substances can be used as **anticrop agents** or **defoliants**.

GRUINARD ISLAND. An island located in the Scottish Highlands, in Gruinard Bay near the mainland along the west coast. During World War II, the **United Kingdom** became concerned that **Germany** might use **anthrax** as a **biological weapon (BW)**. Consequently, British scientists from **Porton Down** tested anthrax-laden bombs on Gruinard Island, then referred to as "X-base." Sheep were tethered nearby to permit the effectiveness of the bombs to be determined. Afterward, all surviving sheep were destroyed and disposed of on the island. Some carcasses managed to get swept away into Gruinard Bay, however, spreading anthrax onto the mainland and resulting in deaths in local livestock. Efforts to decontaminate the island failed, and the island was quarantined.

In 1986, the United Kingdom attempted to disinfect those portions of the island suspected of harboring anthrax spores. This task was accomplished by removing topsoil in the most heavily contaminated areas, then applying a solution of 280 tons of formaldehyde dissolved in some 2,000 tons of sea water. The solution was sprayed across the entire 520-acre island. Subsequent testing showed the island to be free of contamination. On 24 April 1990, a British minister took down the quarantine markers, and civilians were permitted to visit it again.

GRÜNKREUZKAMPFSTOFFE. *See* GREEN CROSS AGENT.

GULF WAR SYNDROME (GWS). Thousands of veterans from the **United States** and the **United Kingdom** who served with the military in the 1991 Persian Gulf War have experienced a collection of symptoms that has been labeled Gulf War Syndrome. These symptoms include chronic fatigue, difficulty concentrating, memory loss, fevers, rashes, diarrhea, sleep loss, heart conditions, nausea, breathing difficulties, and polyarthralgia. A common element among service personnel who suffer from these various conditions is their military service in the Gulf region. No causal link between such service and GWS has been proven, despite more than 10 years of research and analysis. Some observers have suggested that the GWS sufferers are victims of exposure to **chemical weapons (CW)**, **biological weapons (BW)**, or both that were released intentionally or accidentally from **Iraqi** stockpiles later found to have existed at the time of the war.

GUN-TYPE NUCLEAR DEVICE. One design for a **nuclear weapon** involves propelling one subcritical mass of **fissile material** toward a second subcritical mass. The concept is straightforward, although the engineering and physics needed for the design to succeed are complex. Once the two masses are in the proper configuration, **critical mass** is achieved and a nuclear detonation results. In early development of this type of nuclear weapon, an actual gun-tube was used to both separate the masses and provide a path for the one mass to be propelled toward the second. This design was used for the "**Little Boy**" bomb and was thought to be sufficiently straightforward that firing of a test device was not required. Such thinking proved correct, as witnessed by the successful detonation of Little Boy over Hiroshima. *See also* IMPLOSION DEVICE.

– H –

HABER, FRITZ (1868–1934). German-born chemist. Haber is credited with inventing the Haber-Bosch process, permitting ammonia to be synthesized directly from the nitrogen in air. His early 20th-century invention is essential for producing abundant and relatively inexpensive synthetic fertilizers and earned Haber the 1918 Nobel Prize in Chemistry. The process proved essential to **Germany** during World War I by providing a direct means of making explosives, eliminating its dependence on imported nitrates. Haber also played a key role in Germany's development and use of **chemical weapons (CW)** and is seen by some as central to the introduction of CW onto the modern battlefield. Germany's initial CW designs in late 1914 and early 1915 proved ineffective when used in combat, with the releases going largely unnoticed by the intended victims. In early 1915, Haber used his influence with the German government to get the military to adopt a different approach. Rather than incorporating irritating substances, such as xylyl bromide or a sneezing powder, into conventional artillery shells, lethal **chlorine** gas would be released directly from cylinders. In order to be effective, this approach required favorable winds as well as a massive array of cylinders.

Such conditions were achieved near **Ypres**, Belgium, on 22 April 1915, when nearly 6,000 cylinders were opened, and a chlorine cloud caught the French defenders unprepared. Thereafter, Haber continued to play a leadership role in the German CW program, causing him to be named as a prospective war criminal to be tried at war's end. Such a trial never came to pass, and Haber returned to his role as director of the Kaiser Wilhelm Institute for Physical Chemistry and Electrochemistry in Dahlem, near Berlin. He remained in this position until 1933 when the incoming Nazi regime made it difficult for him to continue, owing to his Jewish heritage. He departed Germany, dying in Switzerland in 1934, where he is buried. *See also* HAGUE CONFERENCES OF 1899 AND 1907; PIONEER REGIMENTS 35 AND 36.

HAGUE CONFERENCES OF 1899 AND 1907. An international peace conference was convened in 1899 by Tsar Nicholas II of **Russia** at The Hague, Netherlands, where delegates attempted to reach agreement regarding methods and means of conducting war. Among the topics discussed was chemical warfare (CW), although these words were not the terminology then in use. A final agreement, signed by assorted nations, including **Germany**, and known as the 1899 Hague Convention Respecting the Laws and Customs of War on Land, contained the declaration that all parties to the Convention agreed to "abstain from use of all projectiles the sole object of which is the diffusion of asphyxiating gases." A follow-on peace conference was held at The Hague in 1907. The 1899 Convention was expanded to include a declaration that "it is especially forbidden to employ poison or poisoned weapons." The expanded Convention faltered. When Germany ushered in the modern age of CW in 1915, it was careful to avoid the use of projectiles, choosing instead to use cylinders containing **chlorine**. Apparently Germany felt that this choice would avoid the prohibition contained in the 1899 Convention. Germany's position, however, carried no weight with the Allies, who viewed the 1915 CW attack as a violation of the laws and customs of war. *See also* CHEMICAL WEAPONS CONVENTION (CWC); GENEVA PROTOCOL OF 1925.

HAHN, OTTO (1879–1968). German chemist. In 1938, Hahn and his collaborator, radiochemist Fritz Strassmann (1902–1980), provided the experimental results crucial to the discovery of nuclear **fission**. Their work, coupled with the equally important mathematical proof offered by their colleague **Lise Meitner** and her nephew **Robert Otto Frisch**, greatly influenced efforts by **Germany**, the **United Kingdom**, and the **United States**—among others—to develop **nuclear weapons** and to harness nuclear power for peaceful pursuits. Hahn and Strassmann shared the 1944 Nobel Prize in Chemistry in recognition of their work on nuclear fission, although the seminal contributions of Meitner and Frisch with regard to a rigorous mathematical proof of fission were ignored by the Nobel Prize Committee.

Hahn began his career studying in Germany as a chemist, obtaining a doctorate in organic chemistry at the University of Marburg in 1901. He was greatly influenced, however, by work he undertook in 1904–1905 in the laboratory of Sir William Ramsay at the University of Cambridge in England. Ramsay was interested in the newly discovered phenomenon of radioactivity and set Hahn to work purifying a crude **radium** preparation. While doing so, Hahn isolated a previously unidentified radioisotope, which he labeled "radiothorium." Inspired by this work, Hahn went to McGill University in Montreal, Canada, where he spent 1905–1906 working in the laboratory of Ernest Rutherford, whose recently published text, *Radio-activity*, provided an essential guide to what was then the state-of-the-art in this field. While working at McGill, Hahn discovered another radioisotope, radioactinium. In 1907, he accepted a position at the Kaiser Wilhelm Institute of Physical Chemistry and Electrochemistry, Dahlem. He was joined almost immediately by Meitner, and the two of them would collaborate over the next 30 years until she was forced to flee because of her Jewish heritage.

Hahn's early work on radioactivity was interrupted by World War I, when he served as an officer and **chemical weapons (CW)** specialist, serving on both the Eastern and Western Fronts. However, he was still able to find time during the war to collaborate with Meitner, and this led to the 1917 discovery of the element protactinium, an achievement they shared with two other teams of researchers working independently. Hahn and Meitner had sole claim, however, to the first isolation of the isotope protactinium-231.

The significance of nuclear fission was recognized by the government of Nazi Germany, which set up a group to study exploiting it for military purposes. Hahn, however, was permitted to continue his research on more fundamental problems. At the end of World War II in Europe, Hahn and nine other German nuclear scientists were taken to England and interned at **Farm Hall** in an effort to determine how far the Germans had progressed in developing a nuclear bomb. While interned, he learned of the successful detonation of a nuclear bomb over Hiroshima and was greatly affected by this event.

Returning to Germany, Hahn was elected president of the Max Planck Society for the Advancement of Science, the successor to the Kaiser Wilhelm Society. He became a spokesman for science, campaigning against further development and testing of nuclear weapons. *See also* PIONEER REGIMENTS 35 AND 36.

HALABJA ATTACK. Iraqi forces used **chemical weapons (CW)** against the Kurdish population of the northern Iraqi town of Halabja in March 1988. There are differing views on what toxic chemical or chemicals were used. Some of the victims appeared to show signs of cyanide poisoning. If the Iraqis had used impure **tabun**, this would explain the symptoms seen of exposure to both **organophosphorus nerve agents** and some form of cyanide, because sodium cyanide is used in synthesizing tabun, and an impure final product might have been contaminated with unreacted sodium cyanide. The Iraqis may have also used a nerve agent together with a cyanide compound such as hydrogen cyanide.

HANLON, JOSEPH T. On 28 July 1918, 2nd Lt. Joseph T. Hanlon was the first officer of the U.S. 30th Engineer Regiment to die from enemy action during World War I. The U.S. Army operated a **chemical weapon (CW)** field testing facility near Chaumont, France, during the war and renamed it Hanlon Field following his death. *See also* FIRST GAS REGIMENT.

HD. *See* SULFUR MUSTARD.

HEAVY WATER. A form of water in which **deuterium** replaces ordinary hydrogen. Compared to normal water, water formed from oxygen and deuterium has a greater mass—that is, is heavier. During World War II, scientists working on **nuclear weapon** programs investigated the suitability of heavy water to "moderate" or slow down neutrons as a method of controlling **fission chain reactions**. However, graphite control rods or "piles" were found to be more suitable as moderators than was heavy water, and interest shifted to using these rods instead. *See also* ALSOS MISSION; LIGHT-WATER REACTOR; MANHATTAN PROJECT; NORSK HYDRO PLANT; NUCLEAR PILE.

HEEL. The sludge accumulating naturally inside **chemical weapon (CW)** munitions or storage containers. The presence of heels harms the ballistic and handling characteristic of munitions. Heels also pose engineering and technical challenges when affected munitions and storage containers must be destroyed, as they are often resistant to chemical destruction techniques and form areas in which toxic chemicals might be entrained.

HEISENBERG, WERNER (1901–1976). German physicist. Heisenberg is admired as a brilliant theoretician, but his legacy has become clouded by questions regarding his collaboration with the Nazis on **Germany**'s **nuclear weapon** program. Doubts over what actually transpired during his September 1941 meeting with **Niels Bohr** have added to these questions. Heisenberg is credited as the creator of quantum mechanics, for which he received the 1932 Nobel Prize in Physics, and he is the eponym of "Heisenberg's Uncertainty Principle," which holds that the more precisely the position of subatomic particles is determined, the less precisely their momentum is known. This principle has profound implications for determining the behavior of atoms. In 1937, Heisenberg was branded a traitor in an SS newspaper article for embracing "**Jewish physics**." He was exonerated shortly thereafter by SS leader **Heinrich Himmler**, perhaps owing to their childhood friendship. Heisenberg became prominent in the **Uranium Club** in the late 1930s, and by 1942 he was de facto director of Germany's program to develop a nuclear weapon. However, his brilliance as a theoretician failed to translate into expertise as an experimentalist, and his wartime efforts to make a sustained nuclear **chain reaction** failed, as did Germany's wartime efforts to develop nuclear weapons. *See also* BOHR-HEISENBERG CONVERSATION.

HELSINKI COMMISSION (HELCOM). The Ad Hoc Working Group on Dumped Chemical Munitions of the Baltic Marine Environmental Protection Commission began in 1992 as a series of meetings among countries with an interest in **chemical weapons (CW)** that had been disposed of in the Baltic Sea. The group took the informal name "Helsinki Commission" or "HelCom" after the location of its first meeting and its secretariat. Results of that meeting led to additional sessions to consider the problem of **sea dumping** of CW. The HelCom's national experts found that approximately 40,000 tons of munitions—having an estimated 12,000 tons of toxic chemicals—had been disposed by dumping into the Baltic prior to 1948. The U.S. delegation informed other delegates that there was no evidence for the existence of an agreement between the **United States** and the Soviet Union to dump **German** CW in the Baltic during 1944 to 1948, and the British delegation said that the **United Kingdom** did not dump CW in the Baltic after World War II. The HelCom report recommended that the dumped CW not be recovered, owing to the likelihood that such recoveries might result in large discharges of toxic chemicals if munitions were to break apart.

HERBICIDE. A substance that is toxic to plants and can be used to destroy unwanted vegetation, especially weeds, grasses, and woody plants. Herbicides can be inorganic chemicals, such as **ammonium thiocyanate**, or organic chemicals, such as 2,4-dichlorophenoxyacetic acid (2,4-D) and 2,4,5-trichlorophenoxyacetic acid (2,4,5-T), which were used in **Agent Orange**. Herbicides generally fall outside the regime of **chemical weapons (CW)** controlled by the **Chemical Weapons Convention (CWC)** unless they are used as a method of warfare. *See also* ANTICROP AGENTS.

HIGHLY ENRICHED URANIUM (HEU). Uranium having a uranium-235 **isotope** content of 20 percent or greater is referred to as highly enriched. When the uranium-235 content reaches or exceeds 90 percent, then the material is regarded as **weapons-grade** HEU or, simply, weapons-grade uranium. *See also* LOW-ENRICHED URANIUM (LEU).

HIMMLER, HEINRICH (1900–1945). Nazi German official. Himmler rose to power with the Nazi regime in **Germany**, eventually being named to head the SS (*Schutzstaffel*). He used his power to exonerate physicist **Werner Heisenberg**, who had been accused of practicing **"Jewish Physics"** and was in danger of having to alter his research. The **ALSOS Mission** identified Himmler as someone who was strongly in favor of pursuing an offensive **biological weapon (BW)** program. Most of Himmler's specific activities in this area appear to have been confined to authorizing experimental work to be carried out on concentration camp inmates—despite directions from Adolf Hitler that all BW research was to be for defensive purposes and that experiments were not to be conducted on inmates. *See also* ZYKLON.

HIROSHIMA. *See ENOLA GAY*; LITTLE BOY; NATIONAL PEACE MEMORIAL HALL FOR ATOMIC BOMB VICTIMS.

HIRSCH, WALTER (1897–1950). Austrian chemist and a **German** Army officer during World War II. Hirsch was deeply involved in evaluating **chemical** and **biological weapon (CBW)** activities of the Soviet Union. Following the war, he was tasked by the **United States** to prepare an extensive report on Soviet CBW capabilities. Hirsch died while completing this assignment, but his report became a standard reference for Western intelligence assessments of the Soviet work in this area during the Cold War.

HL. *See* FREEZING-POINT DEPRESSANT.

HN-1; HN-2; HN-3. *See* NITROGEN MUSTARD.

HT-2. *See* TRICHOTHECENE MYCOTOXINS; YELLOW RAIN.

HYDROGEN BOMB. A **thermonuclear** bomb using hydrogen as the explosive. The device functions by **fusion**, requiring temperatures of several million degrees. The explosive yield of a hydrogen bomb is about 58 kilotons of **TNT-equivalent** per kilogram (2.2 pounds) of hydrogen fuel (H-fuel); that is, 1 kg of H-fuel yields a 58-kiloton explosion. This yield is nearly three times that expected from an equivalent mass of **uranium** fuel, which might be used in a **fission**-type nuclear bomb. The first successful test of a hydrogen bomb took place on 11 November 1952 when the **United States** conducted "**Mike**" as part of Operation Ivy. The yield of the blast was equivalent to the explosion of several million tons (megatons) of TNT.

– I –

IAEA SAFEGUARDS. The **Nonproliferation Treaty (NPT)** obliges States Parties to conclude with the **International Atomic Energy Agency (IAEA)** safeguards agreements that specify the nation's obligations to declare nuclear-related activities and to receive inspections and remote monitoring by the IAEA to verify that it is not conducting prohibited activities. These are contained in a nation's bilateral "comprehensive safeguards" agreement with the IAEA, which is modeled on the text of INFCIRC/153. This type of agreement constitutes the legal foundation for the nuclear safeguards system and is based on the concepts of accountancy and control of declared nuclear materials. It gives the IAEA the authority to draft conclusions about both the completeness and correctness of a state's declarations of its nuclear material inventory and fuel cycle facilities.

In 1997, in response to the IAEA's failure to detect under traditional INFCIRC/153-type safeguards the clandestine **nuclear weapon** program in **Iraq**, states began to conclude "Additional Protocol" agreements with the IAEA on the basis of INFCIRC/540. This enhanced the organization's ability to detect undeclared nuclear activities as well as to verify the nondiversion of nuclear material. The IAEA is currently implementing an "integrated safeguards" system that combines traditional safeguards with new measures allowed under the Additional Protocol. A number of verification-related implementation issues remain unclear, including whether and under what circumstances the IAEA has the right to investigate research and development of nuclear weapon–relevant activities, especially where no nuclear materials are present. This could include the development of computer codes for simulation and testing of weapons.

Although the IAEA updated its approach to verification of the first technological stage of nuclear weapon manufacturing (acquisition of nuclear explosive material), developments in **Iran**, Iraq, and **North Korea** have prompted the IAEA to proceed to the verification of what some observers have characterized as the second technological stage—weaponization—and to reassess its role in detecting research and development activities related to nuclear weapons. The Additional Protocol is designed to fill these gaps, partly by allowing IAEA inspectors to access undeclared facilities and sites adjacent to declared facilities, as well as to conduct environmental sampling. *See also* SMALL QUANTITIES PROTOCOL (SQP).

IMPLOSION DEVICE; IMPLOSION WEAPON. A type of **nuclear weapon** whose design features a spherical device that contains a quantity of **fissionable** material slightly below **critical mass** at ordinary pressure. At detonation, the device undergoes implosion, having its volume suddenly reduced by compression brought about by chemical explosives. The compression takes the fissionable material to a **supercritical** mass, and a nuclear explosion ensues. **Plutonium** is often used as the **fissile material** in such a design. "**Fat Man**," the bomb dropped on Nagasaki, is an example of an implosion device.

INCAPACITANT; INCAPACITATING AGENT. In the context of military operations, an incapacitant is any measure that makes it impossible to perform one's military mission but whose effects are transitory, abating or disappearing entirely when the agent is removed. Incapacitants can include biological, chemical, mechanical, and psychological measures. Examples of incapacitating agents include the enteric bacteria responsible for food poisoning; **BZ**, which was used in **chemical weapons (CW)**; loud, unpleasant, or distracting noises, such as those used by the U.S. military during Operation Just Cause, the 1999 mission to capture Panamanian president Manuel Noriega; and propaganda materials. Other chemical incapacitating agents that might be used in CW include those responsible for highly offensive or obnoxious odors, such as skatole and its derivatives, which have potent fecal-smelling properties. *See also* THE DALLES SALAD BAR INCIDENT.

INCENDIARY MATERIAL; INCENDIARY WEAPON. Any substance or combination of substances whose primary intent is to cause fire. An early example of an incendiary weapon is **Greek fire**. A more modern example is napalm, which is a jellied gasoline. As of World War I, military units responsible for using incendiaries have routinely been responsible for military use of **smoke agents** and **chemical weapons (CW)**, and, more rarely, for **biological weapons (BW)**. Examples of such military units include **Germany's Pioneer Regiments 35 and 36**, the **Special Brigade** of the **United Kingdom**, and the U.S. Army **Chemical Warfare Service (CWS)**. An incendiary weapon generally falls outside the definition of a CW provided in the **Chemical Weapons Convention (CWC)**.

INDIA. India has a well-developed nuclear, biological, and chemical (NBC) and ballistic missile defense establishment. It is currently destroying a **chemical weapon (CW)** stockpile in accordance with its obligations under the **Chemical Weapons Convention(CWC)**. India has conducted at least six tests of **nuclear weapons** and was estimated to possess 50 nuclear warheads as of 2006. India is not a party to the **Nonproliferation Treaty (NPT)**. *See also* ATOMS FOR PEACE; SMILING BUDDHA.

INTERCONTINENTAL BALLISTIC MISSILE (ICBM). A ballistic missile is a projectile that has one or more stages with a detachable warhead and, although usually guided during powered flight, is unguided during free flight (that portion of its flight when the path the missile follows is subject only to the external influences of atmospheric drag and gravity). An ICBM is defined as a ballistic missile having a range in excess of 5,500 kilometers (3,410 miles). Immediately after World War II, the **United States** and the Soviet Union exploited the research done in Nazi **Germany** on ballistic missiles, often employing scientists and engineers from the former Nazi program.

The successful detonation of **nuclear weapons** during the war spurred ICBM development, as such missiles held promise of unmanned delivery of nuclear warheads against distant targets. To date, the United States has fielded four major series of ICBMs: Atlas, Minuteman, Peacekeeper, and Titan. As of 2006, the Minuteman III and Peacekeeper were the sole ICBM series remaining in the U.S. inventory, all designed to deliver nuclear warheads. **Russia**, as of 2006, has four operational ICBM systems: the SS-18 Satan (NATO designation; the Russian designation is RS-20 B/V), SS-19 Stiletto (RS-18), SS-25 Sickle (RS-12M Topol), and SS-27 (RS-12M1 Topol-M and RS-12M2 Topol-M). The SS-27 has both a silo-based configuration and a mobile configuration. Similar technology has gone into development of the submarine-launched ballistic missiles (SLBM).

INTERMEDIATE-RANGE NUCLEAR FORCES (INF) TREATY.
In the 1980s, the **United States** and the Soviet Union successfully negotiated a treaty to eliminate their intermediate-range ballistic missiles—those having a range up to 5,500 kilometers (3,410 miles), as opposed to **intercontinental ballistic missiles (ICBMs)**. The Treaty between the United States of America and the Union of Soviet Socialist Republics on the Elimination of Their Intermediate-Range and Shorter-Range Missiles is commonly referred to as the Intermediate-Range Nuclear Forces or INF Treaty. It was signed in Washington, D.C., on 8 December 1987, and entered into force on 1 June 1988, requiring destruction of ground-launched ballistic missiles and ground-launched cruise missiles having ranges between 500 and 5,500 kilometers (310 and 3,410 miles). The INF Treaty also required destruction or elimination of the missile launchers, associated support structures, and support equipment.

Some 2,692 banned missiles were eliminated by May 1991, within the specified three years following the treaty's entry into force. This was followed by a 10-year period during which on-site inspections were conducted to verify compliance. The treaty was the first major arms control breakthrough by U.S. president Ronald Reagan and Soviet leader Mikhail Gorbachev, and its on-site inspection regime was a model for the development of verification measures in subsequent arms control and disarmament agreements. The INF on-site inspection period ended on 31 May 2001.

INTERNATIONAL ATOMIC ENERGY AGENCY (IAEA). The IAEA is responsible for implementing the 1968 **Nonproliferation Treaty (NPT)**, the central international arms control and disarmament legal instrument regarding **nuclear weapons**. The agency was also given primary responsibility for overseeing the nuclear disarmament of **Iraq** following the 1991 Persian Gulf War. Two other significant challenges faced by the IAEA in the 1990s and early 21st century were assessing the compliance with the NPT on the part of **Iran** and **North Korea**. *See also* IAEA SAFEGUARDS.

IPATIEV, VLADIMIR NIKOLAIYEVICH (1867–1952). Russian-born chemist. Ipatiev headed the **chemical weapon (CW)** developments in **Russia** during World War I, rising to the rank of major general in the tsarist army. Despite his background of serving the monarchy, he became an important figure in the military-chemical department of the Union of Soviet Socialist Republics (USSR) and was a principal party in the negotiations over **Bersol**. In 1931, Ipatiev defected to the **United States**, where he worked jointly as a lecturer at Northwestern University in Chicago (1931–1945) and a researcher with Universal Oil Products. In 1939, Ipatiev founded the Ipatieff Catalytic Laboratory (later renamed the Ipatieff High Pressure Synthesis Laboratory) at Northwestern and directed this laboratory until his death. He is best known among chemists for his contributions to high-pressure chemistry, such as his discovery of methods for alkylation of paraffins with olefins, which had previously been considered impossible. This breakthrough, as well as his pioneering work on catalytic dehydrogenation, isomerization, and polymerization, made possible the production of high-octane fuels and synthetic rubber.

Ipatiev's achievements earned him election to full membership in the Russian Academy of Sciences, the Soviet Academy of Sciences, and the U.S. National Academy of Science—the only person to have been honored by election to all three bodies. But along with his contributions to chemistry, Ipatiev also contributed to the development of tsarist Russia's and the USSR's offensive and defensive chemical warfare capabilities. He is credited with suggesting the establishment of **DobroKhim**, a volunteer society that promoted the chemical industry and chemical defense. He was intimately involved with **Germany** in the post–World War I period when the Weimar Republic and the USSR collaborated on CW developments, such as **Tomka**.

IRAN. There has been long-standing concern about Iran's nuclear activities and whether the country has complied with its obligations under the **Nonproliferation Treaty (NPT)**, including the commitment not to develop **nuclear weapons**. Since about 2002, the **International Atomic Energy Agency (IAEA)** has been involved in an extensive effort to verify Iran's compliance with the comprehensive nuclear safeguards agreement it concluded with the agency as part of the normal procedure by which member states fulfill their NPT commitments. The IAEA has been largely able to verify the "correctness" of Iran's declarations; however, the arguably more important verification of the "completeness" of the declaration (i.e., the absence of undeclared nuclear materials and activities) has proved to be much more difficult. A range of political factors and related initiatives have contributed to the complexity in the understanding of and efforts to resolve the problem. They have had the effect of obscuring the question of whether Iran is actively pursuing a nuclear weapons program or merely wishes to keep open the option to develop nuclear weapons in future and is for now solely interested in developing nuclear energy for peaceful purposes.

In February 2006, the agency voted to report Iran to the **United Nations** Security Council (UNSC) for being in possible breach of its NPT commitments. The underlying concern is that Iran has been attempting to develop a nuclear weapon by putting into place all necessary elements of a **nuclear fuel cycle**. This concern was heightened when negotiations in 2005 between Iran and **France**, **Germany**, and the **United Kingdom** (the so-called EU-3) to consider how to guarantee Iran's access to nuclear energy in the future became bogged down, mainly over the modalities of whether and how Iran should suspend nuclear enrichment activities. Iran reacted to the IAEA move by, among other things, removing IAEA seals and monitoring equipment.

IAEA concerns and assessments tend to be politically acceptable to all UN member states and to carry greater weight than statements and assessments by individual countries. The issues of IAEA concern may be divided according to activities in the four following areas:

1. Enrichment program
2. **Uranium** metal work
3. Transparency visits and discussions
4. Modalities for whether and how Iran should suspend nuclear enrichment activities

IAEA inspection teams have taken samples at various Iranian nuclear facilities, leading to questions being raised by the agency about the origin and significance of some **low-enriched uranium (LEU)** and **highly enriched uranium (HEU)** particles found on centrifuge components. In some instances, samples indicate that undeclared nuclear enrichment activities have taken place. Iran has shown agency officials documentation from ostensible foreign intermediaries offering centrifuge and other equipment. The offers of nuclear equipment to Iran are generally understood to include equipment, materials, and specifications offered by the **A. Q. Khan** network.

Iran has apparently suggested that any contamination indicating enrichment would have occurred outside Iran before delivery of the equipment. In particular, this includes the taking of delivery by Iran of 500 sets of P-1 centrifuge components in the mid-1990s. Iran has denied taking delivery of P-2 centrifuge components; however, it has acknowledged to the IAEA that it purchased magnets suitable for the P-2 centrifuge design. Iran has also allowed IAEA inspectors to review assorted documentation, including a document that describes procedures for the casting of enriched and **depleted uranium (DU)** metal into hemispheres. Such information would be useful for fabricating the nuclear warhead (i.e., the "pit") of an **implosion device** nuclear weapon. The document was placed under IAEA seal (although it is not clear whether this was still the case as of 2007). IAEA transparency concerns include clarifying whether Iran carried out studies for the production of **green salt**. Iran has also removed topsoil from some sites prior to IAEA inspections, ostensibly for environmental health and safety reasons. This implies to some that Iran wishes to limit the possibility of IAEA inspectors detecting and analyzing nuclear **isotopes**. Finally, the modalities of whether and how Iran should suspend nuclear enrichment activities have been intricate.

It has been observed the political leadership of Iran may not be fully aware of the activities carried out by the military and religious leadership. Iran has expressed dissatisfaction with the de facto division between the "haves" and the "have-nots" of nuclear weapons under the NPT and has experienced instances where the delivery of nuclear materials has been denied. Prior to the 1979 Islamic Revolution, the **United States** had reportedly undertaken to provide fuel for an Iranian research reactor. Iran was also a shareholder in a multinational French uranium enrichment company. The postrevolutionary government apparently never received the fuel from the United States nor any enriched uranium from the multinational consortium.

In 2006 and early 2007, there were press reports that **Israel**, the United States, and possibly the **United Kingdom** were planning to destroy Iran's nuclear infrastructure through a short and focused campaign of air strikes and commando raids. There were also reports that military planners within the U.S. Department of Defense have serious concerns about whether such an attack could successfully eliminate Iran's nuclear infrastructure and that the geopolitical consequences of such a campaign might, on balance, worsen international peace and security. Iran's current president, Mahmoud Ahmadinejad, publicly stated in 2005 that Israel must be "wiped off the map."

In July 2006 the UNSC adopted Resolution 1696 by a vote of 14–1 (with Qatar voting against) demanding that Iran suspend nuclear enrichment by 31 August 2006 or face economic and diplomatic sanctions. Iran refused to do so and, on 23 December 2006, the UNSC adopted Resolution 1737 imposing sanctions. The IAEA director general, Mohamed ElBaradei, reacted by saying that he hopes for a longer-term comprehensive agreement that will "allow for the development of relations of cooperation with Iran based on mutual respect and the establishment of international confidence in the exclusively peaceful nature of Iran's nuclear programme."

The United States has questioned the completeness of Iran's declaration to the **Organization for the Prohibition of Chemical Weapons (OPCW)**, partly because Iran did not declare having a **chemical weapon (CW)** stockpile (although the United States has never lodged a formal accusation of Iranian noncompliance within the framework of the OPCW). Iran has declared a past CW production capability and does possess a CW defense establishment that has specialized expertise in the treatment of CW casualties. It has also indicated that it can assist with the treatment of CW casualties in case an OPCW member state is attacked with such weapons (the treaty has provisions for mutual assistance and cooperation against CW). Furthermore, Iran is periodically cited, mainly by the United States, as having an offensive **biological weapon (BW)** program. *See also* CALUTRON; IRAN-IRAQ WAR; SMALL QUANTITIES PROTOCOL (SQP).

IRAN-IRAQ WAR. During the 1980–1988 Iran-Iraq War, **Iraq** used **chemical weapons (CW)**, especially **sulfur mustard** against Iranian forces. Although allegations have been made that Iran also used CW against Iraq, they have not been conclusively proven. Investigative teams sent to the region by the **United Nations** secretary-general provided proof of Iraqi use of CW, however. In 2006 criminal proceedings were continuing in Iraq against members of Saddam Hussein's regime that included charges of use of CW in **Halabja** and elsewhere.

IRAQ. Following the 1991 Persian Gulf War, the **United Nations** Security Council (UNSC) adopted Resolution 687, which required Iraq to end its extensive nuclear, biological, and chemical (NBC) weapon programs and activities and to destroy any existing stockpiles of such weapons and related material and equipment. Iraq was also required to destroy missiles with a range of greater than 150 kilometers (93 miles). The **United Nations Special Commission on Iraq (UNSCOM)** and later the **United Nations Monitoring, Verification, and Inspection Commission (UNMOVIC)** and the **Iraq Survey Group (ISG)** carried out inspections and analysis to try to conclusively determine Iraq's compliance with this and later UNSC resolutions.

Biological Weapons Program. Iraq engaged in a covert program to develop **biological weapons (BW)** that, according to UNSCOM, was under way by 1973 and ran through at least 1991. The nature and scope of the BW program came to light as a result of the 1995 defection of **Hussein al-Kamal**, a son-in-law of Iraqi dictator Saddam Hussein.

Iraq succeeded in producing the biological pathogens and **toxins** aflatoxin (a **mycotoxin**), **anthrax**, **botulinum toxin (BTX)**, *Clostridium perfringens* (the causative agent for gas gangrene), **ricin**, and wheat smut (an **anticrop agent**). Iraq was also working on other pathogens and toxins, although on a more modest scale. The earliest BW research and development center was al-Hazen Institute, where work took place involving anthrax, BTX, cholera, *Shigella* bacteria (responsible for shigellosis), and certain viruses. This institute closed on 16 January 1979 owing to fraud by its chairman and senior staff. The program was reconstituted elsewhere, including dedicated BW research and development sites at al-Hakam, al-Muthanna, and al-Salman. Of these, al-Hakam became a primary facility for production. Iraq initially claimed al-Hakam, which was set up in 1988, produced food for animals and pesticides for plants. Following the 1995 defection of al-Kamal, though, Iraq admitted that this facility had produced 8,500 liters of anthrax, 19,000 liters of BTX, and experimental quantities of *C. perfringens*. In 1990, Iraq took over the Daura **Foot-and-Mouth Disease (FMD)** Vaccine production facility and converted it for the BW program. The facility took on the additional name of al-Manal, and both it and al-Hakam were used for the field testing of aerial bombs, helicopter-mounted spray tanks (such as the **Zubaidy device**), rockets, and other BW-type munitions.

The ultimate fate of the BW pathogens and toxins and of the munitions is uncertain, whether due to mere incompetence on the part of the personnel involved in the BW program, inaccurate claims made by the BW program personnel to Saddam Hussein, or deliberate efforts to conceal such materials. *See also* AMMASH, HUDA SALIH MAHDI.

Chemical Weapons Program. Iraq had a significant program to produce **chemical weapons (CW)** during the regime of Saddam Hussein. Iraq's possession of such weapons came to light with their use during the **Iran-Iraq War**, and the use of CW was feared by military planners responsible for Operation Desert Storm that followed Iraq's 1990 invasion of Kuwait. UNSCOM and the follow-on UNMOVIC documented the extent of this CW program and attempted to verify the ultimate disposition of the bulk chemicals as well as the stockpiled CW. The Muthanna State Establishment near Samarra was the principle Iraqi CW research, development, and production facility. **Sulfur mustard**, **tabun**, **sarin**, and **cyclosarin** were produced here and loaded into rockets, aerial bombs, 155-mm artillery projectiles, and al-Hussein missile warheads. Iraq also attempted production of **VX** but that effort apparently met with little success. *See also* CHEMICAL ALI; HALABJA.

Nuclear Weapons Program. During the regime of Saddam Hussein, Iraq had a covert program to develop a **nuclear weapon** that came to light in the aftermath of the 1991 Gulf War. UNSC Resolution 687, adopted in April 1991, gave the **International Atomic Energy Agency (IAEA)** the mandate to conduct the inspection and verification activities necessary to discover the program and verify its dismantlement. In carrying out its mandate, the IAEA established the Iraq Nuclear Verification Office (INVO) to lead the effort.

INVO has issued findings regarding what was discovered about the nuclear weapons program in the wake of the 1991 War as well as in the aftermath of the 2003 invasion of Iraq led by the **United States** and the **United Kingdom**. According to INVO, there was no evidence that Iraq succeeded in producing nuclear weapons, despite significant attempts. These attempts include design, development, construction, and limited operation of **gas centrifuges** and **gaseous diffusion** plants. Additionally, Iraq was judged to be on the threshold of producing **highly enriched uranium (HEU)**. In March 2003, IAEA personnel completed a round of inspections and found no evidence that Iraq's nuclear weapons program had been revived during the forced absence of INVO from 1998 through 2002. *See also* OSIRAQ REACTOR BOMBING.

IRAQ SURVEY GROUP (ISG). A fact-finding mission established by the coalition forces that attacked **Iraq** in 2003. Under the leadership of David Kay, the ISG was tasked to uncover weapons and programs prohibited by the 1991 **United Nations** Security Council (UNSC) Resolution 687, which prohibited Iraq from having or developing **nuclear weapons**, **chemical weapons (CW)**, **biological weapons (BW)**, or ballistic missiles with a range of more than 150 kilometers (93 miles). The ISG was also given a number of secondary tasks, including determining the status of a U.S. Navy pilot shot down during the 1991 Persian Gulf War and other intelligence gathering. In January 2004, Kay was succeeded by Charles A. Duelfer, formerly deputy director of the **United Nations Special Commission on Iraq (UNSCOM)**. Shortly after his resignation, Kay stated that there was "no doubt" that most Western intelligence services assessments of Iraq's CW and BW capabilities were wrong. In October 2004, Duelfer confirmed that Iraq did not have an active CW or BW program and that the country's stockpiles of such weapons had been destroyed. He added, however, that there were indications that Saddam Hussein had taken measures to retain expertise in these weapons in order to restart the programs once international sanctions had been lifted. The October 2004 ISG report was based on numerous interviews with Iraqi officials and approximately 40 million pages of documents.

ISHII SHIRO (1892–1959). Japanese microbiologist and physician. Ishii was a key figure in the **Japanese chemical weapon (CW)** and **biological weapon (BW)** programs, starting in the 1930s and continuing until the end of World War II. Ishii joined the Japanese Imperial Army early in his career, working on such problems as water purification for military units. He apparently believed that CW and BW must be effective weapons, because otherwise the Great Powers would not have attempted to limit or ban their use by concluding the **Geneva Protocol of 1925**. This belief stimulated his involvement in developing and testing such weapons. Following the Japanese occupation of Manchuria in 1937, Ishii supervised the construction and operation of various test and research facilities, especially **Unit 731**. He was actively engaged in the use of BW, including its employment in 1938 against the Soviet Red Army during the Russo-Japanese conflict in the Kholgan-Gol region of Mongolia.

Ishii rose to the rank of major general prior to the end of the war. He avoided prosecution for possible war crimes largely by agreeing to be debriefed by the **United States** about his work. However, his openness and the value of the information he provided have been questioned.

ISOTOPE. A unique form of an element. The isotopes of an element share the same chemical properties but different nuclear properties. In particular, one isotope may be radioactive while another isotope of the same element is stable. For example, hydrogen has three isotopes: hydrogen-1 (or simply "hydrogen"), hydrogen-2 (**deuterium**), and hydrogen-3 (**tritium**). All three have the chemical properties, but the mass of deuterium is double that of ordinary hydrogen, while that of tritium is triple that of hydrogen. Furthermore, tritium is radioactive, while the other two are stable.

ISRAEL. Israel is widely believed to possess **nuclear weapons**. It also has a well-developed chemical and biological warfare (CBW) defense capability as indicated by its scientific and technical publications. There has been periodic speculation that the country might also have an offensive **chemical weapon (CW)** or **biological weapon (BW)** program; however, definitive public information is lacking. Israel is not a member of the **Biological and Toxin Weapons Convention (BTWC)** or the nuclear **Nonproliferation Treaty (NPT)**. It has signed but not ratified the **Chemical Weapons Convention (CWC)** and the **Comprehensive Nuclear Test Ban Treaty (CTBT)**. Before the entry into force of the latter two treaties, Israeli delegations actively participated in the elaboration of procedures for implementing on-site inspections and the handling of sensitive information by the technical secretariats that implement them. It is generally believed that Israel wishes to keep open the possibility of joining the major arms control and disarmament treaty regimes once it has achieved sufficient success in addressing its regional security concerns.

Biological and Chemical Weapons Programs. Speculation regarding Israel's BW program might be dated to the nation's 1948 founding. On 23 May 1948, the Egyptian military apprehended four Israeli soldiers in the Gaza area. The Israelis were supposedly dressed as Arabs and were found near water wells. The Egyptian Ministry of Defense issued a statement on 29 May accusing these soldiers of carrying a liquid that harbored the bacteria responsible for dysentery and typhoid fever, with the intent of using this liquid to poison artesian wells used by the Egyptians. The soldiers were promptly tried, convicted, and executed. The truth of these allegations has never been determined outside Egypt, and uncertainties regarding the nature of this liquid persist.

Around this same time, Israel founded the Israel Institute for Biological Research (IIBR) at Ness-Ziona. Public statements regarding the IIBR describe it as devoted to the study of biology, medicinal chemistry, and environmental sciences. Considerable speculation, however, points to the IIBR as the center of Israel's BW and CW programs.

This speculation has been fed by various events. In 1983, Marcus Klingberg, then a deputy director of IIBR, was convicted on charges of spying for the Soviet Union. His conviction was kept secret until 1991, and details on his spying did not emerge until 2002, when a book published in Israel alleged that Klingberg had passed secrets regarding Israel's BW and CW programs. Similarly, the 1992 crash of an El Al flight in the Netherlands revealed that its cargo included nearly 200 gallons of dimethyl methyl phosphonate, consigned to IIBR. Israel claimed the chemical was to be used in testing protective equipment, such as masks. But because it is also an essential ingredient in making the **organophosphorus nerve agent sarin**, some speculated its intended use was for CW production.

Nuclear Weapons Program. Conjecture regarding a nuclear weapons program in Israel centers around a nuclear complex at Dimona. Construction of this complex is believed to have begun with the assistance of **France** in 1956. The construction, ostensibly of a research reactor, took place in secret and outside the inspection regime established by the **International Atomic Energy Agency (IAEA)**. By 1958, the **United States** was aware of this construction through overflights by U-2 reconnaissance aircraft. In December 1960, the Israeli government acknowledged the Dimona complex but declared that it was being used for peaceful purposes. A 1968 report by the U.S. Central Intelligence Agency (CIA) concluded that Israel possessed nuclear weapons, but the evidence offered was confined to discussions between a senior CIA official and renowned American physicist Edward Teller. Since then, various reports have surfaced speculating on the Israeli nuclear weapons stockpile, with estimates ranging as high as 400 warheads. The size and composition of such a stockpile, if it exists, remain uncertain. The 1979 **Vela Incident** was viewed by some as a nuclear weapon test conducted jointly by Israel and **South Africa**.

In the mid-1980s Mordechai Vanunu, an Israeli nuclear technician, described to a British newspaper what he said was nuclear weapons–related work being carried out at Dimona. Vanunu was abducted in October 1986 in Rome and was transported to Israel, where he was put on trial on charges of revealing state secrets. During the trial, he wrote on the palm of his hand that he had been kidnapped in Rome and placed his hand against the side window of the vehicle that was transporting him to court. The message was captured by international television news crews. Vanunu was convicted and imprisoned. He was released from prison in 2004 but is still not permitted to travel outside Israel.

Israel has traditionally maintained a policy of ambiguity as to whether it possesses **nuclear weapons**. However, on 12 December 2006 Israeli prime minister Ehud Olmert caused this policy to be called into question when he seemed to state during a German television interview that his country in fact possesses such weapons. *See also* OSIRAQ REACTOR BOMBING.

– J –

JAEGER, AUGUST. On 13 April 1915, Pvt. August Jaeger, an automobile driver attached to **Germany**'s 234th Reserve Infantry Regiment, XXVI Reserve Corps, deserted. Traveling at night, he crossed into **French**-held lines near **Ypres**, Belgium, and turned himself in to troops of the 4th Battalion of Chasseurs. Taken to the French 11th Division headquarters, Jaeger talked freely about German strengths and dispositions along its lines. He also warned of German plans to use an asphyxiating gas, to be released when favorable winds might carry the gas into the French trenches. He advised his captors that three red rockets would be fired as a signal to release the gas. Finally, Jaeger told the French that the German troops had been issued protective gear to use to avoid being harmed by the gas when it was released.

The information regarding a pending release of asphyxiating gas alarmed some Allied officers, especially Edmond Ferry, the commanding general of the 11th Division. He issued orders on 14 April to his own troops to be alert for a gas release and sent similar warnings to both the adjacent British 28th Imperial Division and the Canadian brigade expected shortly to relieve the elements of the 11th. A few days later, Julius Rapsahl, a private in the 4th Landwehr Regiment, XXVI Reserve Corps, deserted and told a similar story to interrogators from the 11th Division. Despite these warnings, the French, Belgian, British, and Canadian forces in the Ypres salient were taken by surprise on 22 April when Germany released **chlorine** against their lines.

In 1930, General Ferry wrote a magazine article of this episode. In it, Ferry revealed Jaeger's name and unit and identified his role in leaking information regarding German intentions to use toxic chemicals during the second Battle of Ypres. This news robbed Jaeger of his anonymity. Eventually, he was found by German authorities and, under the newly installed Nazi regime, charged with desertion and betrayal. He was convicted by the Reich Supreme Court and sentenced to 10 years' imprisonment. Jaeger would remain in custody throughout the Nazi regime. Deemed a traitor and security risk, he was confined to concentration camps at Buchenwald, Malthusen, and Dachau, where he was finally freed on 24 April 1945 by the advancing Red Army. The fate of Rapsahl—the other deserter who also spoke of German intentions to use **chemical weapons (CW)**—is unknown.

JAPAN. *Biological Weapons Program.* Japan had a robust and extensive **biological weapons (BW)** program dating to the 1930s. For most of its existence, the program was led by **Ishii Shiro**, who centered his operations on facilities known collectively as **Unit 731**. These facilities were largely located outside Japan on the Asian mainland. Various attempts were made at using BW, but the results are difficult to measure. Following World War II, the Soviet Union placed 12 Japanese military personnel from Unit 731 on trial for BW-related crimes. The **United States**, **United Kingdom**, and other World War II Allies were invited to participate in the trial, which was conducted in Khabarovsk, but they declined. None of the Unit 731 personnel who fell into U.S. hands was placed on trial for any BW-related crimes. Instead, they were granted immunity in return for sharing details of their work with the U.S. military. *See also* OPERATION PX; PLAGUE.

Chemical Weapons Program. Japan began developing **chemical weapons (CW)** after World War I and used such weapons during the conflict on mainland Asia, starting in the late 1930s. There is no evidence that Japan continued development of such weapons after World War II. Among the chemical warfare agents produced by Japan during World War II were diphenylcyanoarsine, diphenylchloroarsine, hydrogen cyanide, **sulfur mustard**, **lewisite**, and **phosgene**. Its battlefield use of CW was apparently confined to mainland **China**. At least 700,000 CW have been discovered in China, mostly in the northeastern regions formerly part of the Japanese puppet state of Manchukuo (Manchuria). The Chinese attribute them to Japan and claim Japan is responsible for the safe, secure, and environmentally benign disposal of these **abandoned chemical weapons (ACW)**. Their destruction is expected to take place over the next several years and will be verified by the **Organization for the Prohibition of Chemical Weapons (OPCW)**, the body that implements the 1993 **Chemical Weapons Convention**.

Nuclear Weapons Program. During World War II, Japan undertook a program to develop **nuclear weapons**. The program was conducted on a small scale and was poorly financed, similar to **Germany**'s program. There is no evidence Japan succeeded in developing a nuclear device, despite rumors to that effect. Japan currently is party to the **Nonproliferation Treaty (NPT)** and has a declared nuclear energy program subject to inspection and monitoring by the **International Atomic Energy Agency (IAEA)**.

The World War II–era effort by Japan to develop nuclear weapons consisted of two programs. The government approved the first program in July 1941 at the Institute for Physical and Chemical Research (Rikagaku Kenkyusho, RIKEN), near Tokyo. The RIKEN program was led by Yoshio Nishina (1890–1951), an eminent physicist whose professional associates included **Niels Bohr** and **Albert Einstein**. By the mid-1930s, Nishina had grasped the significance of nuclear physics as a source for energy, including its possible use in weapons, and had strongly advocated a Japanese program to counter any effort by the United States to develop such a weapon.

In 1942, the Japanese Navy began a second program on nuclear weapon development. This program, given the code name "F-Go," began with the goal of harnessing nuclear reactions as an energy source, so that the navy might be less dependent on oil for propulsion. The need to counter the threat of an American nuclear weapon caused the program to alter its goal, in effect duplicating the work at RIKEN. The group working on the navy's program included Hideki Yukawa, who would win the 1949 Nobel Prize in Physics for his work on the fundamental nature of the atomic nucleus.

Japan appealed to Germany for assistance, and at least one such appeal is known to have been answered. The German submarine *U-234* was dispatched with a cargo of 560 kilograms (1,230 pounds) of some form of **uranium**, plus other items of military hardware. Also aboard the submarine were German scientists and at least two Japanese military officers. The U.S. Navy intercepted the *U-234* on 14 May 1945, following Germany's surrender. The cargo and crew were seized, but the Japanese officers had already committed suicide. The uranium oxide was labeled "U-235," leading to speculation that the contents were the **fissile isotope** uranium-235. This possibility seems unlikely, however, given the quantity involved, and most authorities believe the cargo was uranium oxide rather than **highly enriched uranium (HEU)**.

"JEWISH PHYSICS." During the rise of **German** nationalism following World War I, some German physicists denounced **Albert Einstein**'s theory of relativity as "Jewish physics" and a fraud. Instead, they preached "Aryan physics" (*Deutsche Physik*) as the only acceptable approach for true Germans. They equated relativity in physics to relativism in morals, branding both as frauds and morally corrupt. This rejection of relativity and the insistence that German scientists follow more classical approaches to nuclear science would ultimately prove incompatible with quantum mechanics and similar concepts vital to achieving nuclear **fission** and developing **nuclear weapons**.

Two Nobel laureates were prominent in the Aryan physics movement and the denunciation of relativity and related ideas as Jewish physics: Philipp Lenard (1862–1947), a Hungarian-born scientist who later received German citizenship, and Johannes Stark (1874–1957), awardees of the 1905 and 1919 Physics prizes, respectively. In 1937, Stark wrote an article for the Nazi SS newspaper *Das Schwarze Korps* in which he branded 1932 Nobel Prize in Physics winner **Werner Heisenberg** a "White Jew" for his embrace of relativity. He implied that the Bavarian-born Heisenberg was a traitor to Germany for using such non-German ideas in his theories. Stark also wrote an admiring book about Adolf Hitler and served as one of Hitler's science advisors.

The nationalist attitude toward physics inherent in Aryan physics and the rejection of Jewish physics might have contributed to Germany's failure to develop a nuclear weapon, by discouraging younger scientists from studying relativity or accepting its precepts as part of their research into nuclear fission.

JOE (JOE 1; JOE 4). On 29 August 1949, the Union of Soviet Socialist Republics (USSR) conducted its first successful detonation of a nuclear device. The Americans gave this device the nickname "Joe," after Soviet leader Joseph Stalin; the nickname for this first test was modified to "Joe 1" after the Soviets conducted other successful nuclear tests. The Soviets conducted the test in secrecy, and the **United States** was unaware of the test at the time. However, a U.S. detection system using "**sniffers**" onboard weather reconnaissance aircraft provided the evidence that would both detect and date this detonation, informing the West that the USSR had perfected a nuclear weapon.

On 12 August 1953, the Soviets successfully detonated their first **thermonuclear** device. Its estimated yield was 400 kilotons. The U.S. government dubbed this device "Joe 4," in line with designations used for prior Soviet nuclear devices. *See also* ALARM CLOCK; RUSSIA; SAKHAROV, ANDREI DMITRIYEVICH.

JOINT RESEARCH DEVELOPMENT BOARD (JRDB). After World War II, the U.S. government established the Joint Research Development Board to consider technical aspects of biological warfare (BW). Various factors caused the Joint Chiefs of Staff and other government officials to assess the threat posed by BW as well as U.S. policy toward this threat. These officials worried that uninformed or misleading information regarding U.S. policy on BW was periodically put into the public domain. Their worries were fed by a proposal put forward in the **United Nations (UN)** by the **United States** and **United Kingdom** to put atomic energy under international control. These officials feared that the perceived linkage among **nuclear, biological**, and **chemical (NBC) weapons**, which were all seen as **weapons of mass destruction (WMD)**, would mean that discussions on the atomic energy proposal in the United Nations could be extended to include BW. In 1947, Secretary of Defense James V. Forrestal, together with the secretary of the navy, asked the JRDB to undertake a study of the technical aspects of BW. In 1948, the Joint Chiefs of Staff, and the government generally, appeared to have been operating on the understanding that biological weapons had "probable value as a military weapon."

JUGLONE. Juglone is a nonproteinaceous **toxin** occurring naturally in the *Juglans* genus such as walnut and butternut trees. It was isolated as early as 1905 from walnut shells. During World War I, juglone was investigated by the **United States** as a potential biological warfare (BW) agent. The investigation was carried out by the U.S. Army's **Chemical Warfare Service (CWS)** at its Offensive Unit, located at the **Catholic University of America**, and was prompted by intelligence suggesting that **Germany** was already developing it for BW purposes. The intention of the work of the CWS was to fill the toxin into toxic bullets, although it is unclear whether such bullets were actually produced. The quality of the intelligence was subsequently deemed to be questionable by the U.S. government. Juglone is a solid and sees commercial use in combating bleeding.

JUMBO. U.S. plans for the 1945 **Trinity test** of the **implosion**-type nuclear device called for two explosions. The first would be a conventional explosion involving TNT, which would implode a **subcritical mass** of **plutonium**. If the implosion worked as designed, a second explosion would occur within a fraction of a second when **critical mass** was attained and a **chain reaction** occurred. If the implosion failed to achieve the desired chain reaction, however, the blast of TNT would throw the plutonium into the air and over the countryside. Because plutonium was both precious and toxic, those designing the Trinity test wanted to safeguard against such a loss. The solution was "Jumbo," designed to contain the force of the TNT blast and secure the plutonium in the event the intended chain reaction failed.

Built by the Eichleay Corporation of Pittsburgh, Pennsylvania, Jumbo was sent by train to a railhead in Pope, New Mexico. Measuring 25 feet long and 10 feet in diameter, the steel-constructed Jumbo weighed 214 tons. It would not fit onto an ordinary trailer, so a specially built trailer having 64 wheels was used to move it 25 miles from Pope to Alamogordo, where it was placed at the Trinity Test Site. As development of the plutonium bomb progressed, confidence grew that the design would work and that a nuclear detonation would be achieved. Plans to use Jumbo were therefore scrapped. On 16 July 1945, the Trinity test took place, with Jumbo suspended in a steel tower 800 feet from the **zero point**. The blast vaporized the tower, but Jumbo survived. Although damaged in some follow-on testing, Jumbo remains at the Trinity Test Site as a National Historical Landmark accessible to the public.

– K –

KABACHNIK, MARTIN ISRAELIVICH (1908–1997). Russian chemist. Kabachnik made fundamental and practical contributions to the **chemical weapons (CW)** program of the Soviet Union. He specialized in the chemistry of organoelement compounds, as did his colleague **Ivan Knunyants**. In September 1944, Kabachnik prepared **sarin** while working at the University of Kazan. His synthesis of this **organophosphorus nerve agent** was independent of Gerhard Schrader's synthesis, which had taken place in **Germany** in 1939 and was most likely unknown to the Soviets at the time because of World War II. In 1946, Kabachnik received the Stalin Prize, First Class, in recognition of this work. Following the war, Kabachnik relocated to Moscow, where he spent the remainder of his career on theoretical and applied problems related to organoelement compounds. He received the Lenin Prize, the highest honor in the USSR, in 1974 for developments related to V-type nerve agents.

KAMAL, HUSSEIN AL-. A son-in-law of Saddam Hussein whose 1995 defection to Jordan apparently caused Saddam Hussein to decide to admit to the **United Nations Special Commission on Iraq (UNSCOM)** that **Iraq** had pursued an offensive **biological weapon (BW)** program. Iraqi government officials claimed that Kamal had unilaterally oversaw the program in secret without authorization. In 2004, the **Iraq Survey Group (ISG)** concluded that Kamal's defection resulted in a decision by Saddam Hussein to reorganize the Iraqi BW-related infrastructure. Kamal was killed immediately upon his return to Iraq, despite his having been promised clemency for his 1995 defection.

KAPLAN, MARTIN (1915–2004). U.S.-born veterinarian. Kaplan spent much of his career working for the **World Health Organiza-**

tion (WHO) in Geneva, Switzerland, and with the **Pugwash** movement, where he became a noted advocate for chemical, biological, and nuclear arms control and disarmament. Kaplan joined WHO in 1949, becoming chief of veterinary public health and, later, chief of medical research. He joined the Pugwash movement shortly after its founding in 1957 and served as its secretary-general from 1976 to 1988. He was instrumental in organizing the first Pugwash conference on **chemical** and **biological weapons (CBW)**, held in August 1959.

KATIE. In September 1953, the U.S. military began developing a **nuclear weapon** to be used in the 16-inch guns of the U.S. Navy's *Iowa*-class battleships. This device, nicknamed "Katie," became the Mark-23 naval shell. Katie was placed in the U.S. stockpile in December 1956 and remained part of the stockpile until October 1962. Each shell was slightly over 5 feet long and weighed nearly a ton. Its suspected explosive yield was 15 to 20 kilotons **TNT-equivalent**. There is no record that any U.S. battleship ever carried Katie on board while at sea. *See also* ATOMIC ANNIE.

KHAN, ABDUL QADEER (1935–). Pakistani physicist. Khan is an engineer widely viewed as the founder of the **nuclear weapons** program in **Pakistan**. Born in Bhopal, **India**, he was educated in Pakistan and Europe, earning a doctorate in 1972 from the Catholic University of Leuven in Belgium. He is the central figure in the "A. Q. Khan nuclear technology smuggling network," which included the participation of individuals from **China, Iran, Libya, North Korea**, and Saudi Arabia. His official career came to an end in 2001 when he was dismissed as director of a nuclear laboratory on the orders of Pakistani president Pervez Musharraf. However, the government of Pakistan decided to overlook any improprieties Khan may have committed in the nuclear weapon technology smuggling network and has not allowed him to be prosecuted or questioned by other governments or the **International Atomic Energy Agency (IAEA)**. The existence of the network and of his role in it came to light largely as a consequence of Libya's 2003 decision to renounce **nuclear, biological**, and **chemical (NBC) weapons** and longer-range ballistic missiles.

KHARITON, YULI (1904–1996). Russian physicist. Khariton was among the founders of the Soviet **nuclear weapon** program. His influence was greatest through his position as director of **Arzamas-16**, the secret nuclear weapon complex that he established in 1946. In the 1920s, Khariton studied under the famed British physicist Ernest Rutherford. *See also* KURCHATOV, IGOR VASILIEVICH; SAKHAROV, ANDREI DMITRIYEVICH; SEMIPALATINSK.

KING TUT BLOCK. A barrier positioned within or outside a bunker used for storing **chemical weapons (CW)** and possibly other high-value materials. The "King Tut block" is designed to drop across the entrance area, thereby preventing the easy removal of the weapons (for instance, by a vehicle) if a forced entry should succeed.

KLIEWE, HEINRICH. During World War II, Kliewe was the director of the Hygiene Institute at Giessen, **Germany**, and was the chairman of the **Blitzableiter Committee**. He was a disinfection and **aerosol** specialist. Following the war, he was detained by the **ALSOS Mission** and questioned regarding his knowledge of Germany's **biological weapons (BW)** program. Kliewe proved useful to ALSOS, as his memory was excellent and he had kept meticulous files.

KNUNYANTS, IVAN LUDVIGOVICH (1906–1990). Soviet chemist. Knunyants was born in Shusha, in the Nagorno-Karabakh region of present-day Azerbaijan, and rose to prominence as an internationally famed academic chemist. His fundamental contributions to organophosphorus and organosulfur chemistry were valuable to the Soviet **chemical weapons (CW)** program. Knunyants's brilliance was recognized early in his career, and he rose rapidly, being elected an academician (the highest rank) in the Academy of Sciences of the USSR at age 47. His work on organofluorine chemistry aided Soviet development of **organophosphorus nerve agents**, especially **sarin** and **soman**. In 1972, this work was recognized by his receipt of the Lenin Prize, the most prestigious award in the USSR. Knunyants devoted much effort to understanding the relationship between molecular structure and physiological activity. Although his interests were principally theoretical and basic research, the results heavily influenced development of novel CW agents.

KOCH'S POSTULATES. A set of conditions that must be fulfilled in order to determine whether a given pathogen is the causative agent for a given disease. The postulates are named after German biologist and physician Robert Koch (1843–1910), who is credited with their development. The four conditions are as follows:

1. A given microorganism must first be present in every instance of disease to be considered as the probable causative agent.
2. It must be possible to then isolate and culture the microorganism in every case.
3. Samples of the cultured microorganism must cause the same disease when used on test animals.
4. The microorganism can be recovered once more and recultured.

KRYTON. The type of ultrafast electrical switch used to cause detonation of a **nuclear weapon** or other nuclear device. Krytons function in less than one-tenth of a millionth of a second ($<10^{-7}$ sec), directing electric current to the chemical explosives wrapped around **plutonium** in an **implosion weapon**. *See also* SHAKE.

KUNTSEVICH, ANATOLY DEM'YANOVICH (1934–2003?). Soviet and, later, Russian military officer, scientist, and government official. A physical chemist by training, Kuntsevich was a corresponding member of the Soviet Academy of Sciences Division of General and Technical Chemistry from 29 December 1981 until 23 December 1987 when he was elevated to academician of the division. He commanded the **Shikhany** military chemical establishment from 1975 to 1983.

Following the dissolution of the Soviet Union, Kuntsevich was named by **Russian** president Boris Yeltsin to serve as chairman of the Presidential Committee on Problems of Chemical and Biological Weapon Conventions (also known as the "**Conventional Committee**"). Kuntsevich was also a key participant in negotiations with the **United States** on the **Bilateral Destruction Agreement (BDA)**. In early 1995, Kuntsevich was dismissed as chairman of the Conventional Committee amid allegations that he had been involved in assisting Syria with materials or information for a suspected **chemical**

weapon (CW) production program. The Russian government later dropped the charges.

There was significant institutional conflict between Kuntsevich's committee and the Department of Chemical Troops of the Russian Ministry of Defense, in part over the question of delineation of control and oversight over the Russian CW stockpiles and in part owing to personality conflicts between Kuntsevich and some members of the leadership of the department. Kuntsevich is reported to have died in 2003 during an airplane trip between Russia and Syria, although some mystery surrounds this report. According to a 2004 Russian news source, he had a role in developing the fentanyl-related opiate used by Russia in ending the **Moscow Theater Incident** in 2002.

KURCHATOV, IGOR VASILIEVICH (1903–1960). Soviet physicist. In 1943, Soviet leader Joseph Stalin ordered a small-scale project to be started aimed at developing a **nuclear weapon**. He placed the respected Kurchatov in charge. On 25 December 1946, Kurchatov and his team in Moscow succeeded in achieving a nuclear **chain reaction**, using an experimental graphite-moderated natural **uranium**-fueled **nuclear pile** called the Fursov Pile or F-1. Kurchatov is widely seen as the father of the Soviet nuclear weapon program, and his Moscow Institute of Atomic Energy was renamed the I. V. Kurchatov Institute of Atomic Energy in his honor. *See also* ARZAMAS-16; KHARITON, YULI; SAKHAROV, ANDREI DMITRIYEVICH.

– L –

LABYRINTHIC. Describing any chemical warfare (CW) agent that affects the labyrinth of the ear, thus interfering with the sense of equilibrium and causing those affected to stagger and otherwise be unable to maintain their balance. During World War I, the French used the term (in French, *labyrinthique*) for chemicals such as *bis*(bromomethyl) ether and *bis*(chloromethyl) ether, which were used as fills in French **chemical weapons (CW)**.

LACHRYMATOR. A substance that causes tears to flow from the eyes. A synonym is "tear gas," although this term is misleading because a lachrymator can also be a liquid, such as xylyl bromide, or a solid, such as **CS**. In addition to affecting the eyes, lachrymators can irritate other parts of the body on contact, especially the skin, throat, and nasal passages. Lachrymators were among the first **chemical weapons (CW)** used during World War I. The distinguishing features of a lachrymator are that the physiological effects normally disappear rapidly (that is, within minutes) upon removal from exposure and that medical treatment for these effects is rarely required. *See also* T-SHELL; WHITE CROSS AGENT.

LEAGUE OF NATIONS. The League of Nations was established by the Allied Powers in 1919. Its charter, also referred to as the Covenant of the League of Nations, was approved as part of the **Treaty of Versailles** and entered into force on 10 January 1920. U.S. president Woodrow Wilson was awarded the 1919 Nobel Peace Prize for his role in helping to establish the body. The League was increasingly seen to be weak and ineffective, partly as a consequence of its failure to respond effectively to complaints of **chemical weapon (CW)** use that were lodged with the League in the 1930s by the governments of **China** and **Ethiopia**, respectively. For example, the League agreed to impose sanctions against Italy for invading Ethiopia (then often called Abyssinia). However, in so doing it exempted two categories of materials: oil and steel. The League of Nations was officially dissolved on 18 April 1946. The **United Nations (UN)** took over the League's assets, including its archives.

LEGEND. A cover story used to obscure or keep hidden secret activities. For example, legends were reportedly employed during the post-1972 Soviet **biological weapon (BW)** program. According to **Vladimir Pasechnik**, a former **Biopreparat** employee who defected to the **United Kingdom** in 1989, workers in the **antiplague system** were given one of four legends, depending on their personal level of security clearance. The first level was an "open legend," which denied that there was a BW program. The second, a "closed legend," acknowledged BW work but said it was solely defensive in nature. The third level involved providing the individuals with limited information about some aspects of offensive work. Finally, individuals cleared for the fourth and highest level of legend were permitted to know the true nature and scope of the program. *See also* ALIBEK, KENNETH.

LEWIS, WINFORD LEE. *See* LEWISITE.

LEWISITE. A group of three closely related chlorovinyl arsine chemicals: lewisite-1 (2-chlorovinyl arsine dichloride, $C_2H_2AsCl_3$), lewisite-2 (*bis*[2-chlorovinyl] arsine chloride, $C_4H_4AsCl_3$), and lewisite-3 (*tris*[2-chlorovinyl] arsine, $C_6H_6AsCl_3$). Lewisite-1 was the intended product of lewisite production, but the other two were often present as by-products. Therefore, "lewisite" is commonly used to refer to lewisite-1 alone. The name honors Winford Lee Lewis (1878–1943), who took credit for their original synthesis and characterization in April 1918.

While serving in the U.S. Army's **Chemical Warfare Service (CWS)** during World War I, Lewis was working at its **Catholic University of America** branch when he synthesized these three chlorovinyl arsine chemicals from arsenic trichloride and acetylene. When he noted strong **vesicating** properties and high human toxicity in these chemicals, the army believed it had discovered a novel and extremely useful **chemical weapon (CW)**. Lewisite was immediately rushed into production at a factory in Willoughby, Ohio. A shipment of lewisite CW was en route to Europe when word was received that the Armistice had been signed, which resulted in the dumping of the cargo into the Atlantic Ocean.

The identity of lewisite was kept secret by the **United States** during and immediately after World War I. A paper in the April 1921 *Journal of the Chemical Society* by British scientists revealed a method for lewisite production, however, making it impossible to keep the identity secret any longer. The publication ignited a controversy over the right of first discovery of lewisite, with claims being made by the United States, the **United Kingdom**, and **Germany**. Eventually, Lewisite was found to degrade rapidly, causing its military effectiveness to be questioned.

Lewisite was produced and stockpiled by various nations, including **Japan**, the United States, and the Soviet Union. Lewisite saw use, too, in mixtures with **sulfur mustard**, where lewisite acted as a **freezing-point depressant**. The Japanese might have used lewisite in combat during its operations on the Asian mainland, but there are no other records of combat use of lewisite despite extensive production and stockpiling. *See also* CONANT, JAMES BRYANT; SEA DUMPING.

LIBYA. Reports that Libya was pursuing **nuclear**, **biological**, and **chemical (NBC) weapons** programs began to surface in the late 1970s. The country was subjected to one of the most stringent sanctions regimes ever, largely because of its failure to cooperate with international criminal investigations into, among other things, the 1988 bombing of a Pan Am airliner over Lockerbie, Scotland, and the 1989 bombing of a UTA French airliner that crashed in Niger.

In 2003 a series of secret contacts among British, Libyan, and U.S. officials resulted in a December 2003 joint statement that Libya had agreed to renounce NBC weapons and longer-range missiles as well as associated programs. During this trilateral process, British and U.S. officials visited sites of concern in Libya and interviewed Libyan officials and technical experts. They uncovered no concrete evidence of an existing biological weapon (BW) program. The **United Kingdom** and the **United States** nevertheless reportedly believe that certain agricultural and pharmaceutical facilities were established with BW in mind.

In 2004 Libya declared to the **Organization for the Prohibition of Chemical Weapons (OPCW)** 3,563 empty chemical weapons (CW) airborne bombs and 23.62 metric tons of **sulfur mustard** and other chemicals that could be used in the production of CW. Libya stated that it had never transferred CW. In March 2004 Libya completed the destruction of the bombs. That December, the OPCW approved Libya's request to convert a former sulfur mustard production facility at Rabta into a pharmaceutical production facility to produce drugs to treat acquired immune deficiency syndrome (AIDS), malaria, and tuberculosis. While it is evident that Libya stockpiled air-droppable CW and sulfur mustard, the exact nature of its work with other agents is less clear. For example, Libya reportedly carried out some experimental work with **sarin** and **soman**.

Most of Libya's ballistic missile stockpile prior to the December 2003 agreement consisted of a limited number of aging FROG and Scud-B missiles that had been imported from the former Soviet Union (FSU).

Libya had violated its **International Atomic Energy Agency (IAEA) safeguards** agreement by covertly pursuing a nuclear weapons program. However, the country was prevented from developing nuclear weapons partly because of the long-standing international sanctions and a lack of indigenous technical and scientific expertise. Libya's nuclear efforts also suffered setbacks because it paid large sums of money to the informal nuclear weapons smuggling ring known as the **A. Q. Khan** network, which consisted of individuals in **China**, **North Korea**, **Pakistan**, and elsewhere secretly assisting others with developing nuclear weapons. Libya was frustrated in its dealings because it felt that it had paid a great deal of money for incomplete or unnecessary equipment and materials, many of which remained unused in their original packaging. The bulk of the critical components and material for the nuclear weapon program was shipped to the United States as a consequence of the trilateral process.

LIGHT-WATER REACTOR (LWR). A nuclear reactor that uses ordinary water (as opposed to **heavy water**) as the moderator and coolant. **Low-enriched uranium (LEU)** is commonly used as the fuel in such reactors.

LIMITED TEST BAN TREATY (LTBT). The Treaty Banning **Nuclear Weapon** Tests in the Atmosphere, in Outer Space, and under Water, commonly referred to as the Limited Test Ban Treaty, was negotiated by the **United Kingdom**, **United States**, and Soviet Union and was signed by those three nations in Moscow on 5 August 1963. It entered into force on 10 October 1963. Since then, more than 100 nations have signed this treaty, and another 23 have acceded to it. The LTBT bans the testing of nuclear explosives above ground and underwater. It does not ban underground testing of nuclear explosives, unless such testing will cause radioactive debris to be spread outside the territorial limits of the nation under whose jurisdiction or control the test is conducted. In August 1988, six nations (Mexico, Indonesia, Peru, Sri Lanka, Venezuela, and Yugoslavia) proposed amending the LTBT to extend its prohibitions to all environments. This proposal, if it had been accepted by the three original signatory nations, would have transformed the LTBT into a comprehensive test ban treaty. However, the United States opposed using the LTBT as a vehicle for negotiating a comprehensive test ban, and the proposal failed to achieve the consensus needed for adoption. *See also* COMPREHENSIVE NUCLEAR TEST BAN TREATY (CTBT).

LITTLE BOY. The first **nuclear weapon** used in warfare. The bomb, nicknamed "Little Boy," was dropped over Hiroshima, **Japan**, by the **United States** on 6 August 1945. It used **uranium** as the fuel for its explosive. Little Boy was designed as a **gun-type nuclear device**, which called for a small wedge of uranium to be fired at a larger piece of uranium. On impact, the two pieces fused briefly, forming a **supercritical** mass. The resulting nuclear detonation was equivalent to exploding 20,000 tons of **TNT**, yet the bomb itself weighed less than 4.5 tons and was a mere 10 feet long and slightly over 2 feet in diameter. The design of the Little Boy bomb was officially designated the Mark-1 (Mk-1). Despite the successful bombing of Hiroshima, the U.S. military preferred the design of the "**Fat Man**" bomb, and production of that bomb overshadowed production of the Mk-1. A few Mk-1 bomb casings (perhaps 30) were constructed, but no nuclear explosive cores were made. By 1951, the Mk-1 Little Boy bomb was no longer in the U.S. nuclear weapon stockpile. *See also* AMOS; ARCHIE; GADGET; THIN MAN.

LIVENS PROJECTOR. The search for an effective means of achieving a high concentration of a lethal chemical warfare (CW) agent on an enemy's position produced one of the more clever yet simple weapons of World War I. In 1916, William Howard Livens, a civil engineer serving as a captain in Royal Engineers as commander of Z Company, **Special Brigade**, designed a mortar-like weapon consisting of a metal tube and a drum. The tube was emplaced in the ground at a 45-degree angle and pointed toward its target. Firing charges were placed inside the tube, followed by the drum. When fired, the drum was launched and discharged its contents onto or over the target. This drum-and-tube system was known as the "Livens projector" and offered advantages of large payload (a 65-pound drum held a 30-pound payload), easy emplacement, the ability to strike a target with little or no advance warning, and the ability for many to be fired simultaneously or in quick succession. This last advantage meant that a single target could be saturated in toxic chemicals or **incendiaries** with little or no dependency on favorable winds to carry a toxic gas cloud onto a target, as was required for cylinder gas discharges. A single drum provided a 10- to 20-fold enhancement over the chemical payload of a typical artillery shell. The system was an area weapon, having an effective range of 800 to 2,000 meters (0.5–1.2 miles). While it was not a precision-fired munition, its ability to saturate a target through rapid fire and large payloads compensated for the lack of precision in aiming any single drum.

Livens's design first saw combat use in fall 1916 and came into common usage the following year. It continued to be employed throughout World War I, and its success inspired the **Germans** to design a similar weapon.

A related weapon was the Stokes trench mortar. Also designed by the British in 1916, the 4-inch (diameter) Stokes mortar saw extensive use during the war, including by the U.S. Army's **First Gas Regiment**, following U.S. entry into the war. As with the Livens projector, the Stokes mortar used a drum for delivering CW agents. A 25-pound drum contained 7 pounds of the CW agent. Both weapons could also be used to fire conventional explosives, incendiary agents (mainly thermite), and **smoke agents** such as white phosphorus. While the Livens projector offered a significantly higher payload, it required extensive work and significant time to be reloaded. Once emplaced, a Stokes mortar could be fired at a rate of 10 to 20 drums per minute.

LOW-ENRICHED URANIUM (LEU). Uranium that has been processed to increase the uranium-235 content (that is, has been "enriched") but still contains less than 20 percent of that **isotope**. LEU can sustain a **chain reaction** under certain conditions and, thus, is used as fuel in **light-water reactors (LWR)**. Further processing is required, however, to make the material **weapons-grade** suitable for use as a nuclear explosive. *See also* HIGHLY ENRICHED URANIUM (HEU).

– M –

M687 155-MM ARTILLERY PROJECTILE. In 1976, the U.S. Army approved the design for the M687 155-mm artillery projectile, which became the first modern **binary chemical weapon** to be adopted by the U.S. military. The projectile had two canisters, each containing relatively nontoxic chemicals. One was filled with an organophosphorus chemical, methyl phosphonic difluoride, which was given the code name "DF." The other canister contained "OPA," a mix of isopropyl alcohol and isopropylamine. Because the two canisters were separately nontoxic, they allowed for safe storage and shipment. When the projectile was fired, setback and spin forces caused disks in each canister to rupture. The contents mixed within the shell, forming **sarin** ("GB"). To distinguish sarin formed by this binary process, it was given the code name "GB2." Although the M687 155-mm artillery projectile was approved in 1976, a decade would pass before all the necessary steps were finalized for full-scale production of the DF and OPA canisters and stockpiling of the munitions. *See also* BIGEYE.

MADDISON, RONALD. British Royal Air Force (RAF) Leading Aircraftsman Ronald Maddison joined five other British service personnel on the morning of 6 May 1953 at **Porton Down**. They were to be human subjects used in a test with chemical warfare (CW) agents—in their case, the **organophosphorus nerve agent sarin**. Similar tests had been conducted many times previously without serious mishap. The six personnel entered an airtight chamber, and each was issued a respirator for protection against toxic vapors and had a patch of two fabrics—one army flannel, the other battle dress serge—taped onto an arm. Approximately 200 milligrams of sarin were dropped onto each patch, and the six human subjects were observed. After about 30 minutes, Maddison complained of feeling "queer." Shortly thereafter, he went quiet, and then fell over. He was promptly evacuated from the test chamber, but despite the best efforts of medical personnel, Maddison could not be revived. He died, age 20.

The near-term consequences of this tragedy were modest. An inquest was held in secret and concluded that Maddison died of accidental mishap. Porton Down suspended nerve agent tests on human subjects. The family was informed of his death, although details were withheld from all but his father, who was admonished to refrain from sharing what he had learned. Some months later, a newspaper reporter found Maddison's death certificate, however, and details of the circumstances surrounding his death began to emerge. His death continues to attract attention, more than a half-century later. In 1999, the Wiltshire Constabulary, whose district includes Porton Down, launched a criminal investigation. That investigation continues, and as recently as June 2006 the British government stated that the Crown Prosecution Service was considering cases against former members of the Porton Down staff.

MANHATTAN PROJECT. In June 1942, the U.S. War Department decided to initiate a plan to develop a weapon using the newly discovered process of nuclear **fission**. In part, this decision grew out of the findings issued in the **MAUD Committee** report. To maintain secrecy, the plan was placed under the Army Corps of Engineers. **Leslie R. Groves**, the Corps official who had overseen the construction of the Pentagon outside Washington, D.C., was placed in command of the Manhattan Engineering District (MED), the code name selected for the effort to build the first **nuclear weapon**. The effort would later become known as the Manhattan Project.

Scientists, engineers, and others from Canada, the **United Kingdom**, and the **United States** contributed to the Manhattan Project, working out of more than 30 locations. The major sites involved were

- Alamogordo, New Mexico, designated the **Trinity Test Site**, where the first successful detonation of a nuclear device would take place on 16 July 1945.
- Berkeley, California, where the Radiation Laboratory made fundamental contributions to nuclear physics.
- Chicago, Illinois, where Italian-born physicist Enrico Fermi led the team at the Metallurgical Laboratory that achieved the first sustained **chain reaction**.
- Los Alamos, New Mexico, known as **Site Y**, where much of the research and design of nuclear weapons took place.
- Oak Ridge, Tennessee, known as **Site X**, which become home to the Headquarters, MED, as well as the Clinton Engineering Works, where **uranium** was enriched for use in weapons.
- Richland, Washington, known as **Site W** and home to the Hanford Site that produced **plutonium** for use as a fuel in a nuclear explosive.

- Wendover, Utah, where the U.S. Army Air Corps airfield was used by the **509th Composite Group** as part of "Project Alberta."
- Many distinguished scientists contributed to the Manhattan Project, including **Niels Bohr** and **Robert Otto Frisch**. U.S.-born nuclear physicist Robert Oppenheimer supervised research into **fast neutrons** and directed much of the work at Los Alamos, causing many to view him as father of the American nuclear bomb.

Although World War II ended with the formal surrender of **Japan** on 2 September 1945, the work of the Manhattan Project continued for another 16 months. In January 1947, the Manhattan Project ceased when its work was transferred to the newly established **Atomic Energy Commission (AEC)**. *See also* BUSH, VANNEVAR; FAT MAN; FIFTH WASHINGTON CONFERENCE ON THEORETICAL PHYSICS; FUCHS, KLAUS EMIL JULIUS; GADGET; GERMANY; JUMBO; NATIONAL DEFENSE RESEARCH COMMITTEE (NDRC); OFFICE OF SCIENTIFIC RESEARCH AND DEVELOPMENT (OSRD); STAGG FIELD.

MARBURG VIRUS. *See* USTINOV, NIKOLAI VASIL'YEVICH.

MARK-9 AND MARK-19 280-MM PROJECTILES. The U.S. military fielded two nuclear projectiles for **Atomic Annie**, its 280-mm atomic cannon. The Mark-9 (Mk-9), having a range of about 15 miles, was test-fired successfully on 25 May 1953 during **Shot Grable** at Frenchman Flats, Nevada. Its weight and poor aerodynamics spurred development of a replacement, the Mark-19 (Mk-19), which was 200 pounds lighter and had a range of nearly 19 miles.

MATERIALS UNACCOUNTED FOR (MUF). The amounts of **radioactive materials** lost or imbedded in equipment incident to normal operating procedures at a nuclear reactor. The nuclear industry and the military use "MUF" to denote gains or losses of materials relative to prior inventories. Explanations for MUF include uncertainty in the measurement techniques, measurement bias, human error, unknown or unmeasured flow streams, and unknown and often immeasurable holdup (such as residue collected within pipes). Determining whether missing nuclear materials are caused by MUF or are the result of diversion for undeclared nuclear activities, such as for the construction of **nuclear weapons**, is an important verification issue confronting the **International Atomic Energy Agency (IAEA)**.

MAUD COMMITTEE. Set up by the British government in spring 1940, the Military Application of Uranium Disintegration (popularly known by its acronym, MAUD) Committee studied the possibility of developing a **nuclear weapon**. Its conclusions greatly influenced both the British and U.S. governments. A July 1941 MAUD Committee report estimated that a **critical mass** of 10 kilograms (22 pounds) of **uranium**-235 would be sufficient to produce a large explosion unlike any obtained by conventional explosives. The report went on to suggest that a nuclear bomb could be loaded into existing aircraft. Finally, it concluded that such a bomb could be completed in about two years.

The MAUD Committee report erred in some of its conclusions, especially its dismissal of both **plutonium** production and the use of centrifuges as a means of **isotopic** enrichment. But the report carried great credibility with U.S. officials considering the possibly of nuclear warfare, including **Vannevar Bush**, **James Conant**, and President Franklin Delano Roosevelt. Further, it highlighted **German** achievements in nuclear science, especially the 1938 discovery of **fission** by German scientists **Otto Hahn** and Fritz Strassmann, as well as the fact that a large part of the Kaiser Wilhelm Institute in Berlin had been devoted to uranium research since spring 1940. Overall, the work of the MAUD Committee strengthened the resolve of the **United States** to develop a nuclear bomb, both out of a concern that the Nazi regime in Germany might succeed in its work on such a bomb and from a belief that such a bomb was technically feasible.

MAY-JOHNSON BILL. On 3 October 1945, a special message from President Harry S. Truman was communicated to the U.S. Senate and House of Representatives. In his message, Truman advocated swift passage of the May-Johnson Bill, legislation drafted by the War Department that laid out procedures governing the security, handling, and development of atomic energy. The bill was named for its cosponsors, Rep. Andrew May and Sen. Edwin Johnson. If the legislation had been adopted as proposed, then control of atomic energy would have been placed firmly under the control of the military, overseeing a newly created **Atomic Energy Commission (AEC)**. Although many U.S. scientists associated with the **Manhattan Project**, as well as its leader, **Leslie R. Groves**, supported the legislation, others in the scientific community expressed concerns. In particular, they viewed the proposed penalties for security violations as particularly onerous: 10 years' imprisonment and a $100,000 fine for each violation. Support for the May-Johnson Bill eroded as scientific opposition heated up, and in late 1945, Truman withdrew his support. A substitute bill, the McMahon Bill, was introduced as a replacement and eventually was enacted as the **Atomic Energy Act of 1946**.

McMAHON ACT; McMAHON BILL. *See* ATOMIC ENERGY ACT OF 1946.

M DEVICE. An apparatus developed by the **United Kingdom** at **Porton Down** during World War I as a means of disseminating certain chemical warfare (CW) agents. The device was officially termed a "thermogenerator," but a simpler description would be to call it a candle. Once the M Device was activated, a pyrotechnic mixture would burn, dispersing the CW agent as a particulate. This approach to dissemination was found to be especially effective for particulate materials, such as **adamsite** and diphenylchloroarsine. Because these agents are solids having high melting and boiling points, dissemination as a gas from a cylinder was impossible. Furthermore, conventional explosively driven munition designs failed to suspend a militarily significant portion of the solid in the air.

The M Device overcame these limitations. Although the device was developed too late for use during World War I, it was used by the United Kingdom in 1919 during its intervention in the **Russian Civil War**. British forces operating in the far north near Murmansk and along the frontier between Finland and **Russia** used M Devices on many occasions. Reliable reports on its effectiveness in combat are lacking, but the historical record of the fighting in this region suggests the M Device failed to prove decisive. The apparatus inspired other nations to adopt similar approaches for dissemination of CW agents, and candle-type munitions were used repeatedly by the **Japanese** during the fighting on mainland Asia in 1937–1945.

MEITNER, LISE (1878–1968). Austrian-born physicist. With her nephew **Robert Otto Frisch**, Meitner was the first to provide a mathematical explanation for the results of **Otto Hahn** and Fritz Strassmann and correctly identify that these results confirmed the process of nuclear **fission**. Meitner's private communication of their findings to **Niels Bohr** in December 1938 spurred U.S. development of a **nuclear weapon**.

After receiving her doctorate in physics at the University of Vienna, Meitner joined the Kaiser Wilhelm Institute of Physical Chemistry and Electrochemistry, Dahlem, in 1907, where she collaborated with Hahn. In 1917, they were one of three teams of researchers that independently discovered the element protactinium (Pa, atomic number 91). Their collaboration in the field of radiochemistry continued until 1938, when the **German** annexation of Austria made it difficult for Meitner, who was born into a Jewish family although she later converted to Christianity, to continue working in Nazi Germany. She immigrated to Sweden, where she got some space but little other support at Manne Siegbold's institute in Stockholm.

Meitner continued to correspond with Hahn, taking a particular interest in the Hahn-Strassmann experiments in which they bombarded **uranium** with neutrons. On 13 November 1938, Hahn and Meitner met secretly in Copenhagen, Denmark, to discuss the results. Meitner enlisted her nephew to help analyze and explain these results. They succeeded, naming the process "fission" and publishing their mathematical proof in the 11 February 1939 issue of *Nature*. But Meitner had already communicated these results, as well as her and Frisch's proof, to Bohr. This proof of nuclear fission, as well as the fact that scientists in the Nazi regime in Germany were engaged in such work, had a profound influence on American and British planning for the development of a nuclear weapon.

The 1944 Nobel Prize in Chemistry was awarded to Hahn and Strassmann. This award omitted any mention of the seminal contributions of Meitner and Frisch, whose work both recognized that fission had occurred and provided its mathematical proof. Although the failure to recognize their contribution was rationalized by many, especially Hahn, a feeling developed among many following Meitner's death that her role had been underrecognized. In 1997, the International Union of Pure and Applied Chemistry (IUPAC) provided some of that recognition when it approved the name "Meitnerium" (Mt) for the newly discovered element 109. *See also* FIFTH WASHINGTON CONFERENCE ON THEORETICAL PHYSICS.

MELTDOWN. Melting of the core materials in a nuclear reactor. Meltdown is of serious concern because its occurrence can lead to breaching of the reactor vessel and result in venting of **radioactive materials** into the atmosphere. *See also* CHINA SYNDROME.

MERCK, GEORGE W. (1894–1957). Merck served as special assistant to the U.S. secretary of war during World War II. He also headed the War Research Service (WRS), a civilian agency established in May 1942 within the Federal Security Agency, and directed the Branch for War Research in Chemistry. In his capacity as chairman of the U.S. Biological Warfare Committee, he submitted a final report to Secretary of War Robert P. Patterson on 24 October 1945 that summarized various countries' **biological weapon (BW)** activities during World War II. The report, which concluded that the **United States** should maintain a BW program, had a significant impact on U.S. policy after the war and helped provide the basis for funding BW research. From 1925 to 1955, Merck worked for Merck & Company, a pharmaceutical firm founded by his family.

MIGHTY MITE. An air compressor–based dispersal system employed by U.S. forces during the Vietnam War to deliver **riot-control agents (RCA)** into tunnels and cave systems.

MIKE. On 1 November 1952 (before midnight 31 October in the United States), the **United States** conducted the first successful detonation of a staged **thermonuclear** device at **Enewetak Atoll**. This device, given the code name "Mike," had an estimated yield in excess of 10 megatons and used the "**fission-fusion-fission**" design concept. The overall device was nearly 7 feet in diameter and 20 feet long and weighed 82 tons. This bulk, plus the requirement for cryogenic equipment to cool the **deuterium**, a component of the secondary portion of the explosive, meant Mike was not a deliverable **nuclear weapon**. *See also* BRAVO; GEORGE.

MILITARILY CRITICAL TECHNOLOGIES LIST (MCTL). A comprehensive listing of technologies whose acquisition by a nation is judged by the **United States** as capable of significantly enhancing that other nation's military capability, to the detriment of U.S. national security. These capabilities include programs to develop **weapons of mass destruction (WMD)**.

MILITARY ACADEMY OF CHEMICAL DEFENSE. *See* S. K. TIMOSHENKO MILITARY ACADEMY OF RADIOLOGICAL, CHEMICAL, AND BIOLOGICAL DEFENSE.

MILITARY UNIVERSITY OF RADIOLOGICAL, CHEMICAL, AND BIOLOGICAL DEFENSE. *See* S. K. TIMOSHENKO MILITARY ACADEMY OF RADIOLOGICAL, CHEMICAL, AND BIOLOGICAL DEFENSE.

MIRZYANOV, VIL SULANOVICH. Mirzyanov worked as a chemist at Moscow-based **GosNIIOKhT** during the time of the Union of Socialist Soviet Republics (USSR). On 10 October 1991, his article "Inversion" appeared in the newspaper *Kuranty*, in which Mirzyanov warned of continuing work in the USSR on novel **chemical weapons (CW)**. In his article, he hinted at a novel class of CW, later revealed to be the **novichoks**. Immediately after the December 1991 dissolution of the USSR, Mirzyanov was dismissed from GosNIIOKhT. He was arrested by Russian authorities on 22 October 1992 and charged with revealing state secrets. His arrest and imprisonment attracted international attention, with calls for his release and for the charges to be dropped. On 22 February 1994, his case was closed, due to the absence of any evidence of a crime. Mirzyanov subsequently immigrated to the United States, where he continued to speak and write about the novichoks and other activities represented as circumventing or contravening the **Chemical Weapons Convention (CWC)**. In 2002 Mirzyanov published his memoirs, *Vyzov* [The Call], in which he discusses general aspects of the Soviet CW defense research establishment and the circumstances of his arrest.

MISSILE TECHNOLOGY CONTROL REGIME (MTCR). An effort on the part of 34 participating states to counter proliferation of missiles capable of delivering **nuclear weapons**. The MTCR applies to missile technologies as well as the missiles themselves and includes unmanned missiles, rockets, and cruise missiles having a payload of at least 500 kilograms (1,100 pounds) and a range of at least 300 kilometers (186 miles).

MISSION-ORIENTED PROTECTIVE POSTURE (MOPP). The U.S. military uses MOPP as a means of categorizing the carrying and wearing of personal protective equipment (PPE) to be used in response to the actual or expected presence of toxic chemicals, biological pathogens, and **radioactive materials**. Five levels of MOPP exist:

1. At Level 0, the lowest level of MOPP, individuals will have protective clothing and equipment (such as a protective mask, gloves, and overboots) available, but not worn.
2. At Level 1, personnel must don a protective overgarment and helmet and carry the other PPE items.
3. At Level 2, personnel must don protective overboots.
4. At Level 3, personnel must don protective (gas) masks and hoods.
5. At Level 4, the highest level of MOPP, personnel must don butyl rubber gloves and glove liners.

MOPP levels provide uniform and clear guidance for U.S. military operations.

MONTEBELLO DECISION. In a communication issued by the NATO ministers at the conclusion of the alliance's autumn 1983 meeting, the ministers declared that the policy of NATO was to preserve the peace through the maintenance of forces at the lowest level capable of deterring the threat posed by the Warsaw Pact. Consistent with this policy, the ministers announced that the Nuclear Planning Group had decided on 27 October 1983 to reduce the number of nuclear warheads in Europe by 1,400. Because the ministers were meeting in Montebello, Canada, the decision became known as the Montebello Decision. The reduction was carried out. Among the nuclear warheads removed from Europe was the stockpile of U.S. **atomic demolition munitions (ADM)**, which were returned to the **United States** and ultimately dismantled.

MOROCCO. In 1908, Spain invaded Morocco, attacking from Spain's two historical enclaves on the north Moroccan coast, Ceuta and Melilla. This conflict would continue for several decades, but it was especially fierce in the 1920s. It also witnessed significant use of **chemical weapons (CW)**, especially air-droppable chemical bombs, which were then something of a novelty. In 1918, King Alfonso XIII of Spain sent requests to **Germany** for samples of CW and for information regarding their manufacture. Following the armistice ending World War I, negotiations between Spain and the Weimar Republic intensified, and Germany ultimately provided extensive technical support on the use of CW, culminating in a contract to a German entity based in Hamburg to construct a CW production facility. This facility would become the Maestranza facility in Melilla. Spanish forces bombarded Moroccan rebels with **chloropicrin**, **phosgene**, and **sulfur mustard**, beginning as early as November 1921. CW use continued until at least 1927. The Moroccan rebels had scant protection against these weapons, but it is unclear whether their use proved decisive for the Spanish. *See also* STOLTZENBERG, HUGO.

MOSCOW THEATER INCIDENT. On 23 October 2002 Chechen terrorists took hostage the audience and actors of the Dubrovka Theatrical Center in Moscow during an evening performance. The crisis ended 56 hours later in the early morning hours of 26 October when **Russian** special forces dispersed what was initially described as "sleeping gas" into the theater about 30 minutes prior to entering the theater. The scene was secured within about 15 minutes after the forces went in. The Chechen terrorists killed two hostages, but another 129 perished as a consequence of exposure to the chemical used by the Russian Special Forces. All the hostage takers died at the scene. Subsequently, the chemical used in the operation was reported to have been an **aerosolized** form of carfentanil or etorphine, drugs typically used to sedate big game animals. This episode focused attention on how such incidents as this one might be treated with respect to the provisions of the **Chemical Weapons Convention (CWC)**.

MUBTAKKAR. An Arabic term variously translated as "device" or "invention." The term is reported to have been used in literature, including design specifications, circulated among al-**Qaeda** operatives to refer to a type of crude dispersion device to disseminate toxic chemicals. As such, a mubtakkar is taken to be an improvised form of a **chemical weapon (CW)**. Further details regarding the toxic chemicals and effectiveness remain to be verified in the open literature.

MULTIPLE INDEPENDENTLY TARGETABLE REENTRY VEHICLE (MIRV). A single missile weapon system having several warheads, each of which can be programmed separately. A weapon system having a MIRV capability can strike more than one target or strike a single target repeatedly. Examples of weapon systems that can be designed and built to be MIRV capable include **intercontinental ballistic missiles (ICBM)** and submarine-launched ballistic missiles (SLBM).

MUSTARD GAS. An enduring but flawed name for the chemical *bis*(2-chloroethyl)sulfide, a chemical warfare (CW) agent that causes blisters and burns. A preferred term is **sulfur mustard**. This substance is neither a mustard (in the sense used by chemists) nor, under ordinary conditions, a gas. The substance was discovered repeatedly and independently by chemists in the 19th century, and one of these chemists, Frederick Guthrie, remarked in 1859 that the chemical had an odor resembling that of "oil of mustard" and that it tasted like horseradish. In its pure state, mustard gas is a straw-colored liquid, although impurities can cause it to appear reddish-brown to black. In any event, the liquid bears little resemblance in color, odor, or taste to the condiment mustard.

When sulfur mustard first appeared on the battlefield in July 1917, soldiers were in the habit of referring to all chemical warfare agents as "gases," regardless of their physical state. It might be that this habit, plus the aromatic resemblance it bore to oil of mustard, account for the soldiers' labeling this chemical "mustard gas." The label endures and has been adopted in the names used for related substances, such as chemical analogues (e.g., bromine mustard, half-mustard, oxygen mustard) and substances causing similar blisters and burns (in particular, **nitrogen mustard**).

MYCOTOXIN. A **toxin** produced by fungi. Such toxins include the **trichothecenes** implicated in the **yellow rain** episode and aflatoxin, a potent cancer-causing substance associated with fungi that infest food products such as corn, milk, and peanuts. Mycotoxin contamination can have important consequences for military operations. In a memoir, Soviet premier Nikita Khrushchev wrote the following:

> In early 1939 . . . horses were dropping dead on farms all over the Ukraine, along the Polish border. We figured that the **Germans**, who were then preparing for war against us, might be trying to sabotage our economy and our military capabilities. You see, horses weren't just livestock in those days; they were what tanks, airplanes and jeeps are today. . . . [We] decided German agents were poisoning the horses. . . . [But a commission] came to the conclusion the horses were being made sick by a fungus that grew on wet hay. Recommended method for stamping out the disease was simple—keep hay dry.

– N –

NAGASAKI. *See BOCK'S CAR*; FAT MAN; NATIONAL PEACE MEMORIAL HALL FOR ATOMIC BOMB VICTIMS.

NATIONAL DEFENSE RESEARCH COMMITTEE (NDRC). On 12 June 1940, President Franklin Delano Roosevelt signed an executive order establishing the National Defense Research Committee and appointing **Vannevar Bush**, president of the Carnegie Foundation, as its director. Roosevelt was reacting to concerns expressed by scientists and government officials that the **United States** needed to organize its scientific research for service in a national emergency. The NDRC, whose members were appointed by the president, was instructed to supplement the work of the departments of the army and navy in developing instruments of war. Consistent with this instruction, the NDRC took responsibility for the **Uranium Committee**.

The following year, the president established the **Office of Scientific Research and Development (OSRD)**, with the NDRC as one of its units. Bush moved from the NDRC to head OSRD and was replaced by **James B. Conant**, who served as the NDRC's chairman until 31 December 1947, at which time its activities were taken over by the newly established Department of Defense. During its existence, the NDRC recommended to OSRD suitable projects and research programs and administered the technical and scientific work of relevant contracts. Initially, the NDRC was set up with five divisions, each headed by an NDRC member. In fall 1942, the NDRC reorganized its activities into 23 divisions, panels, or committees. For example, Division 9, Chemistry, headed by Walter Kirner, was primarily devoted to problems of offensive and defensive chemical warfare.

NATIONAL PEACE MEMORIAL HALL FOR ATOMIC BOMB VICTIMS. The **Japanese** government has established two National Peace Memorial Halls for Atomic Bomb Victims. They are located in the two cities that experienced nuclear explosions in August 1945: Hiroshima and Nagasaki. Each hall includes an exhibit with names and photographs of victims. To be included in the exhibit, the victim must have been exposed directly during the bombings on 6 and 9 August 1945; exposed by entering either city within two weeks of the bombing; affected by radiation as a result of relief work or similar activity; or exposed in the womb. Whether the victim died of the exposure is irrelevant to inclusion in the exhibit.

At least five U.S. servicemen are included in the Hiroshima exhibit, including Norman Brissette, John Long, Julius Molnar, and Ralph Neal. These men were being held as prisoners of war in Chugoku Military Police Headquarters, Hiroshima. They died in the bombing or shortly thereafter. Japanese government records suggest as many as 20 Allied POWs may have been in Hiroshima when it was bombed, but verifying dates and causes of deaths for those POWs who might have been there has proven problematic.

NATIONAL RESEARCH COUNCIL (NRC). During World War I, the National Research Council was established to coordinate research by scientists and universities with the needs identified by the various departments of the U.S. government and the NRC itself. In April 1917, the NRC established a Committee on Noxious Gases to carry out this function in the area of **chemical weapons (CW)**. Difficulties experienced in ensuring that the work done by academic scientists matched the needs of the military inspired **Vannevar**

Bush to propose the creation of the **National Defense Research Committee (NDRC)** as the **United States** prepared for its entry into World War II.

NATURALLY OCCURRING RADIOACTIVE MATERIAL (NORM). Sources of radiation that occur naturally and, hence, whose presence should have a benign explanation. For example, **radium** is a NORM because all of its **isotopes** are radioactive. Detecting radium is not necessarily indicative of any suspicious activity, as its presence can be mere happenstance. On the other hand, **plutonium** is a man-made element. All its isotopes are **radioactive material** and many are useful for making a **nuclear weapon**. Consequently, any detection of plutonium would be cause for further investigation.

NE. *See* BIGEYE.

NERVE GAS. A misleading but frequently encountered term used for an **organophosphorus nerve agent**. The common organophosphorus nerve agents **tabun, sarin, soman, V-gas,** and **VX** are liquids rather than gases under ambient conditions such as those to be expected in combat. The term "nerve gas" persists, but its use should be avoided.

NEST. *See* NUCLEAR EMERGENCY SEARCH TEAM (NEST).

NEUROTOXIN. A **toxin** that acts specifically on nervous tissues. Examples include **aconitine, botulinum toxin (BTX),** and the venom of black widow spiders.

NEUTRON BOMB. Secretary of State John Foster Dulles stated in October 1957 that "recent tests point to the possibility of possessing **nuclear weapons**, the destructiveness and radiation effects of which can be confined substantially to predetermined targets." Dulles was referring to the neutron bomb, which uses prompt radiation effects (principally from neutrons) to destroy living organisms but which has modest conventional-weapon effects such as blast and high temperatures. The neutron bomb would have relatively little radioactive **fall-**

out, meaning that an area hit by a neutron bomb could be entered safely soon afterward. The concept of a neutron bomb likely came from Edward Teller, a primary participant in the **Manhattan Project** and a leader in U.S. efforts to develop a **hydrogen bomb**. No public record exists of the successful development of a neutron bomb. The concept, however, received serious consideration, especially during the administration of President Jimmy Carter (1977–1981).

NEVADA TEST SITE (NTS). In 1950, the **United States** redesignated the Las Vegas Bombing and Gunnery Range as the Nevada Test Site and established it as the nation's continental area for testing of nuclear devices. Previously, most **nuclear weapon** tests were conducted in Pacific Ocean regions. This arrangement proved costly, logistically cumbersome, and time consuming. The range north of Las Vegas, Nevada, was selected because it was already government property and had few residents nearby. The first nuclear test conducted at NTS took place on 27 January 1951, when a one-kiloton bomb was dropped from an airplane. By 2006, the United States had conducted 896 nuclear weapon tests at NTS, including 24 tests conducted jointly with the **United Kingdom**. NTS was also the site of another 29 nuclear detonation tests conducted as part of the **Plowshare Program**.

NIKOLSKY'S SIGN. The condition in which a person's outer layer of skin is easily rubbed off by slight injury or contact. In many cases, the condition leads to complications, such as infection of the exposed area. In the context of chemical warfare (CW), a peculiar complication is the prospect of forming secondary blisters resulting from the transfer of a **vesicant**, such as **sulfur mustard** or **nitrogen mustard**, from skin that is rubbed off onto unaffected surfaces, such as nearby skin.

NI-SHELL. In fall 1914, as World War I settled into a war of attrition, each side looked for means of gaining the advantages needed to achieve decisive victory. **Germany** considered various technical innovations, one of which was to use chemicals that could be launched into the enemy's trench and force them to expose themselves to the lethal effects of artillery shells and small-arms fire. Walther Nernst

(1864–1941), a distinguished scientist who would receive the 1920 Nobel Prize in Chemistry, suggested *o*-dianisidine chlorosulfonate, an intensely irritating substance dubbed "sneezing powder" (German: *Niespulver*). The Germans took up Nernst's suggestion, incorporating this sneezing powder along with conventional explosives into 105-mm artillery shells. The shells, designated *Ni-schrapnells* or "Ni-shells," were used against British and Indian troops at Neuve-Chapelle, France, on 27 October 1914. The results were inconsequential, and the British military diaries from that time have no indication that anything unusual was detected in the air following the explosion of these Ni-shells along their lines. The ineffectiveness of Ni-shells was dramatically demonstrated by the son of German general Erich von Falkenhayn, chief of the general staff, who reportedly won a wager of a case of Champagne by remaining unprotected for five minutes in a cloud of *o*-dianisidine chlorosulfonate. Thus, this episode of early use of **chemical weapons (CW)** appears to have gone unnoticed. Disappointed in these results, the Germans discontinued use of Ni-shells, although the search for an effective chemical warfare agent continued. *See also* CHLORINE.

NITROGEN MUSTARD. Any of a group of chemical warfare (CW) agents similar to **sulfur mustard** in the physiological effects caused by exposure but having nitrogen as a key constituent in place of sulfur. The nitrogen mustard group is most closely associated with a series of alkyl di(2-chloroethyl)amines, whose discovery was reported in the scientific literature in the mid-1930s. The primary members of the nitrogen mustard series are ethyl di(2-chloroethyl)amine ("HN-1"), methyl di(2-chloroethyl)amine ("HN-2"), and *tris*(2-chloroethyl)amine ("HN-3"), which are explicitly mentioned in the **Chemical Weapons Convention (CWC)**. The **United States** produced about 100 tons of HN-1 during World War II, first at **Edgewood Arsenal** and later at Pine Bluff Arsenal, Arkansas. **Germany** produced 2,000 tons of HN-3 during the war and created a stockpile of 105-mm and 150-mm artillery shells and 150-mm rockets filled with it. There is no evidence any nitrogen mustard has ever been used in combat. Nitrogen mustards are **vesicants**; certain nitrogen mustards have been used successfully to treat cancer.

NIVALENOL. *See* TRICHOTHECENE MYCOTOXINS; YELLOW RAIN.

NODDY SUIT. British slang for a chemical warfare (CW) protection suit. *See also* MISSION-ORIENTED PROTECTIVE POSTURE (MOPP).

NONPERSISTENT AGENT. *See* CLASSES OF CHEMICAL WEAPONS.

NONPROLIFERATION TREATY (NPT). The 1968 Treaty on the Nonproliferation of Nuclear Weapons, commonly referred to as the "Nonproliferation Treaty," forms the legal foundation for the global nuclear nonproliferation regime. The treaty, which entered into force on 5 March 1970 and has 189 States Parties, obliges its members not to "assist, encourage or induce" non–nuclear weapon states (NNWS) in manufacturing or acquiring **nuclear weapons**, nuclear explosive devices, or "control over such weapons and explosive devices." The treaty also obliges each NNWS to place **International Atomic Energy Agency (IAEA) safeguards** on various nuclear activities carried out under its control.

NORSK HYDRO PLANT. In 1911, the world's then largest hydroelectric facility opened in Norway. Known as the Norsk Hydro Plant and situated at the base of a waterfall, the facility took on special significance following the Nazi occupation of Norway in 1940. The plant was already the world's sole commercial source of **heavy water** (water enriched in **deuterium**, an **isotope** of hydrogen), and the Nazis forced Norsk Hydro to increase monthly heavy water production from 10 kilograms (22 pounds) to 100 kg (220 pounds), with the product being shipped to **Germany** for use in its nuclear program. For technical reasons, German scientists had concluded that only heavy water would be satisfactory as a moderator in their design for a nuclear reactor, which was a necessary step toward producing **plutonium** for use in a **nuclear weapon**. The Allies learned of this situation and decided to sabotage the plant.

In late 1942, a sabotage operation ("Operation Freshman") was mounted, and two gliders carrying 41 British commandos were released near the plant. Both gliders crashed, killing several of the commandos. The rest of the force surrendered, believing, because they were in uniform, that they would be treated as prisoners of war. However, Adolf Hitler had already issued orders calling for the extermination of all commandos, and all the prisoners were executed.

Another sabotage attempt, "Operation Gunnerside," was launched in February 1943, and this operation succeeded. Nine commandos were involved. All were Norwegians, trained in the **United Kingdom**. Explosives destroyed 18 heavy water cells, and the entire stockpile of heavy water from five months' work drained away. All nine commandos succeeded in escaping. Repairs were completed by April 1943, and full production was restored by August. On 15 November 1943, U.S. bombers hit the plant, causing little damage to the heavy water equipment but extensive damage elsewhere.

The Germans thereafter elected to dismantle the plant and relocate it to Germany, along with its stockpile of 14 tons of heavy water. This relocation effort failed, however, when one of the Norwegian commandos from Operation Gunnerside, assisted by two local residents, placed explosive charges on a ferry carrying 49 drums of heavy water. The charges detonated, sinking the ferry and 45 of the drums. Thereafter, the Germans had no real chance of achieving a self-sustaining nuclear reaction prior to the end of the war.

NORTH AMERICAN AEROSPACE DEFENSE COMMAND (NORAD). An air defense command and control center, commonly known as NORAD, operated jointly by Canada and the **United States**. NORAD is tasked to detect and monitor man-made objects over North America, including in outer space. The facility is hardened against **nuclear weapon** attack and is deeply buried within Cheyenne Mountain near Colorado Springs, Colorado. Although it was established primarily to detect possible nuclear attacks and to coordinate an appropriate response, the facility has also been used to assist with the interdiction of narcotics smuggling.

NORTH KOREA. The Democratic People's Republic of Korea (DPRK), commonly referred to as North Korea, is known to have a **nuclear weapons** program and is assessed by various intelligence agencies as having **chemical** and **biological weapons (CBW)** programs. North Korea also is known to be developing ballistic missiles that might give it capability of launching nuclear, biological, or chemical (NBC) weapons against neighboring countries. It has test-launched intermediate-range ballistic missiles in the direction of **Japan**.

In 1993 North Korea expelled inspectors from the **International Atomic Energy Agency (IAEA)** and withdrew from the **Nonproliferation Treaty (NPT)**. These actions were prompted by a dispute over indications documented by the agency that North Korea had secretly diverted nuclear fuel and had carried out undeclared enrichment work. The North Korean withdrawal prompted negotiations that resulted in a 1994 Agreed Framework between North Korea and the **United States**. The framework, which the two parties are careful not to characterize as an "agreement," aims to achieve peace and security on a nuclear-free Korean Peninsula partly by allowing North Korea to replace its older graphite-moderated reactors with more proliferation-resistant **light-water reactors (LWRs)** and reaffirming a commitment by both sides to work toward strengthening the international nonproliferation regime, including by adhering to the NPT. **China**, Japan, North Korea, **Russia**, South Korea, and the United States have worked together to implement aspects of the agreed framework. However, it has only been partially implemented and its utility has been seriously questioned.

North Korea has periodically indicated that it would like to obtain a comprehensive security guarantee that the United States will not attack it and points out that a peace treaty was never concluded following the end of the Korean War. It would also like the United States to withdraw its military forces from the Korean Peninsula. There are widespread press reports about North Korean government-sponsored criminal activities, such as kidnappings of Japanese and South Korean nationals, as well as money counterfeiting and narcotics trafficking that are designed to help raise hard currency and to obtain access to luxury goods. China has been the main conduit for economic trade into North Korea and is concerned that if North Korea were to collapse, it would face serious challenges maintaining stability along its border and have to readjust to possible regional security changes.

North Korea has also been implicated in the work of the so-called **A. Q. Khan** network, which may have aided the country's acquisition of nuclear weapon technology and knowledge. In 2005 North Korea publicly stated that it possessed nuclear weapons. It is estimated to have between 5 and 10 nuclear warheads. On 9 October 2006, North Korea exploded a nuclear device. Seismic and other monitors confirmed the explosion, but experts estimated the explosive yield to be only between 500 and 1,000 tons of **TNT-equivalent**. This yield is considered low, fueling speculation that the device suffered from **preinitiation** and leading Richard L. Garwin, a key designer of the U.S. **hydrogen bomb**, to describe it as a "waste of **plutonium**." In October 2006 the **United Nations** Security Council (UNSC) unanimously voted to impose economic and political sanctions on North Korea.

As of May 2007, the so-called six-party talks, consisting of representatives from China, Japan, North and South Korea, Russia, and the United States, appeared stalled but are expected to resume once North Korea shuts down its Yongbyon nuclear reactor. The talks are designed to offer North Korea a combination of economic, security, and diplomatic incentives to forgo its nuclear weapon program. In particular, the parties are discussing what security guarantees North Korea should receive that it will not be attacked; the modalities for whether and how the construction of LWRs that were planned to be constructed under the 1994 Agreed Framework should proceed, for how North Korea should rejoin the NPT and be provided access to nuclear energy for peaceful purposes, and for normalizing diplomatic relations and trade; and the measures North Korea must take to achieve verifiable and irreversible disarmament.

NOVICHOK. A term typically translated from the **Russian** новичок as "newcomer," Referring to a class of novel **chemical weapons (CW)**. Open-literature reports regarding the novichoks can be traced to the early 1990s, although their development dates to work begun in the Union of Soviet Socialist Republics (USSR). According to articles by **Vil S. Mirzyanov**, the novichoks were developed by Moscow-based **GosNIIOKhT**. He describes a series of innovative CW with designations such as A-230, A-232, Novichok-5, and Novichok-7. There is no authoritative, publicly available information, however, on the existence and precise chemical nature of the novichoks. No such CW agents have been declared by Russia as being in its CW stockpile. *See also* OPERATION SHOCKER.

NUCLEAR EMERGENCY SEARCH TEAM (NEST). A special unit in the National Nuclear Security Administration (NNSA) of the U.S. Department of Energy (DOE). NEST was established in 1974 and is tasked with handling technical aspects of nuclear or radiological terrorism, including searching for and assisting in the rendering safe of an improvised nuclear device (IND) or a **radiological dispersal device (RDD)**. *See also* NUCLEAR WEAPON.

NUCLEAR FUEL CYCLE. The steps involved in producing fuel for nuclear reactors include the following; namely,

1. mining
2. refining
3. enrichment
4. fabrication of fuel
5. recovery of **fissionable** materials from spent fuel
6. final disposal or reuse of such materials

Most of the technologies, materials, and equipment used in the nuclear fuel cycle may also be used to support a **nuclear weapon** program, prompting concerns over potential diversion or misuse of such technologies. *See also* INTERNATIONAL ATOMIC ENERGY AGENCY (IAEA); SMALL QUANTITIES PROTOCOL (SQP).

NUCLEAR PILE. The early nuclear reactors, such as the one at **Stagg Field**, were fashioned from stacks or piles of graphite blocks interspersed with slugs of natural **uranium**. This construction led to such reactors being dubbed "piles" or "nuclear piles." The preferred term currently is *nuclear reactor*. During World War II, the **ALSOS Mission** uncovered an unworkable pile constructed by **Germany**.

NUCLEAR REGULATORY COMMISSION (NRC). *See* ATOMIC ENERGY COMMISSION (AEC).

NUCLEAR SUPPLIERS GROUP (NSG). A consortium of 45 nations, together with the European Commission, that coordinate, through nonbinding guidelines, their national export controls on dual-use materials, technology, and equipment, such as nuclear fuel, that could be used to support a **nuclear weapon** program. The NSG was established following **India**'s 1974 **peaceful nuclear explosion (PNE)**. The Indian nuclear device used imported **plutonium**, and such use is generally considered a misuse of nuclear material that was transferred to India for peaceful purposes. The NSG's guidelines were first made public in 1978. *See also* ATOMS FOR PEACE.

NUCLEAR WEAPON. An explosive device that uses **radioactive materials** as the primary fuel for the explosion. This fuel undergoes either a **fission** or **fusion** reaction, resulting in the release of an enormous amount of energy. A weapon using a fusion reaction is more commonly called a **thermonuclear** bomb or sometimes a **hydrogen bomb**. At least nine countries are known or believed to possess nuclear weapons: **China**, **France**, **India**, **Israel**, **North Korea**, **Pakistan**, **Russia**, the **United Kingdom**, and the **United States**. **South Africa** is believed to have had nuclear weapons but to have destroyed them prior to its transition from an apartheid regime.

As of 2006, the total world stockpile of nuclear weapons is estimated to be approximately 27,000. Of these, about 12,500 are considered to be operational. At the height of the Cold War, the total number of nuclear warheads peaked at about 70,000.

Russia and the United States possess over 95 percent of all nuclear weapons. Russia has an estimated 16,000 warheads, of which some 5,800 are active or operational, while the United States has approximately 10,000 warheads, with around 5,700 active or operational. France is thought to have about 350 nuclear warheads, the United Kingdom somewhat fewer than 200 operational, and China an estimated 145. India has reportedly produced sufficient **fissile material** to construct 100 or so nuclear warheads, but may have only about 55. Regional rival Pakistan is believed to have produced enough fissile material for some 90 nuclear warheads, with perhaps 50 to 60 currently available. Both India and Pakistan are believed to be increasing the size of their respective nuclear weapon stockpiles. Israel, which follows a policy of ambiguity as to whether it possesses nuclear weapons, reportedly has produced between 60 and 80 nuclear warheads and has sufficient fissile material to produce 115 to 190 warheads in total. North Korea, which publicly stated in 2005 that it possesses nuclear weapons and which conducted a nuclear test in October 2006, could, depending on its technical capability, have 5 to 15 operational warheads.

While Russia and the United States are committed to further substantial reductions of their nuclear weapon stockpiles, all countries that have openly declared stockpiles are pursuing a variety of stockpile stewardship programs to retain nuclear weapon expertise and nuclear deterrence. The United States has considered developing low-yield, deep-penetrating nuclear warheads for use as "bunker busters" against deeply buried or hardened suspected nuclear, biological, and chemical (NBC) facilities, while India and Pakistan have indicated that they are committed to having a credible nuclear "triad" consisting of land-based, sea-based, and air-launched nuclear weapons. "Subcritical experiments"—essentially combinations of chemical explosives and fissile materials that are detonated in such a manner that there is no sustained nuclear fission reaction—continue to be carried out by a number of the nuclear weapon possessors, including Russia and the United States. Such tests are permitted by the **Comprehensive Nuclear Test Ban Treaty (CTBT)**.

The **Nonproliferation Treaty (NPT)**, the principal international legal instrument against nuclear weapons, requires the eventual and complete nuclear disarmament by all of the parties. Monitoring for nuclear explosions is possible through the use of hydroacoustic, infrasound, radionuclide, and seismological techniques. Certain techniques permit nuclear explosions to be distinguished from earthquakes and other seismic events. However, it is possible that seismic monitors would not detect **decoupled** nuclear explosions. *See also* RADIOLOGICAL DISPERSAL DEVICE (RDD).

NUNN-LUGAR PROGRAM. *See* COOPERATIVE THREAT REDUCTION (CTR) PROGRAM.

– O –

OBSCURANT. *See* SMOKE AGENT.

OFFICE OF SCIENTIFIC RESEARCH AND DEVELOPMENT (OSRD). Preparations by the **United States** for its eventual entry into World War II got a boost on 28 June 1941 when President

Franklin Delano Roosevelt approved the creation of the Office of Scientific Research and Development. **Vannevar Bush** moved from his position as chairman of the **National Defense Research Committee (NDRC)** to head OSRD, reporting directly to the president. This move enhanced Bush's ability to work with other federal agencies and lessened military influence over many research and development programs involving instruments of war. Most importantly, OSRD took over the **Uranium Committee**, making it the OSRD Section on Uranium. Results of this committee could now be communicated directly from Bush to the president. The NDRC became more of an advisory body, making its recommendations to OSRD. This arrangement remained in place, with Bush as director, until 31 December 1947, when the OSRD and NDRC were abolished and their functions taken over by the newly established Department of Defense.

OGARKOV, VSEVELOD IVANOVICH (1926–1987). Soviet microbiologist. Ogarkov, a major general as well as a corresponding member of the Soviet Academy of Medical Sciences, served as the first head of **Biopreparat**, which was also known as "Ogarkov's System."

OLD CHEMICAL WEAPONS (OCW). The **Chemical Weapons Convention (CWC)** defines *old chemical weapons* as **chemical weapons (CW)** produced before 1925, or those produced between 1925 and 1946 that have been determined to be unusable. Official statements to the effect that a state "does not possess chemical weapons" sometimes cause confusion because the CWC makes distinctions among **abandoned chemical weapons (ACW)**, old chemical weapons, and chemical weapons.

OPA. *See* M687 155-MM ARTILLERY PROJECTILE.

OPERATION ALADDIN. In January 1942, the British War Cabinet approved developing an offensive **biological weapon (BW)** capability, ostensibly for retaliation in kind against **Germany**. Operation Vegetarian, later renamed Operation Aladdin, was launched immediately thereafter. The operation involved the production and stockpile of linseed cakes containing **anthrax** spores. Some five million cakes were made in an Old Bond Street, London, soap factory and then shipped to **Porton Down**. The cakes, known as "buns," went to the "bun factory," where women injected them with spores. The anthrax-laden cakes were placed in cardboard boxes and stored for military use. The concept was that aircraft would drop the anthrax-laden cakes over the German countryside, where cattle might feed on them.

The effects were calculated to be several-fold. Anthrax-infected cattle would die or be slaughtered, depriving Germany of the meat, dairy, and leather products needed to feed and clothe its people and military. The spores would survive in the fields, reinfecting cattle and other foraging livestock for years to come. Failure to diagnosis anthrax infection in livestock would increase the likelihood that anthrax-contaminated meat, milk, and leather would be passed along to consumers, thereby adding to the medical burden in wartime Germany and further reducing its ranks of workers and soldiers. Finally, fears over anthrax contamination would erode public confidence in Germany in the safety of meat products (hence, the original Operation Vegetarian code name). The cattle cakes, as they came to be called, were never used. Most were destroyed immediately following the war. A few were kept as part of culture collections, but these had been destroyed by 1972.

OPERATION BIG DEW. In 1951–1952, the **United States** carried out Operation Big Dew, a biological warfare (BW) **aerosol** study. It involved the study of 250 pounds of fluorescent tracer released from a minesweeper off the southeast U.S. coast and was designed to estimate the vulnerability of the United States to a covert offshore release of a BW agent.

OPERATION BIG ITCH. Operation Big Itch involved a series of U.S. field tests conducted at **Dugway Proving Ground (DPG)** in 1954. The tests called for E-23 and E-14 munitions loaded with *Xenopsylla choepis* fleas that had been infected with the **plague** bacterium to be dropped over DPG test grids, releasing their contents onto guinea pigs stationed in the grids. Technical difficulties with the E-23 munition, however, allowed fleas to escape into the plane, with the result that the bombardier, observer, and pilot were all bitten. It is uncertain whether any of these personnel became ill as a result. *See also* SKULL VALLEY INCIDENT.

OPERATION BLUE SKY. The U.S. **Chemical Corps (CmlC)** conducted Operation Blue Sky, a public relations project designed to convince the U.S. public and Congress of the humanity of using "nonlethal" chemical and biological warfare (CBW) agents. It operated in the 1960s, although it may have begun a decade earlier.

OPERATION CHASE. In Operation CHASE, the U.S. Navy sank a number of ships loaded with obsolete munitions off the U.S. East Coast. CHASE is an acronym for "Cut Holes And Sink 'Em." Four of the exercises involved sinking ships loaded with **chemical weapons (CW)**. The first scuttling of a CW-laden ship occurred on 15 June 1967, and the fourth and final one on 18 August 1970. CW materials disposed through this operation included containers of **sulfur mustard**, **sarin**, and **VX**, as well as M-55 rockets filled with sarin and VX.

Concern over the appropriateness of this operation (and over **sea dumping** of CW generally) resulted in a request by the U.S. Army to the National Academy of Sciences (NAS) to evaluate the hazards associated with sea dumping. The resulting 1969 NAS report recommended that other CW destruction technologies, including neutralization-based technologies, be pursued and that sea dumping, open-pit burning, and land burial not be used as methods of destruction. Operation CHASE and the NAS report represented a major turning point in U.S. policy regarding destruction of chemical weapons. Thereafter, dumping at sea, burial, and open-pit burning were no longer employed as methods of destruction, and starting in the early 1970s the U.S. Army began testing and evaluating a variety of CW destruction technologies. *See also* HELSINKI COMMISSION (HELCOM).

OPERATION CROSSROADS. In July 1946, the U.S. military tested Mk-III **"Fat Man"** nuclear bombs near Bikini Atoll in the South Pacific. Given the name Operation Crossroads, the tests witnessed the successful detonation of two **plutonium** bombs. The first test, referred to as "Shot Able," took place 1 July and involved the dropping of a bomb from a B-29 aircraft. This test was judged successful because the bomb detonated as planned, but the bomb missed its intended target, a battleship, by some 1,000 feet owing to wobble—a significant design defect that would plague the Mk-III Fat Man bombs. The second test, "Shot Baker," took place on 25 July and involved an underwater detonation. Because this test was static, the bomb could not drift off-target. This test revealed the extent to which ground and underwater nuclear blasts could produce **fallout**, adding to the potentially harmful effects from nuclear bombs.

OPERATION HARNESS. A British **biological weapon (BW)** sea trial carried out off the coast of Antigua in 1948–1949. The agents, which included *Bacillus anthracis*, *Brucella suis*, and *Francisella tularensis* (the causative agents of **anthrax**, **brucellosis**, and **tularemia**, respectively), were tested on animals placed onto small boats. Among the problems experienced was that some of the test animals were eaten by sharks before the trials could be initiated.

OPERATION LARGE AREA COVERAGE (LAC). A U.S. project to estimate the path, spread, and duration of **biological weapons (BW)** when released in the atmosphere. Operation LAC, carried out in 1957–1958, involved the release of fluorescent zinc cadmium sulfide particles as a **simulant** for BW. The tests were carried out over the central part of the **United States**, and results showed that the particles traveled distances in excess of 1,000 miles, effectively covering large segments of the United States. This demonstrated the vulnerability of the United States, or any nation, to an atmospheric release of BW.

OPERATION PX. During the closing months of World War II, **Japan** initiated Operation PX, a plan for attacking the West Coast of the **United States** using submarine-launched aircraft loaded with rats and insects infected with biological pathogens. Specially designed submarines were outfitted for the task of carrying the Seiran ("Mountain Haze") bombers, whose cargo would spread diseases such as **plague**, cholera, dengue fever, and **typhus** across America. The war ended, however, before Operation PX could be implemented, mostly likely because the infected animals and insects were unavailable. In March 2005, one of the submarines designed for this task, I-401, was recovered off the Hawaiian coast. *See also* VECTOR.

OPERATION RANCH HAND. *See* AGENT ORANGE.

OPERATION RED HAT. In 1971, the **United States** relocated its **chemical weapon (CW)** stockpile from Okinawa to the Johnston Atoll, located in the Pacific Ocean southeast of Hawaii. The relocation was given the code name "Operation Red Hat" and was also known as the "Kalama Express." Operation Red Hat was prompted by public disclosure of the existence of the CW stockpile on Okinawa, which generated opposition to its presence by locals and others, who deemed such a U.S. stockpile on the heavily populated island to be risky. *See also* OPERATION STEEL BOX.

OPERATION SHIPBOARD HAZARD AND DEFENSE. *See* PROJECT 112.

OPERATION SHOCKER. A disinformation program reportedly operated by the **United States** against the Soviet Union during the 1960s and 1970s. As part of Operation Shocker, the U.S. government is believed to have passed the Soviets some 4,500 official documents on U.S. research into a new type of **organophosphorus nerve agent**. While the documents were genuine, the research was bogus. The United States intended by passing these documents about nonexistent research to encourage the Soviets to waste resources by attempting to conduct similar research. However, there is speculation that Operation Shocker may have proved counterproductive to U.S. interests. In particular, some believe that this program may have spurred Soviet development of the **novichok** agents.

OPERATION STEEL BOX. In 1990, the U.S. Army successfully transferred more than 100,000 **chemical weapons (CW)** from West Germany to the Johnston Atoll in the Pacific Ocean. The transfer was given the code name "Operation Steel Box" but was known by some as "Operation Golden Python." *See also* OPERATION RED HAT.

OPERATION VEGETARIAN. *See* OPERATION ALADDIN.

ORALLOY. A World War II–era code name for **uranium**-235. The "OR" in ORalloy referred to Oak Ridge (**Site X**), the Tennessee facility where much of this **isotope** was produced. The "alloy" imitated the British use of a "**Directorate of Tube Alloys**" to refer to **nuclear weapon** developments.

ORGANIZATION FOR THE PROHIBITION OF CHEMICAL WEAPONS (OPCW). The OPCW, based in The Hague, Netherlands, is an international agency responsible for implementing the **Chemical Weapons Convention (CWC)**. The organization consists of three organs: the Conference of the States Parties (CSP), the Executive Council (EC), and the Technical Secretariat (TS). The CSP is the primary decision-making body. It delegates specific powers and functions to the EC and TS. The CSP meets in regular session once per year. Its duties include appointing the director-general and approving the annual budget. The EC, which consists of 41 members from five geographical groupings, is the organization's executive body. It supervises the activities of the TS and cooperates with member states' national authorities. It meets in regular session four or five times per year, considers specific implementation-related matters, and prepares recommendations for consideration and possible adoption by the CSP. Finally, the TS implements the treaty on a day-to-day basis. It receives annual declarations from CWC States Parties and conducts on-site inspections, including inspections of former **chemical weapon production facilities (CWPF)** and chemical industry facilities to confirm the nonproduction of **chemical weapons (CW)**.

ORGANOPHOSPHORUS NERVE AGENT. A chemical in which phosphorus is bonded to one or more organic radicals and which disrupts the normal mechanisms by which nerves communicate with muscles, glands, and other nerves. The nerves are overstimulated, which causes hyperactivity. If the hyperactivity persists, the systems being stimulated will become fatigued and eventually cease functioning. If enough systems shut down, death ensues. Within the context of **chemical weapons (CW)**, the term *nerve agent* (or the inaccurate term *nerve gas*) is used exclusively for those chemicals that act by inhibiting enzymes known as **cholinesterases**. While other chemicals, such as **botulinum toxin**, also disrupt nerve communications and thus could be considered nerve agents, the term is associated exclusively with the anticholinesterase chemicals.

Although organophosphorus chemicals had been known to chemists for decades prior to World War II, the extreme effects of some of them was recognized only shortly before the war, as a result of research by **German** chemist **Gerhard Schrader**. His work created intense interest by Germany in producing weapons containing

tabun, sarin, and **soman.** The Allies learned that Germany had discovered a novel class of CW, but the precise nature of its discoveries remained uncertain until after the war. As the **United States, United Kingdom,** and Soviet Union learned the full scope of the German arsenal of organophosphorus nerve agents, each undertook to produce them and to search for improved nerve agents. This search was aided in the United Kingdom by the discovery of **Amiton,** which became the basis for a new class of organic compounds of phosphorus and sulfur and led to the discovery of **VX** (in the United Kingdom and United States) and **V-gas** (in the USSR).

Despite stockpiling of millions of CW containing organophosphorus nerve agents, there is no evidence that any of these weapons were ever used in combat. All stockpiles of organophosphorus nerve agents declared to the **Organization for the Prohibition of Chemical Weapons (OPCW)** are being or have been destroyed.

OSIRAQ REACTOR BOMBING. Osiraq, **Iraq,** is the site where a nuclear power reactor was to be constructed. The reactor was ostensibly to be used solely as a source of electricity for civilian purposes, and it was to operate within the framework of the **International Atomic Energy Agency (IAEA) safeguards** program administered by the IAEA. Nevertheless, in 1981, the **Israeli** Air Force mounted an air strike against the reactor and, in a feat of precision bombing, destroyed it. This action was taken from the Israeli belief that the reactor was to be diverted to support a **nuclear weapons** program in Iraq. Later findings issued by the IAEA support the conclusion that Iraq had such a program.

OSOAVIAKhIM. OsoAviaKhim is an acronym from the **Russian** for the General Society for Aviation and Chemistry (*Obshchoi Soyuznoe Obshchestvo Aviatsy i Khimy*). The Cyrillic acronym is ОсоАвиаХим. It was a voluntary patriotic military organization that existed in the Union of Soviet Socialist Republics (USSR) from 1927 to 1948. Its activities included training and competitions that emphasized defensive preparations against chemical warfare (CW), such as the proper wearing of protective equipment and effective means of decontaminating individuals, equipment, and areas. OsoAviaKhim was established 23 January 1927 by merging **AviaKhim** and the USSR Society of [Military] Defense. It was disestablished on 16 February 1948, and its functions were transferred to three newly created organizations.

Absent from these organizations, however, was any volunteer society that expressly emphasized the chemical industry or defense against chemical attacks. *See also* DOBROKHIM.

OVCHINNIKOV, YURI A. Soviet official. Ovchinnikov was involved in the expansion of the Soviet **biological weapons (BW)** program. In the early 1970s, he served as vice president of the Academy of Sciences of the Union of Soviet Socialist Republics (USSR) and, reportedly, as a consultant to the Military-Industrial Commission of the USSR Council of Ministers Commission on the Problem of Providing for the Development through Fundamental Research of New Types of Biological Weapons. Ovchinnikov is notable for advocating fundamental and applied research into genetics and molecular biology. These fields had been neglected and were largely forbidden topics in the USSR owing to the influence of Trofim Lysenko (1898–1976), a **Russian** biologist who rejected genes as determining heredity but held that new species of crops and other organisms could be created by altering their environment and that these changes would be passed to the next generation. Lysenko became a favorite of Soviet dictator Joseph Stalin, making it nearly impossible for Soviet scientists to question his views.

OXIMES. *See* CHOLINESTERASES.

– P –

PAKISTAN. Pakistan is known to possess **nuclear weapons**, having conducted its first successful test on 28 May 1998. It also has a significant medium-range ballistic missile capability, fueling concerns that it might use nuclear weapons against a neighboring country, especially **India**. As of 2006, Pakistan was estimated to have 50–60 assembled nuclear warheads. It has neither signed nor ratified the **Comprehensive Nuclear Test Ban Treaty (CTBT)**. *See also* KHAN, ABDUL QADEER.

PASECHNIK, VLADIMIR ARTEMOVICH (1937–2001). Soviet microbiologist. A former director of the Institute of Highly Pure Biopreparations in Leningrad, Pasechnik defected to the **United Kingdom** in 1989. He revealed to the West the actual nature of **Biopreparat**, a network of civilian research institutes that was really established in the early 1970s to assist the Soviet military in its offensive **biological weapon (BW)** program. It was largely on the basis of information provided by Pasechnik that the United Kingdom and the **United States** decided to carry out secret demarches against Soviet premier Mikhail Gorbachev and Foreign Minister Eduard Shevardnadze requesting clarification on Soviet activities and programs. This highly secret diplomatic process was subsequently formalized as the **trilateral process**, in which each country agreed to receive on-site inspections at national defense–related and other sites.

PASH, BORIS T. (1901–1995). U.S. Army intelligence officer. Pash was best known for having headed the World War II scientific intelligence **ALSOS Mission** field unit. During World War I, Pash, who was born in the **United States**, served in the **Russian** Imperial Army as an artillery officer-cadet and fought in the Ikskul Bridgehead and Dvina River campaigns. Following the Bolshevik Revolution in 1917, he fought with Russian White Army forces under the command of generals Anton Deniken and Petr Wrangel. In 1919 Pash was part of an assault group that captured the battle cruiser *Kagul* at Sevastopol. He later worked as a famine relief worker in southern Russia for the American Red Cross and Young Men's Christian Association (YMCA). In 1924–1940 he worked as a physical education instructor at Hollywood High School in Los Angeles.

Pash joined the U.S. G-2 Army Intelligence reserves as a second lieutenant in 1930. During the early part of World War II, he oversaw some U.S. Army intelligence-gathering operations along the border with Mexico whose purpose was to uncover possible **Japanese** activities to secure landing sites for their aircraft and submarines for an attack on the continental United States. Pash was later made responsible for the security of the Berkeley Radiation Laboratory, which performed work for the **Manhattan Project. Leslie R. Groves**, the head of the project, recommended Pash to head the ALSOS Mission.

After the war, Pash served on Gen. Douglas MacArthur's Tokyo staff as military liaison to the Soviet Mission to Japan. There he was given responsibility for countering Soviet intelligence operations, including Soviet efforts to place intelligence operatives disguised as priests within the Japanese branch of the Russian Orthodox Church and various efforts to influence Japanese elections in favor of Japan's Communist Party. Pash held several other positions within the U.S. Army and worked for a time for the Central Intelligence Agency (CIA) before retiring in the early 1960s. In the early 1970s Pash published an account of his work as head of the ALSOS Mission.

PEACEFUL NUCLEAR EXPLOSIONS (PNE) TREATY. The PNE Treaty places limits on the size of nuclear explosions conducted for peaceful purposes, such as large earth-moving operations during the construction of a dam. It also establishes that each state must comply with the **Limited Test Ban Treaty (LTBT)** when conducting a PNE. Any single PNE cannot have a yield exceeding 150 kilotons, but aggregate explosions totaling 1.5 megatons are permitted if each individual explosion can be verified to be less than 150 kilotons. The PNE Treaty prohibits explosions exceeding 1.5 megatons for any purpose and in any manner. The treaty was signed by the United States and the Soviet Union in Moscow on 28 May 1976 and entered into force on 11 December 1990.

PENKOVSKY, OLEG VLADIMIROVICH (1919–1963). Soviet intelligence officer. Lieutenant Colonel Penkovsky of the GRU (Soviet military intelligence) spied for the **United Kingdom** and **United States**. Before being caught and executed for treason, he provided information on a wide range of topics, including Soviet attitudes and work in the area of **chemical** and **biological weapons (CBW)**. A compendium of information that he passed on was published as *The Penkovsky Papers* (1965).

PERMISSIVE ACTION LINK (PAL). During the 1950s, the U.S. government grew concerned that a **nuclear weapon** might be detonated without presidential authorization. This concern resulted in development of the permissive action link, a system intended to prevent a nuclear weapon from being armed until a prescribed code or combination is inserted. The PAL ensures that a weapon can be used when authorized and lessens or eliminates the prospects for unauthorized use. The U.S. Air Force took delivery of the first PAL systems in 1961 and installed the hardware into Jupiter intermediate-range ballistic missiles, which were equipped with W-49 **thermonuclear**

warheads. In June 1962, the U.S. government mandated installation and use of PAL systems in all land-based nuclear weapons with U.S. forces in Europe.

PERSISTENT CHEMICAL AGENT. *See* CLASSES OF CHEMICAL WEAPONS.

PHOSGENE. An easily liquefied gas that has featured prominently as a **chemical weapon (CW)**. Liquid phosgene (carbonyl chloride, CCl_2O) is colorless to light yellow. When diluted in air, phosgene vapors have an odor resembling newly mown hay. **Germany** introduced use of phosgene as a CW on 19 December 1915 during an attack against British positions around Nieltje, Belgium. **Chlorine**, which was familiar to the British, was also released in this attack, and for this reason, the presence of phosgene received little attention initially. Phosgene and chlorine are both **choking agents**, but the effects of exposure to phosgene may be delayed by hours to days. Soldiers who appeared to have survived the chemical attack collapsed suddenly. These delayed casualties prompted further investigation and new fears by the Allies, who sought to retaliate in kind. **France** was the first to do so, using a phosgene-filled artillery shell against Germany in February 1916. The **United Kingdom**, **United States**, and **Russia** also produced phosgene for use as a CW. The United Kingdom and United States gave phosgene the code name "CG," perhaps taken from "choking gas." The chemical and physical properties of phosgene, plus its relative ease of production, caused it to be used extensively until the end of the war, leading one observer to write that it "was the principal offensive battle gas of the Allies. . . . More than 80 percent of the gas fatalities in the World War were caused by phosgene." *See also* GREEN CROSS AGENT.

PILE. *See* NUCLEAR PILE.

PIONEER REGIMENTS 35 AND 36. In early 1915, the **German** military took steps to organize for waging chemical warfare (CW). Soldiers having scientific backgrounds were selected and placed into units that were eventually designated Pioneer Regiments 35 and 36. The regiments were commanded by career officers, but chemist **Fritz**

Haber, who had earlier been promoted from the enlisted ranks to captain, was designated their technical advisor. In this role, he recruited distinguished scientists from throughout Germany, including future Nobel Prize Laureates **Otto Hahn** (Chemistry, 1944), James Franck (Physics, 1925), and Gustav Hertz (Physics, 1925), as well as physicist Hans Geiger, famed as developer of the Geiger counter. These scientists and others would serve throughout the war as the German military's chemical specialists, providing exceptional technical expertise at the front lines where the weapons were used.

PLAGUE. A disease caused by *Yersinia pestis*, a **Gram-negative** bacillus. Prior to the introduction of antibiotics, the disease in humans was often fatal. Even with modern treatments, recovery is uncertain. The disease has three primary clinical manifestations: bubonic plague (invasion of the lymph nodes), pneumonic plague (invasion of the lungs), and septicemic plague (invasion of the bloodstream). Transmission of *Y. pestis* to humans typically occurs through the bite of an infected carrier, most often a flea, or through contact with infected animals or humans. Carriers such as fleas serve as hosts for the bacterium but do not develop the disease. If the disease progresses to the pneumonic stage, then the organism can be exhaled by an infected person and thus spread from human to human by the inhalation. The ability of plague to be spread through insect hosts and in an **aerosolized** form may account for the interest shown in developing **biological weapons (BW)** that would spread plague.

Various accounts exist regarding the deliberate spread of plague by an attacking force catapulting the corpses of plague victims into fortified cities. These reports typically cite this tactic as having been used successfully in 1346 during the Tartar siege of Kaffa (modern-day Feodosia, Ukraine) and go on to speculate that it led to the Black Death that overtook Europe in following decades. Such accounts are difficult to verify, although the story endures as a supposed example of early biological warfare (BW). More verifiable, if less well known, is **Japan**'s use of *Y. pestis*–infected fleas as a means of spreading plague on the Asian mainland, beginning in 1937. These efforts were centered on **Unit 731** near Harbin, where scientists are known to have developed ceramic bombs that were used to deliver the fleas against targets, mostly in northeastern China. The effectiveness of this and other Japanese-developed plague weapons is difficult to assess, as precise records have been lost or were never kept by those who were targeted. Unit 731 included buildings that housed breeding colonies of *Y. pestis*–infected fleas, as well as rats to be used with these fleas. These buildings survived the destruction of Unit 731 at the end of World War II and are part of the Unit 731 exhibit operated by the Chinese in Harbin. *See also* ANTIPLAGUE SYSTEM; OPERATION PX.

PLAYFAIR, LYON (1818–1898). British chemist, educator, and politician who offered proposals for novel **chemical weapons (CW)** and **incendiaries**. In 1855, Playfair, then director of science in schools for London, suggested two new munitions to the British Admiralty. At the time, the British were engaged in the Crimean War and were anxious to find anything that might give their forces an advantage. Playfair believed that CW might aid in reducing the defenses of Sevastopol, then under siege. His first proposed CW combined phosphorus, **carbon disulfide**, and a fuel, with the result being both incendiary and toxic. A second proposed CW is variously reported to have called for cyanide or **cacodyl cyanide** or a mix of **cacodylic acid** and **cacodyl**. Although the British Ordnance Department rejected his proposals, Playfair's career nevertheless prospered. He was appointed to the chemistry faculty at Edinburgh University, was elected to Parliament, and in 1892 was created the first Baron Playfair of St. Andrews and lord-in-waiting to Queen Victoria.

PLOWSHARE PROGRAM. In addition to setting off nuclear detonations to test weapon designs and effects, the **United States** also investigated using nuclear detonations for peaceful purposes. The Plowshare Program set off 35 nuclear detonations at five sites to test the use of nuclear devices for extracting natural gas and oil and for earth-moving. The tests were conducted at Carlsbad and Farmington, New Mexico (one test each); Grand Valley (one) and Rifle (one test involving three simultaneous detonations), Colorado; and the **Nevada Test Site** (29). *See also* PEACEFUL NUCLEAR EXPLOSIONS (PNE) TREATY.

PLUM ISLAND. An island located off the northeastern fork of Long Island, New York. Its relative isolation resulted in its selection for work with exotic animal pathogens (that is, biological pathogens not found in the **United States** that are harmful to animals but seldom to humans). Following World War II, Plum Island was selected by the U.S. Army **Chemical Corps (CmlC)** as the site for a research and testing facility to support selected aspects of the U.S. **biological weapons (BW)** program. That facility was built but immediately transferred to the U.S. Department of Agriculture. Presently, it is home to the Plum Island Animal Disease Center, which houses the North American repository of vaccine for **foot-and-mouth disease (FMD)**.

PLUTONIUM. A man-made element, with atomic number 94 and symbol "Pu." There are no stable **isotopes** of plutonium; hence, all isotopes are radioactive. The most significant radioisotopes in the context of nuclear security are plutonium-238, plutonium-239, and plutonium-240. Plutonium-238 is used as a power source in satellites. Plutonium-239 is a **fissile material**. It has both **thermal neutrons** and **fast neutrons**, making it useful in both **nuclear weapons** and electric power production plants. Plutonium-239, which can be produced by neutron bombardment of **uranium**-238, is the primary isotope used in U.S. nuclear weapons. This isotope has a half-life of 24,360 years, meaning that any released as **fallout** or otherwise will persist in the environment for a lengthy period—which may account for the plutonium found in October 2006 among snails from areas associated with the 1966 **Spain hydrogen bomb incident**. Plutonium-240 is often present at 15 to 20 percent in plutonium used for electric power production. However, plutonium-240 has a high rate of spontaneous **fission**, and its presence increases the chances of **preinitiation**. For this reason, the plutonium used in nuclear weapons normally contains 7 percent or less plutonium-240.

P.O. BOX A-1968. Certain Soviet organizations were given post office (P.O.) box numbers, thereby concealing the city or region where the organizations were actually located or what might be the work of these organizations. P.O. Box A-1968 was assigned to the **15th Directorate**, the section of the Soviet Ministry of Defense that operated the **biological weapon (BW)** program of the Soviet Union.

POLONIUM. A naturally occurring element, with atomic number 84 and symbol "Po." There are no stable **isotopes** of polonium; hence, the element is naturally radioactive. Trace amounts of polonium occur in **uranium**-containing ores. In the context of **nuclear weapons**, the polonium-210 isotope is significant. It is considered a strong emitter of **alpha particle** radiation, and a single milligram of polonium-210 gives off as much alpha radiation as do five grams of **radium**. This highly radioactive nature is sufficient to cause a blue glow in the air around polonium-210. The element is highly toxic in all its forms. The toxicity of polonium was noted in the events surrounding the 23 November 2006 death under suspicious circumstances of Alexander Litvinenko, a former agent of the Russian Federal Security Service (FSB).

PORTON DOWN. Initiation of chemical warfare (CW) during World War I prompted the British to search for a site suitable for testing of such weapons. In early 1916, a site was selected in Wiltshire, near Salisbury. Initially designated the War Department Experimental Ground, Porton, it is commonly referred to as "Porton Down" or merely "Porton." The first personnel reported to Porton Down in spring 1916. Work was concentrated on testing of possible **chemical weapons (CW)** so that the **United Kingdom** might have an effective means of retaliating in kind to the use of **chlorine** and other toxic and irritating substances by **Germany**. Eventually, Porton Down became home to laboratories for exploring novel CW agents and designing protective measures, such as gas masks and other garments. In 1940, **biological warfare (BW)** became an official part of the activities at Porton Down with the establishment of the "Biology Department, Porton." The site has gone through various names, including Chemical Defence Experimental Establishment (1948–1970) and Chemical and Biological Defence Establishment (1991–1995). Currently designated the Defence Science and Technology Laboratories (Dstl), Porton Down, the site remains in use for defensive studies related to chemical and biological warfare (CBW) materials.

PREINITIATION. The sequence and timing of events is critical to proper functioning of a **nuclear weapon**. Preinitiation occurs when the **fissile material** of a nuclear weapon initiates a **chain reaction** prior to attaining maximum compression or complete assembly. When preinitiation occurs, the result is either no nuclear explosion or an explosive yield far less than expected based on theoretical calculations. Concerns over preinitiation caused the **United States** to cease development of the "**Thin Man**" bomb design, switching instead to the "**Little Boy**" design. The 6 October 2006 detonation of a nuclear device by **North Korea** is reported to have suffered from preinitiation. An alternative term used for preinitiation is *fizzle*.

PROJECT 112. The **United States** conducted a series of **chemical** and **biological weapon (CBW)** dispersion tests from the early 1960s and 1970s under Project 112. These tests included Operation Shipboard Hazard and Defense (SHAD), which was carried out at sea. Land-based Project 112 tests were conducted on the territory of at least three countries: Canada, the **United Kingdom**, and the United States. Some veterans of Project 112 have complained of ailments similar to those experienced by people suffering from **Gulf War Syndrome (GWS)**.

PROJECT BIOSHIELD. On 21 July 2004, the U.S. government enacted Project Bioshield, a program under which approximately $6 billion will be spent over 10 years to, among other things, subsidize development and manufacture of improved drugs and vaccines for **anthrax, smallpox,** and **botulinum toxin**, as well as countermeasures against other select pathogens judged to pose a possible **biological weapon (BW)** risk to the **United States**. Project Bioshield has been criticized partly because of liability and patent protection concerns and partly because it funds countermeasures against pathogens that currently cause few or no deaths while efforts against other diseases that *do* result in significant numbers of deaths fail to receive financing under this program. *See also* BIOSAFETY.

PROJECT OBONG. In 1979, the governments of Indonesia and the Netherlands carried out Project Obong, a **chemical weapon (CW)** destruction project. The goal of Project Obong was the safe, secure, and complete destruction of approximately 45 tons of **sulfur mustard** that had been manufactured in Batujajar, West Java, in 1940–1941 by the Dutch colonial government.

PROJECT VELA. The **United States** initiated Project Vela to aid in verifying compliance with the **Limited Test Ban Treaty (LTBT)** of

1963, as well as the **Threshold Test Ban Treaty (TTBT)** of 1974. The project had three major elements. "Vela Hotel" used satellites to detect nuclear explosions in space or on the surface of the Earth. "Vela Sierra" used instrumentation on Earth to detect nuclear explosions in space or in the atmosphere. "Vela Uniform" used seismic equipment to detect, identify, and locate nuclear explosions underground or underwater. The United States carried out seven nuclear tests to characterize, validate, and calibrate the seismic equipment used in Vela Uniform. These tests took place near Amchitka, Alaska (one test); Fallon, Nevada (one); and Hattiesburg, Mississippi (two), and at the **Nevada Test Site** (three). *See also* VELA INCIDENT.

PROLIFERATION SECURITY INITIATIVE (PSI). An initiative established in 2003 as a response to the proliferation of **weapons of mass destruction (WMD)**. PSI helps to implement the **United Nations** Security Council Presidential Statement of January 1992, which states that the proliferation of all WMD constitutes a threat to international peace and security. PSI involves a group of like-minded states that have agreed upon a set of "interdiction principles" with the objective to prevent the shipment of WMD, their delivery systems, and related materials.

PUGWASH CONFERENCE ON SCIENCE AND WORLD AFFAIRS. A series of annual meetings of scientists, government representatives, and international organizations who convene to discuss arms control and disarmament questions in their private capacities. The first meeting was held in 1957 in Pugwash, Nova Scotia, and was financed by Canadian-American industrialist Cyrus Eaton and organized in large part by **Sir Joseph Rotblat**. During the Cold War, the Pugwash conferences provided an opportunity for scientists from the Eastern and Western blocks to exchange views on international security matters more informally. Pugwash meetings are generally convened just prior to meetings of international organizations such as the **Organization for the Prohibition of Chemical Weapons (OPCW)** and meetings of delegations to the **Biological and Toxin Weapons Convention (BTWC)**. The organization consists of national chapters that are generally run by individuals who are prominent in the scientific community.

– Q –

QAEDA, AL-. Al-Qaeda is a loosely organized, decentralized, and militant Islamist terrorist network that considers itself to be at war with the **United States** and with most of the Western world. The organization, whose name is usually translated as "the Base" or "the Foundation," traces its roots partly to efforts by the *mujahaddin* to expel Soviet forces from Afghanistan in the 1980s. Individuals and groups that consider themselves to be affiliated with al-Qaeda have periodically demonstrated an interest in acquiring or using **nuclear, biological**, and **chemical (NBC) weapons**. For example, U.S. forces operating in Afghanistan have recovered materials and at least one video of an apparent poisoning of animals with chemical or biological substances. The organization's actions also exemplify the difficulties associated with effectively extending international prohibitions against such weapons below the state-level to so-called nonstate actors. *See also* MUBTAKKAR.

Q FEVER. A disease caused by the rickettsia-like microorganism *Coxiella burnetii*. The disease is seldom fatal, but recovery is often slow, and the disease can re-erupt. A single organism can prove infectious in humans and a wide range of other animals. *C. burnetii* has a spore-like form that is notoriously hardy, with excellent resistance to harsh conditions and many standard antiseptics. The high infectivity and extreme hardiness of *C. burnetii* may account for the interest shown by various nations in using it in **biological weapons (BW)**. Such interest included a U.S. program that studied bulk production of *C. burnetii* (designated at various times as "Agent OU," "Agent MN," and "Agent NT").

There is no evidence of use of *C. burnetii*–laden weapons by any nation. However, reliable information regarding national programs outside that of the **United States** is limited. Natural infections in humans most often arise from contact with infected animals, especially livestock. The organism is shed in the urine and feces of infected animals, making contaminated pastures, soil, clothing, and other inanimate objects possible sources of infection. Q fever infections have been reported in military units that traveled across pastureland or occupied farm buildings that had housed infected animals. The incidence of Q fever may be significantly higher than is reported, however, because infections can be asymptomatic or result in nondebilitating febrile illnesses. *See also* BURNET, FRANK MACFARLANE.

QL. *See* BIGEYE.

– R –

RAD. An acronym for "radiation absorbed dose," an obsolete unit of absorbed doses of radiation. It can be applied to the dose received by any material, from any source of radiation. One rad equals 100 **gray**, the SI (metric) unit for expressing absorbed dose of radiation. *See also* REM; ROENTGEN.

RADIAC. An acronym derived from "radioactivity detection, indication, and computation." RADIAC is used for various types of radiological measuring instruments or equipment.

RADIOACTIVE DECAY. The **disintegration** or breaking up of an atomic nucleus resulting from excess energy in that atom. This decay is accompanied by the emission of radiation (typically in the form of an **alpha particle**, **beta particle**, **gamma radiation**, or neutron radiation), thereby transforming the original nucleus into a different nucleus with a more stable energy state. Radioactive decay will continue, however, until the nucleus achieves a fully stable energy state.

RADIOACTIVE MATERIAL. A substance is labeled *radioactive* when it emits radiant energy resulting from the **disintegration** of atomic nuclei, or **radioactive decay**. The radiant energy can be emitted as **alpha particles**, **beta particles**, **gamma radiation**, or neutron radiation. Some materials are naturally radioactive, such as the elements **uranium** and **radium**. Other radioactive materials are man-made elements, such as **plutonium** and **americium**. *See also* ISOTOPE.

RADIOLOGICAL DISPERSAL DEVICE (RDD). Modifying a conventional explosive device to include **radioactive materials** can enhance its destructive and disruptive effects. Such a device is referred to as a radiological dispersal device or, more colloquially, as a "**dirty bomb**." In addition to any destruction of property and harm to humans caused by the explosive component of the RDD, the presence of radioactive materials means that those materials can be scattered around and carried beyond the scene of the blast. Such radioactivity can make the scene uninhabitable until the radioactivity decays or until steps are taken to remove the radioactive debris. Any radioactive materials might be used for this purpose, including radioisotopes used for legitimate medical, engineering, and research purposes. By contrast, a **nuclear weapon** requires relatively rare **fissile materials** that are supposed to be controlled and monitored. Therefore, construction of an RDD is perceived to be more readily achievable by terrorists than is the construction of a nuclear weapon.

RADIUM. A naturally occurring element, with atomic number 88 and symbol "Ra." In the context of nuclear operations, the **isotope** radium-226 is important. It is **radioactive** and was once used as a source in **gamma radiography** and as a means of making dials and other surfaces glow in the dark. In fact, it is the glow produced by its radiation that inspired Marie Curie to dub the element "radium" for the glow of its rays (Latin: *radius*) that she observed on discovering it.

REACTOR. *See* NUCLEAR PILE.

RECTIFICATION. In chemistry, the process of refining or purifying a compound, especially by distillation. Rectification is important in the context of **chemical weapons (CW)** because many CW agents need to undergo rectification to improve production yield or to enhance their stability. A prime example of this situation is **sulfur mustard**, where distillation was found to both raise the manufacturing yield and extend the storage life.

REM. An acronym for "roentgen equivalent man," a unit of absorbed doses of radiation. The unit applies to any type of absorbed radiation, but it is linked to the biological effect of that radiation and is used exclusively to refer to the dose received in humans. These biological effects vary according to both the type of tissue receiving the radiation and type of radiation. Rem has been the basis for standards of radiation exposure, but is being replaced by the **sievert**. One sievert equals 100 rem. *See also* RAD; ROENTGEN.

RICIN. Ricin is a poisonous substance of botanical origin. It occurs naturally in the castor-oil plant, especially in its seeds (commonly called "castor beans"). Ricin is a delayed-action cytotoxin; that is, exposure (most often by ingestion) seldom produces immediate symptoms of intoxication. Symptoms range from fever, nausea, and diarrhea to respiratory distress and circulatory collapse. No antidote exists, although progress is reported on a vaccine. The castor-oil plant produces ricin; therefore, acquisition of this **toxin** requires refining it from its natural matrix rather than synthesis. Castor-oil plants and seeds are available for commercial and ornamental purposes. Perhaps this availability and the toxicity account for the interest shown by nations, terrorist groups, and individuals in using ricin for military or nefarious purposes. U.S. interest in the military use of ricin dates to World War I. Personnel assigned to the U.S. Army **Chemical Warfare Service (CWS)**, working on the grounds of the **Catholic University of America**, refined ricin for use in **chemical weapons (CW)**. No such CW was used in combat, however.

Interest was renewed during World War II, when the **United States** developed pilot-plant production methods for ricin (code-named "W") and stockpiled 3,800 pounds of relatively pure material. A portion of this cache was used in experimental U.S. and Canadian weapons, which were tested in the United States, Canada, and the **United Kingdom**. Canadian, British, and U.S. interest in ricin might have prompted similar interest by other nations, especially the Soviet Union; reliable information regarding other national programs is lacking, however. There is credible information, though, on the use of ricin as an assassination poison as part of a Soviet-era Bulgarian program to kill dissidents. The most notorious of these efforts was the successful assassination of Bulgarian dissident Georgi Markov. In this incident, a tiny ricin-laden ball was injected into Markov by means of a specially equipped umbrella. Ricin has become notorious, too, as a matter of interest in more small-scale poisonings, including ones associated with domestic terrorists, such as the U.S. experience with the "Patriots Council" in the mid-1990s. There have also been charges of ricin acquisition by international terrorists tied to Islamic extremists. Ricin and **saxitoxin** are the only two toxins specifically called out in schedule 1 (Schedules of Chemicals, Annex on Chemicals) of the **Chemical Weapons Convention (CWC)**. No country has declared possessing ricin stockpiles to the **Organization for the Prohibition of Chemical Weapons (OPCW)**.

RIOT-CONTROL AGENT (RCA). Highly irritating compounds having relatively low toxicity that may be employed to help gain control over violent individuals and crowds without resorting to lethal weapons. Riot-control agents may also be used as part of military operations to facilitate the killing of enemy soldiers by forcing them out into the open away from cover or hiding areas. RCAs, even when used within prescribed guidelines, can cause death, particularly among the young, elderly, and sick. There is a lack of agreement among the States Parties to the **Chemical Weapons Convention (CWC)** on whether, and if so, how, RCAs may be used for purposes other than domestic riot control, including for peacekeeping and counterterrorism operations. Although the CWC allows the use of RCAs for domestic riot-control purposes, it prohibits their use as a "method of warfare." There is concern that some situations where RCAs may be employed, such as counterterrorism operations, cannot be legally understood to be "domestic" or a "riot" and may instead form a part of low-level counterinsurgency operations.

ROENTGEN. A nonmetric unit of radiation dose, abbreviated "R." One roentgen equals the quantity of ionizing radiation that will produce one electrostatic unit of electricity in one cubic meter of dry air at 0°C (32°F). It is used to describe the quantity of radiation given off by a source, but applies to **gamma radiation** only. Its use is considered obsolete, and the preferred unit is **sieverts**. The unit honors **German** scientist Wilhelm Konrad Roentgen (1845–1923). He received the 1901 Nobel Prize in Physics in recognition of his 1895 discovery of x-rays.

ROSEBURY, THEODOR (1904–1976). American biologist. Rosebury was a specialist in biological warfare (BW). During World War II, he was assigned to what became **Fort Detrick**, where he worked on **aerosol** dissemination of BW agents. He is the author of *Peace or Pestilence: Biological Warfare and How to Avoid It* (1949).

ROTBLAT, SIR JOSEPH (1908–2005). Polish-born British nuclear physicist. Rotblat worked on the development of **nuclear weapons** during World War II as part of the Tube Alloys Project. Following the war, Rotblat refused to continue working on nuclear weapons and became one of the most influential advocates of nuclear disarmament. He helped to launch the 1955 **Einstein-Russell manifesto** and was a signatory to it. In 1992 he was awarded the Einstein Peace Prize jointly with Hans Bethe. The 1995 Nobel Peace Prize was awarded jointly to Rotblat and the **Pugwash Conference on Science and World Affairs**, which he helped to found and guided until his 2005 death.

RUSSIA. The Union of Soviet Socialist Republics (USSR) had extensive programs for the development and production of **nuclear, biological**, and **chemical (NBC) weapons**. As a successor state to the USSR after 1991, the Russian Federation has inherited most of the Soviet stockpiles of NBC weapons and much of the infrastructure associated with research, development, and production of these weapons. Russia also took on responsibility for ensuring adherence to various arms control treaties limiting or altogether banning such weapons.

Biological Weapons Program. Setting a precise date for Russia's development of biological weapons (BW) is problematic, given the general lack of verifiable information. Some information suggests an interest in BW dating to the tsarist era. The existence of a state-sponsored BW program by the time **Germany** invaded the USSR in 1941 seems likely, especially in view of a report prepared for the **United States** after the war by **Walter Hirsch**, a former German officer who had specialized in assessing Soviet BW and chemical weapon (CW) capabilities. Additionally, information offered into evidence during war crimes trials of German medical officials conducted immediately after World War II clearly demonstrated Soviet production and use of bullets laced with **aconitine**, a **toxin** derived from biological sources. Allegations of Soviet-inspired use of other toxin weapons surfaced in 1981 during the **yellow rain** episode.

Details on the massive scale of the Soviet BW program became clear with the 1989 defection of **Vladimir Pasechnik** to the

United Kingdom and the 1992 move of **Kenneth Alibek** to the United States. These details helped spur the creation of the **trilateral process**. The USSR engaged in this mammoth BW program despite its being a party to the **Geneva Protocol of 1925** and the **Biological and Toxins Weapons Convention (BTWC)**. Russia has succeeded to the USSR on both these treaties and has publicly stated its intentions to adhere to them. Confidence in its willingness to deal in a transparent manner on BW-related matters was weakened, however, by the 1995 announcement by Russian president Boris Yeltsin that Russia had unilaterally relocated its **smallpox** repository from Moscow to **Vektor**, an institute in Siberia. *See also* ASHMARIN, IGOR PETROVICH; DOMARADSKY, IGOR VALERYANOVICH.

Chemical Weapons Program. Russia initiated a CW program during World War I, in response to Germany's use of **chlorine** in April 1915. This tsarist-era program exploited the existence in Russia of industrial-scale production of chlorine, **phosgene**, and **chloropicrin**. For example, the **antiplague system**, intended to control the spread of **plague** within the tsarist empire, used chloropicrin to exterminate marmots and other animals known to harbor the insect pests that transmitted the bacteria responsible for plague. Facts regarding Russia's World War I experience with CW are meager. However, available records suggest Russia suffered extensive casualties as a result of CW use, which may account for the interest taken by Russian and, later, Soviet officials in developing their own stockpile of CW. CW also figured into the **Russian Civil War**, although few reliable details are available. In any event, use of CW does not appear to have been decisive in that conflict.

Following the civil war, Russia entered into a secret pact with Germany that provided for, among other things, German assistance with the construction of a CW production facility, located near **Shikhany** along the Volga River southeast of Moscow. The USSR, created in December 1922, fostered public interest in CW defense, establishing groups such as **DobroKhim** to encourage individual and group activities such as decontamination and detection. Research into offensive and defensive aspects of CW was promoted under internationally renowned scientists such as **Vladimir N. Ipatiev, Martin I. Kabachnik**, and **Ivan L. Knunyants**.

While a large CW stockpile existed in the USSR when Germany invaded in 1941, no large-scale use of CW took place during World War II. After the war, some details of the Soviet CW program were learned from German sources, especially in the Hirsch report. In general, though, verifiable details on the Soviet CW program, both prior to and after the war, are meager, and much scholarship remains to be done. Russia is a party to the **Chemical Weapons Convention (CWC)** and reports progress on its efforts to destroy its CW stockpile. International assistance, such as the **Cooperative Threat Reduction (CTR)** Program, has been an important element in these efforts. *See also* ANTONOV, NIKOLAI SERAFIMOVICH; FISHMAN, YAKOV MOISEEVICH; KUNTSEVICH, ANATOLY DEM'YANOVICH; MIRZYANOV, VIL SULANOVICH; MOSCOW THEATER INCIDENT; TOMKA.

Nuclear Weapons Program. During the 1930s, the USSR had a significant program conducting basic research in nuclear physics. By early 1939, Soviet physicists had learned of the discovery of nuclear **fission**. They grasped the military significance of this discovery and began research along similar lines to those being pursued in the United States and, to a lesser extent, Germany. In June 1940, the Presidium of the Soviet Academy of Sciences established the Uranium Committee, giving it the mission of researching various aspects of **uranium**, including locating uranium deposits, producing **heavy water** for use as a moderator, developing means of separating **isotopes**, and achieving a **chain reaction**.

Progress slowed following the German invasion on 22 June 1941 but was aided by an extensive network of spies who penetrated the U.S., British, and German **nuclear weapon** programs. In 1943, Soviet dictator Joseph Stalin placed **Igor V. Kurchatov** in charge of scientific aspects of the program. Kurchatov proved an able leader. In spring 1945, he ordered work to begin on a reactor that would produce **plutonium**, which would eventually be used in weapons. The USSR achieved its first chain reaction on 25 December 1946. This milestone was followed by its first successful test of a nuclear device on 29 August 1949, which was dubbed "**Joe**" by the United States. On 12 August 1953, the USSR detonated its first **thermonuclear** device, "Joe 4."

In July 1953, the USSR created the Ministry of Medium Machine Building, and in 1954 this rather innocuous-sounding ministry assumed overall responsibility for research, development, and production of nuclear weapons. By the time the USSR was dissolved in December 1991, it possessed a stockpile of many thousands of these weapons. Four newly formed states were identified as having these weapons on their soil: Belarus, Kazakhstan, Russia, and Ukraine. To ensure the security and facilitate the destruction of these weapons, all four states received international assistance, such as that provided by the United States under the CTR Program. As of 2006, only Russia continues to possess such weapons. *See also* ARZAMAS-16; FUCHS, KLAUS EMIL JULIUS; SAKHAROV, ANDREI DMITRIYEVICH.

RUSSIAN CIVIL WAR. Civil war raged across the former **Russian** Empire from 1918 until at least 1921. As with many civil wars, this conflict witnessed various savageries. On several occasions, the Bolshevik-led Red Army threatened use of **chemical weapons (CW)** against civilians. For instance, in July 1918, the Bolshevik Extraordinary Staff of the Yaroslavl Front issued a written threat: "Our heavy guns will rain the most pitiless hurricane fire of heavy explosives and chemical shells upon the city [of Yaroslavl]. All who have not fled will perish." An attack two days later destroyed this city north of Moscow, but the use of CW in that attack is unconfirmed.

Similarly, Red Army commander Mikhail N. Tukhachevsky (1893–1937) issued a decree on 21 June 1921 warning that CW would be fired into the woods in the Tambov region southeast of Moscow. The intended target was the peasant-led Green forces rebelling against the Bolsheviks and taking refuge in these woods. The rebellion was brutally suppressed, and CW is believed to have played a part.

Use of CW against the Bolshevik forces is confirmed, however. In August and September 1919, British forces fighting in the far north around Archangelsk on the White Sea used aircraft to drop more than 550 **M Devices** on Bolshevik forces on at least 11 occasions. In writing to the War Office in London from General Headquarters, North Russia, an observer wrote, "I think we may confidently say that the recent successes of the Russian Troops on the Railway Front have been due almost entirely to Gas."

RUTHERFORD. A unit of **radioactive decay**, abbreviated "Rd." It has the dimensions **disintegrations** per second, with 1 Rd being equal to 1,000,000 disintegrations per second or 1,000,000 **becquerels**. Becquerels is the SI (metric) unit for radioactive decay and is the preferred unit nowadays for reporting disintegrations. The unit rutherford honors the New Zealand–born physicist Ernest Rutherford (1871–1937), later Baron Rutherford of Nelson and Cambridge. Rutherford is credited as the first person to use the terms *alpha, beta,* and *gamma* to classify types of radiation. He was awarded the 1908 Nobel Prize in Physics in recognition of his discovery of the atomic nucleus.

Rutherford was the first person to observe a nuclear reaction. In 1919, he passed **alpha particles** through gaseous nitrogen. A few collisions (about 1-in-50,000) with nitrogen atoms produced a nuclear reaction resulting in the emission of a proton and transmutation of the nitrogen to oxygen. Despite such pioneering work in nuclear physics, Rutherford was dismissive of the idea of harnessing nuclear power for practical purposes. In a 1933 interview, he labeled such proposals "moonshine." Rutherford died in 1937, a mere year prior to the definitive work by **Otto Hahn** and Fritz Strassmann proving nuclear **fission** and five years before Enrico Fermi's success at **Stagg Field** when a self-sustaining nuclear reaction was safely to generate electric power.

– S –

S-1. During World War II, senior U.S. government officials referred to the project to develop a **nuclear weapon**, as well as the bomb itself, as "S-1." This code was a shorthand designation for the Uranium Section, later designated the S-1 Section, of the **National Defense Research Committee (NDRC)** that oversaw the early work on developing the bomb. *See also* MANHATTAN PROJECT; URANIUM COMMITTEE.

SAADI, AMIR AL-. Iraqi official. Lt. Gen. Amir al-Saadi was scientific advisor to Saddam Hussein. In this position, al-Saadi played a key role in overseeing the development of **Iraq's nuclear weapon**

program. He may also have had some responsibility over **chemical** and **biological weapon (BW)**–related activities. *See also* UNITED NATIONS SPECIAL COMMISSION ON IRAQ (UNSCOM).

SAFEGUARDS. *See* IAEA SAFEGUARDS.

SAKHAROV, ANDREI DMITRIYEVICH (1921–1989). Russian physicist. Sakharov described himself as the father of the Soviet **hydrogen bomb**. His work on controlled **thermonuclear** reactions was essential to successful development of this bomb. Sakharov is better known, however, for his efforts to promote human rights and world peace. His outspoken views in this regard resulted in his arrest in 1980 by Soviet authorities, who exiled him from Moscow to Gorky (now Nizhny Novgorod), **Russia**. His efforts were recognized internationally, most visibly by his selection for the 1975 Nobel Peace Prize. *See also* JOE.

SALTED WEAPON. A **nuclear weapon** to which elements or **isotopes** that capture neutrons have been added in order to produce radioactive products that are not produced by a nuclear weapon of normal design. Therefore, these devices pose hazards unlike those seen with weapons lacking this design feature. *See also* NEUTRON BOMB.

SAN JOSÉ ISLAND, PANAMA. On 9 December 1943, the U.S. Army chief of staff directed the commanding general of the Caribbean Defense Command to lease San José Island from the government of Panama. The U.S. Army selected this island, located off the southern coast nearest Rey Island and Las Perlas Islands in the Gulf of Panama, because its forests "most resemble in important details large areas of forest in Burma, Siam, Indo-China, Malaya, the Philippines and Formosa" (San José Project Miscellaneous Report, 8 December 1944), areas where the U.S. military knew or expected it would be conducting operations during the war with **Japan**. The **United States** was especially interested in having a suitable location for testing various **chemical weapons (CW)** under tropical conditions. Use of an area near Bushnell, Florida, as a CW test range in 1943 and thereafter was deemed generally successful but had failed to address adequately the tropical conditions needed as planning for the war in the Pacific proceeded. In early 1944, the United States and Panama agreed to terms for a lease running for the period of the war plus one year; actual use of the island as a test range continued into 1947, however.

The U.S. military referred to use of this island as the "San José Project," and designated the **Chemical Warfare Service (CWS)** to be responsible, causing it to establish the San José Project Division. From 1944 through 1947, at least 128 CW tests took place on the island, with both the **United Kingdom** and Canada participating in many of these tests. Munitions tested included 1,000-pound AN/M-79 bombs containing cyanogen chloride or **phosgene** and 115-pound M-70 bombs filled with **sulfur mustard**. The total number of munitions tested between 1944 and 1947 is estimated to be in excess of 31,000. The CWS regarded the test results as important to understanding the offensive and defensive phases of chemical warfare in jungle fighting.

One legacy of the San José Island tests is that the Republic of Panama has declared to the **Organization for the Prohibition of Chemical Weapons (OPCW)** that it has **abandoned chemical weapons (ACW)** on its territory. At least four munition bodies originally filled with a toxic chemical have been recovered. However, the identity of the abandoning party or parties has not been officially determined. There is also general uncertainty as to the nature and scope of the problem of retrieving and removing the abandoned CW and of remediating any environmental damage.

SARIN. During his research into **organophosphorus nerve agents**, **German** chemist **Gerhard Schrader** synthesized O-isopropyl methylphosphonofluoridate ($C_4H_{10}FO_2P$) in 1939. He dubbed this substance "sarin," which is taken from the names of <u>S</u>chrader and his colleagues Otto <u>A</u>mbros, Franz <u>R</u>itter, and H. J. von der Li<u>n</u>de. The Soviets became aware of the existence of the German code name for sarin in 1941 when Soviet forces captured documents belonging to the 52nd Chemical Mine Regiment, but they did not know what the code name stood for until the end of the war. However, **Russian** chemist **Martin Kabachnik** independently discovered sarin in 1944. NATO eventually gave sarin the military code name "GB." The Japanese-based religious cult **Aum Shinrikyo** used low-purity sarin to attack the Tokyo subway in March 1995. *See also* SOMAN; TABUN.

SAXITOXIN. A poisonous substance of marine origin. Saxitoxin is rapid acting and among the most potent of all nonprotein **toxins**. It interferes with transmission of nerve impulses, making it a **neurotoxin**. Saxitoxin is produced naturally by microorganisms, especially certain algae, which are ingested by shellfish but cause the shellfish no harm. Humans who eat contaminated shellfish, however, are harmed, with nearly immediate onset of a condition known as paralytic shellfish poisoning (PSP). No antidote is available. The potency and immediacy of saxitoxin made it a subject of research for possible use as a weapon. The **United States**, for example, included it in World War II **biological weapons (BW)** program. Later, the Central Intelligence Agency (CIA) produced and stockpiled modest amounts of saxitoxin for potential use as an assassination weapon. There is no record of its actual use by the United States or any other nation. Perhaps because of this history of development, saxitoxin is one of two toxins explicitly listed in the schedules associated with the **Chemical Weapons Convention (CWC)**, the other being **ricin**.

SCHRADER, GERHARD (1903–1990). German chemist. Schrader is generally credited with the discovery of **organophosphorus nerve agents**. His discovery was the unintended consequence of efforts to try to find substitutes for nicotine. Nicotine is a **toxin**, derived from tobacco plants, that was then in extensive use as an insecticide. As **Germany** prepared for the conflict in Europe, the government became concerned that supplies of nicotine would be disrupted in the event of war, potentially harming German agriculture and causing losses of crops as foodstuffs and in industry. The German chemical industry was encouraged to find alternative insecticides. In 1935 Schrader discovered **tabun**, believed to be the first organophosphorus nerve agent, followed in 1939 by **sarin**. The discoveries were reported to the German government under a law that required the reporting of scientific discoveries of possible military significance.

Germany undertook military development of tabun, sarin, and a third organophosphorus nerve agent, **soman**; however, late in the war, Schrader was diverted from this research to work on a program to development chemical defenses against the Colorado potato beetle. Germany feared an invasion of this insect pest, most likely as a result of deliberate release by the Allies. *See also* ANTICROP AGENTS.

SEABED TREATY. The Seabed Treaty prohibits the implanting on the ocean floor or subsoil of any **nuclear weapons** or other **weapons of mass destruction (WMD)** beyond a 12-mile coastal zone. The treaty also prohibits the emplacement of "structures, launching installations or any other facilities specifically designed for storing, testing or using such weapons." It entered into force on 18 May 1972 and is open to universal membership. Its full title is the Treaty on the Prohibition of the Emplacement of Nuclear Weapons and Other Weapons of Mass Destruction on the Seabed and the Ocean Floor and in the Subsoil Thereof.

SEA DUMPING. In the period from the end of World War I through the early 1980s, dumping of **chemical weapons (CW)** at sea was widespread. **Australia**, various European countries, **Japan**, **South Africa**, the Soviet Union, and the **United States** resorted to sea dumping as a routine method for disposing of excess, obsolete, or unstable CW. Areas affected by this practice include the Arctic Ocean, the Baltic and Black seas, the Sea of Japan, and off the coasts of Australia, Belgium, Denmark, **France**, the **United Kingdom**, and the United States. Although the locations of some sites of sea-dumped CW have been confirmed, others have not. Reasons for this include records having been lost or destroyed, information still being classified or misplaced in national archives, and crews responsible for dumping CW abandoning their cargoes at locations other their intended destination. Fishermen, especially ones working in the Baltic Sea and in Japanese waters, periodically recover sea-dumped CW in their nets, resulting in some injuries and deaths, as well as the loss of the nets and their contents.

Technical experts generally agree that sea-dumped CW should be left undisturbed, because any attempt to move them could result in an explosion or other rupture of the munitions, thereby spilling the contents into the environment. **Organophosphorus nerve agents** hydrolyze readily in sea water into essentially benign degradation products of low toxicity. The primary environmental and human health threats are posed by arsenic-containing CW, such as the World War I–era **blue cross agents** and **lewisite**. Metals and explosives may also present environmental and human health hazards. The quantity of conventional munitions dumped at sea is substantially greater than the quantity of sea-dumped CW. No sea-dumped CW have been declared to the **Organization for the Prohibition of Chemical Weapons (OPCW)**. *See also* HELSINKI COMMISSION (HELCOM).

SEMIPALATINSK. Now located in Kazakhstan, Semipalatinsk was the principal **nuclear weapon** test site of the Union of Soviet Socialist Republics (USSR). It was established in accordance with a 1947 decision by the Soviet Communist Party's Central Committee and the Council of Ministers. The USSR detonated its first nuclear weapon there on 29 August 1949 under the scientific direction of **Igor V. Kurchatov**. It was also the site where the USSR detonated its first **thermonuclear** weapon (12 August 1953) and its first **hydrogen bomb** (22 November 1955). A total of 467 nuclear weapons were detonated at Semipalatinsk from 1949 to 1990. The test facility was shut down in 1991. The site is today occupied by the National Nuclear Center of the Republic of Kazakhstan. The region has experienced serious environmental and human health damage as a result of the nuclear weapon tests. *See also* JOE.

SEMIPERSISTENT AGENT. *See* CLASSES OF CHEMICAL WEAPONS.

SEWER PIPE. The nickname given to the XM-113 **atomic demolition munition (ADM)**. "Sewer Pipe" was one of a series of such ADMs developed by the U.S. military. It was notable because of its relatively small size (slightly over five feet in length and nearly three feet in diameter) and light weight (just under a half-ton). These features would have facilitated its rapid emplacement if military operations had ever required its use. First deployed to Europe in 1961, Sewer Pipe was made obsolete by even smaller, lighter ADMs, such as the Medium Atomic Demolition Munition (MADM), which weighed less than 400 pounds, and the **Special Atomic Demolition Munition (SADM)**, weighing less than 200 pounds. Sewer Pipe was withdrawn from U.S. military service by 1967.

SHAKE. A unit of time. It is used most often in describing atomic or nuclear events. One shake equals 1×10^{-8} seconds. *See also* CHAIN REACTION.

SHARASHKY (*sing.* SHARASHKA). The Soviet Gulag system of prisons had confinement facilities where Soviet scientists and technical specialists serving prison sentences were allowed to continue their professional work. These specialized prisons were called *sharashky* (Cyrillic: шарашкы). Some sharashky were devoted to work on **chemical** and **biological weapons (CBW)**. In some cases, the facilities, including laboratories, were part of a prison complex. In other instances, the prisoners worked at nonprison facilities alongside the civilian population. *See also* FISHMAN, YAKOV MOISEE-VICH; GOSNIIOKHT.

SHEIGEYOSHI MORIMOTO. On 6 August 1945, **Japanese** kite maker Sheigeyoshi was working in Hiroshima. He was in a paint store when the U.S. "**Little Boy**" bomb exploded. The concrete walls of the store shielded him from the explosion, and Sheigeyoshi survived the blast. Afterward, he struggled to return to Nagasaki, his home city. He arrived just as the "**Fat Man**" bomb exploded on 9 August 1945. Gathering his wife and son, they took refuge in a cellar and survived this blast. Sheigeyoshi is believed to be the sole person to have been proximate to both nuclear explosions and yet to have survived. *See also* NATIONAL PEACE MEMORIAL HALL FOR ATOMIC BOMB VICTIMS.

SHIFA PHARMACEUTICAL INDUSTRIES FACTORY, AL-. On 20 August 1998 U.S. warships in the Arabian and Red seas launched satellite-guided cruise missiles toward Sudan. They hit the Shifa Pharmaceutical Industries factory, located in a region of Khartoum, Sudan, destroying the factory but creating a controversy regarding the intelligence used to select this target. The attack, given the code name "Operation Infinite Reach," was carried out for several reasons, including a U.S. assessment that affiliates of **al-Qaeda** leader Osama bin Laden were attempting to use the facility to manufacture **VX**, an **organophosphorus nerve agent**. The U.S. decision in favor of the missile strike reportedly was based in part on laboratory analyses of soil samples suggesting the presence of a precursor chemical involved in the manufacture of VX, namely, O-ethyl methylphosphonothioic acid (EMPTA). However, uncertainty was expressed publicly about the covert sampling and analysis methods used by the **United States**.

In an attempt at disproving U.S. government claims, the Saudi owner of the facility financed an independent study of samples from the site. This study was led by Thomas D. Tullis, then chairman of the Chemistry Department at Boston University, and was executed by three European laboratories and an international engineering firm based in Manchester, England. Their laboratory analyses cast doubts on the claims that the facility had been manufacturing VX or any other chemical warfare (CW) agent. The U.S. government appeared to concede the possibility that it erred in its assessment when it lifted a freeze of the owner's financial assets.

SHIKHANY. The Shikhany Central Scientific-Research and Experimental Institute of Radiological, Chemical, and Biological Defense of the **Russian** Federation is the principal Russian scientific research and test facility for protection against **chemical weapons (CW)**. The facility takes its name from the town of Shikhany, situated on the west bank of the Volga River in the Volsk region southeast of Moscow. Established in 1928, the facility was originally called the Central Military Chemical Proving Ground for the Creation of Domestic Chemical Weapons and Defensive Means. From 1928 to 1929, it was headed by **Yakov M. Fishman**. The establishment of the Shikhany Central Military Chemical Proving Ground was the most lasting result of the **German**-Soviet cooperation in the field of CW that occurred under the terms of the 1922 Treaty of Rapallo.

Although the facility is also responsible for developing and testing methods for the detection of and protection against **radioactive materials** and **biological weapons (BW)**, the focus of its work has always been on CW. A detailed picture of activities of the facility is impossible because the town of Shikhany is "closed." Travel by ordinary Russian citizens to Shikhany is restricted to those having a special invitation from relatives living there. Access to the city by non-Russian citizens is generally not allowed except in cases where special permission is granted by the Russian government. *See also* BERSOL; TOMKA.

SHOT GRABLE. On 25 May 1953, the U.S. military successfully fired a 280-mm **nuclear weapon** from an atomic cannon during "Shot Grable" of the Upshot-Knothole test series. A **Mark-9 280-mm projectile** traveled seven miles and detonated slightly more than 500 feet above ground, with a yield of 15 kilotons. *See also* ATOMIC ANNIE.

SIEVERT. Sievert is the SI (metric) unit for measuring the absorbed or effective dose of radiation received by a human or some other living organism. One sievert (abbreviated "Sv") equals 100 **rem**. The unit honors Swedish physicist Rolf Sievert (1898–1966), whose work on measuring radiation doses used in cancer treatment helped to standardize such measurements. Because the effects produced by radiation vary with the kind of radiation, simply measuring the radiation dose as energy received by the organism fails to give a clear indication of the likely biological effects of that radiation. To account for this variation, the actual dose of radiation (in **grays**, Gy) is multiplied by a factor that accounts for the *type* of radiation to give the effective dose in sieverts. For example, an effective dose of 1 Sv requires 1 Gy of **beta** or **gamma radiation**, but only 0.1 Gy of neutron radiation and just 0.05 Gy of **alpha** radiation.

SIMULANT. A chemical or biological material used in testing to simulate the behavior of chemical and biological warfare (CBW) agents. The ideal simulant is inexpensive and harmless and reproduces all of the chemical and physical properties of the CBW agent of interest for the test. This ideal cannot be fully achieved, so selection of any simulant involves compromises. Frequently, one simulant for a CBW agent is selected for a particular test or type of tests, while other simulants for that same CBW agent are selected for different tests. For instance, zinc cadmium sulfide, an inorganic material, was selected to simulant the aerodynamics of all biological warfare (BW) agents in general during the **Operation LAC** open-air releases. Zinc cadmium sulfide lacks most characteristics of the chemical and physical properties of a BW agent, making it a poor simulant if those characteristics were needed, but they were not. It was selected because of its perceived low toxicity, the ease of measuring its presence in the atmosphere (zinc cadmium sulfide fluoresces, making detection possible), and the relatively low cost of the material.

SITES W, X, Y. In late 1942, **Leslie Groves**, head of the **Manhattan Project**, selected the first sites for what became a nationwide group of laboratories and production facilities for the project's **nuclear weapons** complex. The first locations were designated by the code names "Site W" (near Hanford, Washington), "Site X" (near Oak Ridge, Tennessee), and "Site Y" (near Los Alamos, New Mexico). The three sites were known by these code names throughout World War II as a security precaution. The operations begun at Site W became the basis for the Pacific Northwest National Laboratories and the other facilities important to **plutonium** production; those at Site X, the Oak Ridge National Laboratory; and those at Site Y, the Los Alamos National Laboratory. *See also* Z DIVISION.

S. K. TIMOSHENKO MILITARY ACADEMY OF RADIOLOGICAL, CHEMICAL, AND BIOLOGICAL DEFENSE. The premier educational institute for military specialists in matters pertaining to **nuclear**, **biological**, and **chemical (NBC) weapons**. Located in Moscow, this academy's activities include teaching and research, which includes laboratory work. The academy is divided into various departments, referred to as "faculties." Special Engineering Faculty No. 5, for example, existed between 1967 and 1979 and was designed to train specialists for military and civilian scientific research institutes and enterprises. The school was founded in 1932 and has gone through assorted names. The present name honors Semyon K. Timoshenko (1895–1970), who rose to the rank of marshal in the Army of the Soviet Union.

SKULL VALLEY INCIDENT. On 13 March 1968, ranchers in and near Skull Valley, Utah, noticed that their sheep were ill and dying. Although deaths among sheep are common, these deaths were unusual for the number of sheep affected and the symptoms observed. A subsequent investigation attributed the deaths to an accidental release of **VX** during open-air testing at **Dugway Proving Ground (DPG)**, directly to the west of sparsely populated Skull Valley. The test involved a spray-tank release of 320 gallons of VX from a U.S. Air Force plane over DPG. A valve on one of the tanks malfunctioned and failed to close. As a result, approximately 20 pounds of VX was released accidentally when the plane gained altitude during its exit from the test grid area. The investigation noted that a thunderstorm was forming over DPG as the plane departed the test area and speculated that the developing storm pulled droplets of VX into the atmosphere, carried them to the east as it moved, and deposited them in Skull Valley along with rain, snow, and sleet during the subsequent storm. This finding was greeted with skepticism by DPG and other U.S. military officials, who noted no symptoms of VX exposure in the humans or pets living in the DPG housing area between the test area and Skull Valley.

Eventually, though, the U.S. Army accepted responsibility and reimbursed ranchers for their losses, which were officially recorded as 4,453 sheep from six locations, although an accurate count of dead sheep proved elusive. The incident in Skull Valley had far-reaching and unexpected consequences. It brought public attention to the common practice of conducting open-air releases of **chemical weapons (CW)** and other dangerous materials at DPG. Furthermore, the reluctance of the U.S. government to accept responsibility for the deaths of these sheep eroded public confidence. Ultimately, the incident prompted Congress to enact a requirement that it be notified prior to conducting any open-air releases of chemical and biological warfare (CBW) agents, effectively ending routine open-air testing of these agents by the **United States**.

SLOTIN, LOUIS (1910–1946). Canadian-born physicist. On 21 May 1946, Slotin was demonstrating details of the **Dragon Experiment** to several colleagues at **Site Y**, Los Alamos, New Mexico. Slotin had taken part in the **Manhattan Project** and was familiar with the demonstration, which involved two hemispheres containing subcritical masses of **plutonium**-239. If the masses should come together, a **chain reaction** would ensue. In Slotin's demonstration, the hemispheres were held apart by screwdrivers. As he brought the hemispheres into closer contact, one screwdriver slipped, and the masses of plutonium immediately underwent a chain reaction. Slotin, who had his left thumb in the topmost hemisphere, instinctively raised his arm, causing the hemispheres to separate. The reaction ceased, but it had already unleashed a large burst of radiation. Slotin received a mammoth dose of radiation and died nine days later of acute radiation sickness, becoming the second Dragon Experiment fatality (after **Harry Daghlian**). The others who were present received more modest radiation doses, thanks in part to shielding by Slotin's body.

Slotin was buried in his native city of Winnipeg, Manitoba. In October, 1993, the citizens of Winnipeg dedicated a park in the Luxton Street neighborhood to Slotin. A plaque at the park proclaims the following: "This park is dedicated to the memory of Dr. Louis Slotin who willingly and heroically laid down his life to save seven fellow scientists during an experiment 2 May 1946 at the Los Alamos atomic research project in New Mexico, U.S.A."

SMALLPOX. A contagious disease caused by the *variola* virus. Both *variola major* and *variola minor* give rise to smallpox. *Variola major* is responsible for the classic form of the disease familiar to the public. The disease is unique to humans in that only humans can be host to the virus. Smallpox infections are highly contagious to others who have not been vaccinated or who lack acquired immunity resulting from past infection. The virus is hardy and can be spread readily by the **aerosol** route. Thus, virus-laden exhalations from an infected person can be inhaled and infect another. The virus can also be spread by fomites (inanimate objects), such as clothing and bedding taken from infected individuals. Infection typically has a high mortality rate, and survivors are often permanently disfigured by the pockmarks characteristic of smallpox.

Smallpox might have been spread deliberately during conflicts in the Americas, especially the French and Indian War (1754–1763). One small-scale use took place in 1763 when two blankets and a handkerchief known to have been taken from smallpox victims at Fort Pitt were presented by the British to a group of Native Americans whose loyalty to the British cause was uncertain. Those Indians had little or no immunity to the virus, and smallpox was reported to have broken out among tribes in the Ohio Valley region.

The smallpox vaccination is highly effective but is no longer routinely administered. Therefore, the potential use of variola virus as a **biological weapon (BW)** represents a significant risk to the general population. This may have inspired the Soviet Union to engage in a large-scale program at **Vektor** in Siberia to produce the variola virus. This Cold War–era program included specialized facilities for loading truck-mounted storage tanks that could be driven to airfields for loading virus stocks into aviation spray tanks.

In the 1960s and 1970s, an ambitious effort was undertaken to rid the world of smallpox infections. That effort succeeded, and in 1979 the World Health Organization (WHO) certified that the disease had been eradicated. Shortly thereafter, an international agreement was reached, restricting remaining stocks of variola virus to two locations. Presently, these two sites are in Russia (at Vektor) and the **United States** (at the Centers for Disease Control and Prevention in Atlanta). In keeping with this agreement, these stocks were to be destroyed by 30 June 1999. However, on 22 April 1999, the U.S. government announced its decision not to destroy its stocks of smallpox virus, citing intelligence reports suggesting the existence of the virus outside the two agreed-upon sites. Destruction of all virus stocks continues to be discussed.

SMALL QUANTITIES PROTOCOL (SQP). A part of the Safeguards Agreements that the **International Atomic Energy Agency (IAEA)** concludes with member states of the **Nonproliferation Treaty (NPT)**. Under the Small Quantities Protocol, most of the detailed provisions of a Safeguards Agreement are held in abeyance in cases where a state has little or no declared nuclear material or nuclear activities. Concern that the SQP constitutes a loophole in the **IAEA safeguards** system resulted in moves, starting in 2005, by the IAEA Board of Governors to restrict the eligibility of states to use the protocol. For example, states are prohibited from using the SQP if they plan to construct nuclear facilities. Furthermore, states must also not delay informing the IAEA of such plans. These changes were largely prompted by questions about whether **Iran** was complying with its declaration obligations to the IAEA.

SMILING BUDDHA. The code name **India** gave to its **nuclear weapons** project, which resulted in a nuclear detonation on 18 May 1974. India characterized this detonation as a peaceful nuclear explosion (PNE), but the event likely prompted the neighboring country of **Pakistan** to hasten its own efforts to develop nuclear weapons. *See also* ATOMS FOR PEACE; PEACEFUL NUCLEAR EXPLOSIONS (PNE) TREATY.

SMIRNOV, EFIM IVANOVICH (1904–1985). Russian scientist and military leader. Smirnov graduated from the S. M. Kirov Military-

Medical Academy and the M. V. Frunze Military Academy in the Union of Soviet Socialist Republics (USSR). During World War II, Smirnov was awarded the Order of Kutuzov for his role in evacuating approximately 100,000 wounded from Kharkov prior to the city's occupation by **German** troops. Smirnov headed the Main Military-Sanitary Directorate of the Red Army from 1939 to 1946. A main focus of his work there was to improve military sanitation and develop a system of treating wounded soldiers and expediting their return to service. The name of the directorate was changed in 1946 to the Main Military-Medical Directorate (still headed by Smirnov). In 1947–1953, Smirnov served as the Soviet minister of health. Beginning in 1953, he headed the military-biological research of the Soviet Ministry of Defense (MOD). At about this time, he was also named head of the Kirov Military-Medical Academy. From 1955 to 1960, he headed the Main Military-Medical Directorate of the MOD, and from then until his retirement, he headed the Seventh Directorate of the MOD. This directorate was eventually redesignated the **15th Directorate** and was responsible for directing the Soviet **biological weapons (BW)** program. Smirnov was a member of the Interagency Scientific and Technology Council on Molecular Biology and Genetics, which was involved in coordinating BW-related work.

SMOKE AGENT. Any substance or mix of substances that generates smoke intentionally. "Obscurant" is used as a synonym for "smoke agent," but the applications of smoke agents are more extensive than merely obscuration. Both military and civilian uses of smoke agents exist. Military functions include both signaling, where the smoke designates a position or place, and camouflage, cover, and concealment, where the smoke is used to avoid being seen or to obscure the ability of someone else to see. Civilian uses include detecting leaks, measuring airflow and direction, and visualizing airflow around an object, as is done in a wind tunnel.

In general, smoke agents are nontoxic and fall outside the regime of chemicals controlled by the **Chemical Weapons Convention (CWC)**. Early smoke agents were often blends that included sulfur, tar, and charcoal. However, when sulfur is burned, it forms toxic sulfur dioxide. Fog oil and mixtures with zinc chloride have been used extensively by the military as smoke agents and are relatively safe.

Finally, white phosphorus (WP) has been used as a smoke agent, although it can cause severe burns if unreacted white phosphorus contacts the skin, and it can set objects on fire. *See also* INCENDIARY MATERIAL.

SNIFFER. Concerned that the Soviets were developing a **nuclear weapon**, in the late 1940s the **United States** established a system for detecting a nuclear test. The system included "sniffer" devices installed in U.S. Air Force weather reconnaissance aircraft. Each sniffer pulled air through filters, trapping particulate materials, including radioactive **fallout** from atmospheric testing, if it should occur. The Air Force sent the sniffer filters to a laboratory in Berkeley, California, where the types and distribution of radioactive **isotopes** were measured. In particular, the laboratory measured the rates of **radioactive decay**, thereby determining when each isotope was created. This determination was crucial, because if many or all the isotopes had the same date of creation, then these isotopes must have been produced by a nuclear detonation.

The 375th Weather Reconnaissance Squadron, based in Alaska, regularly patrolled areas downwind of the Union of Soviet Socialist Republics (USSR). On 3 September 1949, an aircraft from this squadron detected high levels of radioactivity while flying a routine mission east of the Kamchatka Peninsula. Analysis of the sniffer filter confirmed that this radioactivity was **fission**-derived. The laboratory estimated that a nuclear device (later to be dubbed "**Joe** 1") had exploded in the USSR on 29 August. This news was communicated by **Atomic Energy Commission (AEC)** chairman David Lilienthal to President Harry S. Truman on 20 September, who informed his Cabinet three days later.

SOMAN. Following the discoveries of **tabun** and **sarin**, **Germany** continued its search for other **organophosphorus nerve agents** during World War II. This search led to the 1944 discovery of O-pinacolyl methylphosphonofluoridate ($C_7H_{16}NO_2P$), which became known as soman. For years, this discovery was attributed to Richard Kuhn (1900–1967), who was selected for the 1938 Nobel Prize in Chemistry for his work on carotinoids and vitamins but declined it. More recent research instead attributes the discovery to Konrad Henkel, a scientist working at the Kaiser Wilhelm Institute for Medical Research, which was directed by Kuhn.

Germany produced soman for use in **chemical weapons (CW)**, although none was ever used in combat. The Allies learned of soman when soman-filled munitions were discovered at the end of World War II. Interviews of captured German scientists and recovered documents added to their knowledge. Soman eventually was selected as a standard CW agent. It was given the military code name "GD" by NATO. The **United States** and the Soviet Union also produced and stockpiled soman-filled CW, but neither country ever used these weapons.

SORT. *See* STRATEGIC OFFENSIVE REDUCTIONS TREATY (SORT).

SOUTH AFRICA. The Republic of South Africa is known to have had a **chemical weapons (CW)** program during the apartheid era. The program focused on developing **incapacitants** rather than more deadly substances such as **sulfur mustard** and **organophosphorus nerve agents**. Substances that were successfully prepared as fills in munitions were as follows: an analogue of the psychochemical **BZ** ("Product B"); a **binary** type of the **lachrymator** CR ("Novel Tear Gas"); the hallucinogen ecstasy; and the sedative methaqualone ("Product M"). The reported intent of these incapacitants was to confuse or otherwise disable victims.

Production of the BZ-analogue ceased when unexpected side effects (not further explained) were detected. Production of ecstasy and methaqualone was modest—approximately 1,000 kilograms (2,200 pounds) of each. However, it remains unclear whether the actual intent for producing these two substances, both of which are notorious drugs of addiction, might have been to undermine the health of persons in targeted communities by sinister introduction of addictive drugs. The precise formulation of Novel Tear Gas and chemical formula of the analogue of BZ are uncertain.

SOVIET UNION. *See* RUSSIA.

SPAIN HYDROGEN BOMB INCIDENT. On 17 January 1966, a U.S. Air Force B-52 bomber and K-135 refueling tanker collided over the Spanish fishing village of Palomares. The crash caused the two planes to break up, killing 7 of the 11 crewmen on board and releasing four of the bomber's cargo of **hydrogen bombs**. Two of these bombs landed intact. The other two underwent high-explosive detonations; no **chain reaction** occurred, but the detonations scattered **radioactive materials** across Spanish territory. Three bombs were promptly recovered by the **United States** from the land territory of Spain, while the fourth was located intact in the North Atlantic Ocean by the submersible *Alvin* of the Woods Hole Oceanographic Institution on 15 March, approximately five miles off the coast of Spain. An estimated 558 acres of territory were contaminated with **uranium** and **plutonium**. The United States removed just under 5,000 barrels of contaminated soil and vegetation to the Savannah River Plant in Aiken, South Carolina, for long-term storage.

In response to the accident, the United States implemented a long-term collaborative technical and financial assistance program known as Project Indal, which includes radiological monitoring for the population of Palomares and the surrounding area. In October 2006, this monitoring found radioactivity among snails, heightening fears regarding residual radioactive contamination.

SPECIAL ATOMIC DEMOLITION MUNITION (SADM). The Special Atomic Demolition Munition was the smallest **nuclear weapon** ever deployed by the **United States**. Precise technical specifications are lacking, but the size of the SADM in its shipping container was estimated to be roughly three feet in length and two feet in diameter, with an overall weight of slightly more than 160 pounds. The modest size of the SADM allowed it to be deployed by U.S. military Special Forces units. Unlike other **atomic demolition munitions (ADM)**, which were intended as defensive weapons, the SADMs were intended for both defensive and offensive use, including being carried behind enemy lines to destroy key facilities. SADMs were stockpiled in Europe, as were other ADMs, but were removed and returned to the United States by 1985. The United States began dismantling its SADMs shortly thereafter, and by 1992, none remained in inventory. *See also* SEWER PIPE.

SPECIAL BRIGADE. Germany's use of **chemical weapons (CW)** in April 1915 prompted the **United Kingdom** to develop capabilities to retaliate. One measure undertaken was the creation of a military unit responsible for waging offensive operations using CW. On 23 May 1915, the British military authorized the "Special Companies" and named **C. H. Foulkes** as its commander. Eventually, the Special Companies would grow to the Special Brigade, having 258 officers and 5,832 enlisted men at its greatest strength. The Special Brigade saw extensive service on the Western Front, conducting 768 CW operations involving the release of approximately 88,000 gas cylinders, 197,000 **Livens projectors**, and 178,000 Stokes mortar bombs. Casualties were high: 5,384, close to 100 percent of total strength. Special Brigade personnel were honored with 557 decorations, including one award of the Victoria Cross, the highest British military honor.

SPECIAL NUCLEAR MATERIAL. The U.S. Atomic Energy Act of 1954 defines special nuclear material (SNM) as any **isotope** of **plutonium**, or **uranium** that has been enriched in either uranium-233 or uranium-235. *See also* HIGHLY ENRICHED URANIUM (HEU); LOW-ENRICHED URANIUM (LEU).

STABILIZER. A substance that prevents or retards the degradation of a chemical warfare (CW) agent and, thus, stabilizes it. Many CW agents are inherently unstable or are contaminated with by-products as a result of the production process. Such degradation limits the shelf life of the agents and detracts from the use of these agents for military purposes. For example, tributylamine is one of several stabilizers that can be added to slow or prevent hydrolysis of **sarin** in storage.

STAGG FIELD. At 3:20 P.M. Central War Time on 2 December 1942, the first self-sustaining **chain reaction** took place in a **nuclear pile** constructed beneath the abandoned west grandstands of Stagg Field at the University of Chicago. The pile, designated "Chicago Pile 1" ("CP-1"), was designed and operated by a team under the leadership of Enrico Fermi, the Nobel Laureate physicist who had fled Fascist Italy for the **United States**. CP-1 consisted of 400 tons of graphite (as the moderator), 6 tons of **uranium**, and 50 tons of uranium oxide. It initially achieved a power output of one-half watt; output increased to 200 watts 10 days later. Fermi's success at Stagg Field was an important milestone in the U.S. quest to harness nuclear power for military and, eventually, peaceful purposes, because it demonstrated that **fission** could be carried out in a controlled and sustained manner. Physicist Karl Compton (1887–1954) represented the **Office of Scientific Research and Development (OSRD)** in witnessing this event and sent fellow OSRD committee member **James Conant** a message that "the Italian navigator has just landed in the new world. . . . Everyone landed safe and happy."

START I. *See* TREATY ON THE REDUCTION AND LIMITATION OF STRATEGIC OFFENSIVE ARMS (START I).

START II. *See* TREATY ON FURTHER REDUCTION AND LIMITATION OF STRATEGIC OFFENSIVE ARMS (START II).

STINKS. British, and possibly other, soldiers used the term *stinks* to refer to foul-smelling but otherwise harmless chemicals fired against enemy positions, with the intent of forcing the enemy to don burdensome protective gear unnecessarily. Substances commonly used as stinks included **balloon dope** and **bone oil**.

STOKES TRENCH MORTAR. *See* LIVENS PROJECTOR.

STOLTZENBERG, HUGO (1883–1974). German chemist. Stoltzenberg devoted his career to **chemical weapons (CW)**. During World War I, he was one of the chemists enlisted by **Fritz Haber** to emplace cylinders of **chlorine** for the 15 April 1915 release near **Ypres**, Belgium, that inaugurated the modern era of chemical warfare. Stoltzenberg lost sight in one eye after a jet of chlorine hit his face when one of these chlorine cylinders burst. Following the war, his Hamburg, **Germany**, firm was awarded the task of disposing of German CW and dismantling certain CW production facilities. Additionally, he set about marketing his CW skills internationally, supervising the construction of CW production facilities in Spain (1921–1927), the Soviet Union (1923–1927), Yugoslavia (1927–1931), and **Brazil** (1937–1942). His production facilities often failed, most spectacularly in the USSR. However, he was able to provide nations with CW, most likely using stocks of World War I German CW that his firm was supposed to have destroyed.

Stoltzenberg's wife, Margarete Stoltzenberg-Bergius, was a bacteriologist and joined him in his lecturing and writing ventures, expanding his coverage to include **biological weapons (BW)**. Their son, Dietrich Stoltzenberg, authored a comprehensive biography of Haber (*Fritz Haber: Chemiker, Nobelpreistrager, Deutsche, Jude*, 1994). This biography details some of Hugo Stoltzenberg's CW ventures during the 1920s and 1930s. *See also* BERSOL; MOROCCO.

STRASSMANN, FRITZ. *See* FISSION; HAHN, OTTO.

STRATEGIC OFFENSIVE REDUCTIONS TREATY (SORT). The Strategy Offensive Reductions Treaty obliges **Russia** and the **United States** to reduce the numbers of their operationally deployed strategic nuclear warheads so that, by 31 December 2012, the aggregate number of such warheads does not exceed some amount in the range of 1,700–2,200 for each party, with the precise number still to be negotiated. After this time, the treaty may be extended if both parties agree. It was signed on 24 May 2002 and entered into force on 1 June 2003. SORT has generated controversy, partly because it allows the parties to redeploy warheads that had previously been removed from operational deployment. *See also* TREATY ON THE REDUCTION AND LIMITATION OF STRATEGIC OFFENSIVE ARMS (START I); TREATY ON FURTHER REDUCTION AND LIMITATION OF STRATEGIC OFFENSIVE ARMS (START II).

SULFUR MUSTARD. The chemical *bis*(2-chloroethyl) sulfide ($C_4H_8Cl_2S$) is referred to as "sulfur mustard," and the group of chemicals similar in structure to *bis*(2-chloroethyl) sulfide can collectively be called "sulfur mustards." *Sulfur mustard* is regarded as a better term than ***mustard gas***, but it suffers from a similar defect in that neither *bis*(2-chloroethyl) sulfide nor its analogues are true "mustards" in the sense used by chemists (that is, chemicals having the general formula R–N=C=S, where R is any alkyl or aryl radical). Sulfur mustards feature prominently in chemical warfare (CW). Various military code names have been used for sulfur mustard. Among the most enduring are "HD," "HS," "Lost," and "Yperite."

Depending on the ambient conditions, sulfur mustard is an oily liquid or a dark solid with an odor resembling that of oil of mustard. This resemblance accounts for the use of "mustard" to describe the substance. Its discovery was reported independently on at least three occasions in the 1800s, and its properties were well known when World War I began. However, both the **United Kingdom** and **Germany** initially decided against its use, perhaps because they were searching for substances that would have more immediate toxic effects. Germany introduced its use in July 1917, and it came to be used extensively thereafter. The Allies wished to retaliate in kind, and **France**, the United Kingdom, and the **United States** all undertook production. By summer 1918, the Allies had sufficient stockpiles to retaliate, and they continued to use sulfur mustard until the end of the war.

The **vesicating** effects of sulfur mustard caused many nations to take an interest in producing and stockpiling sulfur mustard or one of its chemical analogues following the war. The United States and United Kingdom stockpiled sulfur mustard as well as analogues, but none was used during World War II, and production ceased shortly after that war. A substantial stockpile was produced in the Soviet Union, initially with the German assistance. The Soviet stockpile appears never to have been used in combat, although various reports suggest Soviet-supplied sulfur mustard (and possibly other CW agents) was used by Egypt during its intervention in the 1963–1967 **Yemeni Civil War**. Among the nations that did acquire and use sulfur mustard in combat are Spain (for its 1920s offensive against rebels in **Morocco**) and Italy (for its 1935–1937 invasion of **Ethiopia**). **Japan** also produced and stockpiled sulfur mustard and analogues. None of the stockpile appears to have been used against the Allies in World War II, but it remains uncertain whether any of these agents were used during the conflict on the Asian mainland in 1937–1945. *See also* LEWISITE; NITROGEN MUSTARD; STOLTZENBERG, HUGO; YELLOW CROSS AGENT; YPRES.

SUPERCRITICAL. Describing a mass of **radioactive material** greater than a **critical mass**. A typical supercritical mass would be just slightly greater than a critical mass.

– T –

T-2. *See* TRICHOTHECENE MYCOTOXINS; YELLOW RAIN.

TABUN. In 1935, chemists working for IG Farben in **Germany** found promising insecticidal properties for N,N-dimethylamidophosphoryl fluoride. Continuing his systematic research, on 23 December 1936 IG Farben chemist **Gerhard Schrader** synthesized ethyl N,N-dimethylphosphoramidocyanidate, $C_5H_{11}N_2O_2P$. Eventually this substance was renamed "tabun" and became the basis for a novel class of **chemical weapons (CW)**: the **organophosphorus nerve agents.** A sample of tabun was sent to the chemical warfare section of the Army Weapons office in May 1937. Once its military potential was recognized, pilot-scale production was begun at Munster-Lager. Ultimately, full-scale production of tabun was undertaken at Dyhernfurth in Project Hochwerk. Germany gave this substance various code names to help protect its identity, including "Gelan," "Leverkusen 100," "Trilon 83," and "Z-Stoff." NATO would give tabun the military code name "GA." The origin of the name tabun is obscure. *See also* SARIN; SOMAN.

TAILINGS. In the nuclear context, the depleted stream remaining from a **uranium** enrichment process or from uranium milling. In relative terms, the tailings (also occasionally referred to as "tails") are **depleted uranium** reduced in uranium-235, while the enrichment process is enriched in that **isotope.** In general, tailings make poor sources for development of **nuclear weapons** or for use in **radiological dispersal devices (RDD)** because they are low in radioactive uranium-235.

TAMPER. A **nuclear weapon** element designed to hold the weapon together somewhat longer than would occur in its absence. A tamper is used to help achieve a sustained **chain reaction.** It might also serve as a neutron reflector.

TEAR GAS. *See* LACHRYMATOR.

TELLER-ULAM CONCEPT. On 13 January 1950, President Harry S. Truman announced that he was directing the **Atomic Energy Commission (AEC)** to develop a **thermonuclear** weapon. At the time, U.S. **nuclear weapon** designers had failed to develop a successful concept for such a device. In late 1950 and early 1951, physicists Stanislaw Ulam and Edward Teller advanced a concept for such a weapon that would ultimately prove successful. Called the Teller-Ulam Concept, it involves using the x-rays emitted from a primary **fission** event to compress the nuclei in the secondary, **fusion**, core. On 9 March 1951, Teller and Ulam presented a report describing their concept. It was taken up promptly for testing and was validated by the 9 May detonation of the device code-named "**George**."

THE DALLES SALAD BAR INCIDENT. In September 1984, a religious group in Wasco County, Oregon, successfully contaminated salad bars at most of the restaurants in The Dalles by pouring solutions containing *Salmonella enteritica* serotype typhimurium over the salad makings and into the salad dressings. More than 700 persons fell ill with food poisoning as a result of the incident; all recovered. The salmonella outbreaks were not recognized by public health authorities as deliberate until after some cult members informed law enforcement authorities. In fact, a report issued by a group of U.S. public health officials who reviewed the incident deemed it to be due to poor hand-washing and other personal hygiene on the part of food handlers. These officials pointed to the lack of further food poisoning incidents in The Dalles as evidence of their accidental nature.

In reality, the salmonella contamination incident was inspired by wishes of the Baghwan Shree Rajneesh to expand his religious community. This Indian guru had attracted a large following, and he and his cult were living in Wasco County. Relations between cult members and other local residents, however, were difficult, and local zoning regulations were hindering the ability of the cult to expand its compound and membership. Contaminating the salad bars was intended to cause an outbreak of food poisoning that would incapacitate but not permanently harm these county residents. The incident was timed to coincide with a local election. Some cult members hoped to sicken residents such that they would stay home rather than vote, thereby enhancing the chances that the Baghwan and his cult could elect candidates favorably disposed to the Baghwan on zoning matters. The plan to afflict residents with salmonella poisoning was reportedly proposed by the Baghwan's personal secretary in consultation with the nurse who ran the cult's health center. The Baghwan himself appears to have had little or no involvement in approving the plan or its execution. The salmonella bacterial culture was obtained by the Rajneesh Medical Corporation, a seemingly legitimate enterprise. In addition to contaminating the salad bars, cult members were suspected of carrying out other incidents involving use of biological pathogens, including infecting the drinking water of three county commissioners in August 1984. These incidents demonstrate the use of biological pathogens as **incapacitants** to further political, rather than military, objectives.

THERMAL NEUTRON. A neutron having a velocity comparable to that associated with the random motions of atoms in materials. The typical energy of a thermal neutron in a material at 20–25°C is 0.025 electron-volts. *See also* FAST NEUTRON.

THERMONUCLEAR. The process in which rapid **fusion** reactions are made possible by an increase in temperature. A thermonuclear reaction is the basis of the **hydrogen bomb**.

THICKENER. A substance mixed with a chemical warfare agent to increase its viscosity, thereby thickening the mixture. A thickened agent will normally form larger droplets than an unthickened one when sprayed or explosively disseminated. In general, the larger droplets will settle more quickly and more densely, resulting in a dissemination that is more rapid, more accurate, and more concentrated. Various substances have been used as thickeners. Examples of substances used to thicken **sulfur mustard** include the chlorinated rubber Alloprene and a combination of the plastics methyl and ethyl methacrylate. *See also* ADJUVANT.

THIN MAN. The original **nuclear weapon** designs selected by the **United States** were dubbed "Thin Man" and "**Fat Man,**" after U.S. president Franklin Delano Roosevelt and British prime minister Winston Churchill, respectively. Thin Man was to be a **gun-type nuclear device**, while Fat Man would be an **implosion device**. Both would use **plutonium** as the nuclear explosive. The design for Fat Man proved successful, but that for Thin Man encountered technical problems, causing it to be abandoned and an alternate design—"**Little Boy**"—using **uranium** was selected.

Testing of full-scale models of Thin Man and Fat Man began in March 1944. Problems arose with the mechanism for releasing Thin Man from the bomb-bay of the B-29, the U.S. aircraft selected for the bombing mission then being planned against **Germany** and **Japan**. The bomb casing was long and skinny—17 feet long and just under 2 feet in diameter—and full-scale models were found to drop prematurely onto the bomb-bay doors. Testing of the Thin Man models was halted in June 1944 for redesign and repairs. During this pause in testing, scientists discovered that the plutonium-239 to be used as the nuclear explosive in Thin Man was becoming contaminated with plutonium-240. American physicist Glen Seaborg had warned that this contamination might occur. He predicted that, under certain irradiation conditions, plutonium-239 would be likely to pick up an extra neutron, transforming it to plutonium-240. Plutonium-240 in the nuclear explosive was problematic because it increased the likelihood of **preinitiation** or fizzle, resulting in melting of the bullet and target before **critical mass** could be achieved in the gun-tube. Once this situation was recognized in mid-summer 1944, development of Thin Man was terminated, and work shifted to the uranium bomb.

The termination of Thin Man greatly affected the U.S. timetable for having a workable nuclear bomb. While 1943 estimates presented to Gen. George Marshall, the Army chief of staff, made early to mid-1945 a possible date for having one or more workable nuclear bombs ready, the need to switch to the uranium gun-type design pushed that date back to 1 August 1945. **Leslie R. Groves**, chief of the **Manhattan Project**, presented Marshall the revised timetable on 7 August 1944, two months after the successful D-Day landing at Normandy. They predicted that Germany was likely to surrender by summer 1945, making Japan the more probable and sole target for any American nuclear bomb.

THRESHOLD TEST BAN TREATY (TTBT). The Treaty between the United States of America and the Union of Soviet Socialist Republics (USSR) on the Limitation of Underground Nuclear Weapon Tests, commonly referred to as the Threshold Test Ban Treaty, sets a threshold for underground tests of nuclear explosives. Specifically, the TTBT prohibits underground tests having a yield greater than 150 kilotons **TNT-equivalent**. The TTBT was signed in Moscow by the **United States** and the Soviet Union on 3 July 1974, but it did not enter into force until 11 December 1990. The U.S. government delayed submitting the TTBT to the Senate for advice and consent to ratification until July 1976 to allow negotiations on a companion treaty, the **Peaceful Nuclear Explosions Treaty (PNET)**, to be completed.

In 1976, the United States and the USSR separately announced their intentions to observe the TTBT limit of 150 kilotons, pending treaty ratification and entry into force. In November 1987, the two countries initiated negotiations on added verification provisions. Agreement was reached on revised verification protocols in June 1990. The adopted protocols provide for using hydrodynamic yield measurements and seismic monitoring with respect to all nuclear tests having a planned yield exceeding 50 kilotons, plus on-site inspection for tests having a planned yield exceeding 35 kilotons.

TIMOSHENKO, SEMYEN KONSTANTINOVICH (1895–1970). Soviet military leader. Timoshenko was a highly decorated marshal of the Soviet Union. The **S. K. Timoshenko Military Academy of Radiological, Chemical, and Biological Defense**, located in Moscow's Bauman district, is named for him.

TNT-EQUIVALENT. The energy released by the detonation of a **nuclear weapon** is commonly expressed in terms of "TNT-equivalent." This term stands for the amount of trinitrotoluene (TNT) that would be required to release an equivalent amount of energy as that released by the detonation of the nuclear weapon.

TOMKA (TOMKO). A village on the west bank of the Volga River, southeast of Moscow, **Russia**. During the period of Soviet-**German** cooperation on **chemical weapons (CW)** development, Tomka (sometimes spelled Tomko) became the site of a CW proving grounds and training facility. It saw extensive use by Germany, which was forbidden by the **Treaty of Versailles** from engaging in CW-related activities. Germany contributed approximately a million Reich marks in equipment for the Tomka operation, which included four laboratories, two vivaria, a decontamination chamber, and five barracks that served as living quarters for the Germans. The decision on locating in Tomka was influenced by the large local population of so-called Volga Germans, who had settled the region in the 18th century. It was thought that the presence of additional German speakers would not attract undue attention.

The activities at Tomka were concealed through a German-Soviet trade agreement between, on the Soviet side, the Joint Stock Company on the Fight against Vermin and the Use of Synthetic Fertilizers and, on the German side, the Joint Stock Company on the Use of Raw Materials. The Tomka facility was destroyed between 26 July and 15 August 1933. Its destruction was brought about by the ascendancy of Adolf Hitler and the Nazi regime in Germany, which ended all joint military cooperation programs with the Soviets. *See also* BERSOL.

TOXIC INDUSTRIAL CHEMICAL (TIC). Any toxic chemical used for legitimate medical or industrial purposes. In addition to their commercial uses, TICs have been used as **simulants** for chemical weapons (CW), where they can aid in determining the effectiveness of respirators, detectors, and other defensive measures. Concern arises periodically, however, that TICs could be used directly by individuals or groups for chemical terrorism or could be diverted by nations into use in producing CW. TICs are also referred to as toxic industrial materials (TIM).

TOXIN. A poisonous substance that occurs naturally in animals, bacteria, or plants. Examples include **botulinum toxin, ricin,** and the **trichothecene mycotoxins**. Some toxins can be produced artificially through chemical synthesis. The military relevance of toxins was recognized during World War I, when the U.S. Army **Chemical Warfare Service (CWS)** conducted research and production of selected toxins at the **Catholic University of America**. Weapons having toxins as their primary payload are controlled as both **chemical weapons (CW)** (under the **Chemical Weapons Convention [CWC]**) and **biological weapons (BW)** (under the **Biological and Toxin Weapons Convention [BTWC]**). Toxins have also seen use as assassination weapons. *See also* JUGLONE; SAXITOXIN.

TREATY OF VERSAILLES. The treaty ending hostilities between the Allied Powers and **Germany**, concluded on 28 June 1919. Drafted at the Paris Peace Conference, this treaty contains Article 171, which deals explicitly with **chemical warfare (CW)**. The article states in part the following:

> The use of asphyxiating, poisonous or other gases and all analogous liquids, materials or devices being prohibited, their manufacture and

importation are strictly forbidden in Germany. The same applies to materials specially intended for the manufacture, storage and use of the said products or devices.

Although the Allies assumed this article would effectively end CW activities in Germany, they were mistaken. Germany successfully circumvented the CW prohibitions contained in Article 171 through work carried out jointly with the Soviet Union under the 1922 Treaty of Rapallo. *See also* BERSOL; GENEVA PROTOCOL OF 1925; HAGUE CONFERENCES OF 1899 AND 1907; TOMKA.

TREATY ON FURTHER REDUCTION AND LIMITATION OF STRATEGIC OFFENSIVE ARMS (START II). The **United States** and **Russia** signed the Treaty on Further Reduction and Limitation of Strategic Offensive Arms on 3 January 1993. Known commonly as START II, this treaty has not yet been ratified by either country. The treaty required the parties to eliminate **multiple independently targetable reentry vehicles (MIRVs)** attached to **intercontinental ballistic missiles (ICBMs)** and to reduce their respective stocks of deployed strategic nuclear warheads to 3,000–3,500 by 1 January 2003. Although the deadline for destruction was extended to allow time for START II to be ratified by both countries, Russia finally stated in 2002 that it no longer felt itself to be bound to its provisions in view of the U.S. withdrawal from the 1972 **Antiballistic Missile (ABM) Treaty**. *See also* TREATY ON THE REDUCTION AND LIMITATION OF STRATEGIC OFFENSIVE ARMS (START I).

TREATY ON THE REDUCTION AND LIMITATION OF STRATEGIC OFFENSIVE ARMS (START I). The **United States** and the Union of Soviet Socialist Republics (USSR) signed the Treaty on the Reduction and Limitation of Strategic Offensive Arms on 31 July 1991. Known commonly as START I, this treaty entered into force on 5 December 1994. START I obliges the United States and USSR to make reductions in their offensive strategic nuclear forces over a seven-year period. In 1994, Belarus, Kazakhstan, and Ukraine assumed START I obligations when the Protocol to Facilitate the Implementation of the START Treaty (1992 Lisbon Protocol) entered into force. Today none of these three states possesses **nuclear weapons**. *See also* TREATY ON FURTHER REDUCTION AND LIMITATION OF STRATEGIC OFFENSIVE ARMS (START II).

TRICHOTHECENE MYCOTOXINS. A family of structurally related poisonous substances produced by various species of fungi, especially *Acremorium* (*Cephalosporium*), *Fusarium*, *Myrothecium*, *Stachybotrys*, *Trichderme*, and *Verticumonosporium*. Trichothecene mycotoxins are toxic to humans because they inhibit cellular protein synthesis. Prominent examples are deoxynivalenol (sometimes referred to as "vomitoxin" because it induces **vomiting**), diacetoxyscirpenol, HT-2, nivalenol, and T-2. These five toxins gained some notoriety in the so-called **yellow rain** events in Southeast Asia because of allegations that they were associated with Soviet-inspired use of **chemical weapons (CW)**.

TRILATERAL PROCESS. During the early 1990s, the Union of Soviet Socialist Republics (USSR) (and, after its dissolution, **Russia**), the **United Kingdom**, and the **United States** engaged in a secret diplomatic process known as the trilateral process. The United Kingdom and United States used this process in an attempt to clarify the nature of violations of the **Biological and Toxin Weapons Convention (BTWC)** that took place in the USSR and to verify future compliance with the BTWC by Russia. *See also* BIOPREPARAT.

TRINITY TEST SITE. U.S. physicist Robert Oppenheimer selected "Trinity" as the label for the first test of the **plutonium** nuclear device known as "**Gadget**." The name was inspired by the poems of John Donne. The 51,500-acre site where this test occurred on 16 July 1945 became known as the Trinity Test Site. The site itself is in an isolated and barren region of southern New Mexico known as the Jornada del Muerto ("Journey of Death"), approximately 210 miles south of Los Alamos. It was selected because it was already part of the Alamogordo Bombing and Gunnery Range, established in 1942, and was relatively close to Los Alamos, home of **Site Y**.

Trinity Test Site is now part of the U.S. military's White Sands Missile Range, which was established 9 July 1945. In 1975, Trinity Test Site was designated a U.S. National Historic Landmark and is open to the public. The heat of the Trinity blast vaporized the steel tower that had supported Gadget and melted the surrounding desert sand, turning it into a green glassy substance. Dubbed "trinitite," this material littered the site for several years and served as a reminder of the historical test. In 1952, however, the **Atomic Energy Commission (AEC)** hired a contractor to clean up the site, and much of the trinitite was removed. *See also* JUMBO; MANHATTAN PROJECT.

TRITIUM. The **isotope** of hydrogen containing one electron, one proton, and two neutrons, giving it an atomic mass of three. It is an unstable isotope, meaning it undergoes **radioactive decay**. Tritium is added to nuclear warheads to boost their explosive yield by acting as a neutron source. The replacement of tritium inside warheads is an integral part of **nuclear weapon** stockpile maintenance. A longstanding proposed measure to control or restrict nuclear weapons is to prohibit the production and use of tritium for nuclear warhead servicing. *See also* DEUTERIUM; SALTED WEAPON.

T-SHELL. Undeterred by the failure of its first **chemical weapon (CW)**, the **Ni-shell**, **Germany** continued to search for a CW that might enable its forces to achieve superiority on the battlefield in World War I. Hans Tappen, a chemist working for **Fritz Haber** at the Kaiser Wilhelm Institute for Physical Chemistry and Electrochemistry near Berlin came forward in late 1914 with a suggestion. Tappen told his brother, Gerhard, then serving as a colonel on the staff of Field Marshal von Mackensen, that xylyl bromides and related substances were intensely irritating and, hence, ideal for use on the battlefield. Tappen's suggestion was accepted, and the German military produced artillery shells with various isomers of xylyl bromide and xylylene bromide as the fill. The shells were designated "T-shells" in honor of Tappen.

The first combat use of T-shells took place on the Eastern Front, near Lodz, Poland, on 9 January 1915. The weather was extremely cold, limiting the evaporation of the chemical fill, and the use of these shells proved ineffective. A second release took place three weeks later, on 31 January, near Bolimow. Again, results were disappointing, and contemporary records suggest the **Russian** forces subjected to these shells were unaware that the artillery bombardment included anything other than high explosives. Results were more promising when the weather turned warmer. A T-shell release on the Western Front in March 1915 near Nieuwpoort, Belgium, caused irritation and tearing among those receiving the T-shells, now modified to include benzyl bromide to help enhance the vaporization of the irritating chemicals. Shortly thereafter, T-shells, which were distinguished by a large *T* affixed to the munition, came into routine use by Germany. However, their use failed to generate the outrage that would follow the April 1915 release of **chlorine** at **Ypres,** Belgium. *See also* LACHRY-MATOR.

TUBE ALLOYS PROJECT. *See* DIRECTORATE OF TUBE AL-LOYS.

TULAREMIA. A disease caused by *Francisella tularensis*, a nonmotile, **Gram-negative** coccobacillus. The disease is characterized by fever, ulcers on the skin and mucous membranes, and enlarged lymph nodes. Occasionally, the disease progresses to pneumonia, which significantly increases the risk that the infection will prove fatal. A single organism can cause infection, which typically occurs by exposure from skin contact or through inhalation. The organism is hardy and can survive for months in certain natural conditions (for instance, at low temperature in mud or an animal carcass) or in a dried, powdered state. The high infectivity and hardiness of the organism may account for the extensive interest shown in its use in **biological weapons (BW).** There is little verifiable information regarding national programs that called for production of BW containing *F. tularensis*. The United States studied bulk production of *F. tularensis*, designating it at various times as "Agent TT," "Agent UL," and "Agent ZZ."

The Union of Soviet Socialist Republics (USSR) suffered from natural outbreaks of tularemia, especially in rabbits, prompting research into *F. tularensis*. This research reportedly carried over into BW work, including the production of a particularly virulent strain at a facility in Omutninsk, in Kirov Oblast, **Russia.** The fate of any stockpiles from this facility following the collapse of the USSR is uncertain.

During the period 1937–1945, the **Japanese** military conducted experiments with *F. tularensis* on humans held captive at **Unit 731,** near Harbin on the Asian mainland. Any Japanese use of this organism outside such experiments is unknown.

TYPHUS. A group of infectious and contagious diseases caused by the *Rickettsia* genus of bacteria and transmitted by arthropods, such as fleas, lice, and ticks. Typical symptoms of the disease are severe headache, chills, high fever, malaise, and rash. The disease can be fatal in humans; more often, though, it proves debilitating. The ease with which typhus infections can be spread among humans by the bites of fleas, ticks, and lice makes it of particular concern where large crowds are gathered and where personal hygiene is poor. Such conditions are often found during war among both combatants and displaced civilians.

Rickettsia prowazekii is spread by body lice and causes epidemic typhus. It was especially troublesome in Europe in the immediate aftermath of World War I and led to various efforts to halt its spread, including delousing stations in which persons were forced to disrobe and have their bodies, clothing, and luggage sprayed with a chemical disinfectant. The **chemical weapons (CW)** experts from recently defeated **Germany** developed some of these disinfectants, including the group of formulations marketed as **Zyklon**. The high infectivity and ease of transmission of typhus caused it to be studied by various nations for use in **biological weapons (BW)**. **Japan** is known to have used typhus for this purpose during the fighting on mainland Asia in 1937–1945. *See also* UNIT 731.

– U –

UNION OF SOVIET SOCIALIST REPUBLICS (USSR). *See* RUSSIA.

UNIT 731. During World War II, **Japan** had an extensive **chemical** and **biological weapon (CBW)** research and testing program on humans. The most well-known element of this program was designated Unit 731, which was located in Ping Fan, a suburb of Harbin in northeastern China (formerly Manchuria). The Ping Fan complex consisted of more than 150 buildings, including the prison holding cells, a power plant, recreational facilities, and a crematorium. Japan used a number of biological warfare (BW) agents as part of military operations on mainland China, including **typhus** and *Yersinia pestis*, the bacterium that causes **plague**. At the end of the war, the **United States** appears to have agreed to withhold prosecution of personnel in Japan's CBW program in exchange for information on the program's activities.

This apparent understanding has periodically been used to attack the United States as part of **North Korean**, **Chinese**, and Soviet allegations that the United States engaged in BW against North Korea during the Korean War. The fate of the paperwork from Japan's CBW program has also been the subject of continuing uncertainty and dispute. *See also* ISHII SHIRO.

UNITED KINGDOM (UK). The United Kingdom developed **nuclear**, **biological**, and **chemical (NBC) weapons**. Of these, only chemical weapons (CW) were ever used in combat. Britain no longer has a stockpile of any biological weapons (BW) or CW, but it does possess a nuclear weapon stockpile, estimated to be in excess of 200.

Biological Weapons Program. There is no evidence to suggest that the United Kingdom gave serious consideration to the use of BW during World War I. In fact, until early in World War II, most preparations related to BW were solely defensive in nature and were aligned with more general efforts to combat the spread of pathogens under wartime conditions. By July 1940, the British government was considering developing BW as a means of retaliating in kind if the **Germans** should use such weapons, and by September 1940 arrangements had been completed for the necessary research to be done at **Porton Down**. Paul Fildes, a respected microbiologist, was placed in charge and set about exploring possibilities for offensive BW. His work led to several large-scale tests of candidate pathogens, including those conducted with **anthrax** that left **Gruinard Island** contaminated for decades. Fildes oversaw development of anthrax-laden cattle cakes, produced in the millions and stockpiled for possible use against German agriculture as part of **Operation Aladdin**. Other BW designs were considered, but none was used during the war. Eventually, all stockpiles were destroyed, and the United Kingdom reoriented its work toward purely defensive measures against any BW release.

Chemical Weapons Program. During World War I, Germany's April 1915 release of **chlorine** prompted British development of CW. The United Kingdom had considered but rejected CW proposals both earlier in the war and during the 19th century. In the aftermath of the chlorine attack, however, Britain took many measures related to defense against CW, as well as offensive CW use. These measures included establishing Porton Down as a center for research and development of CW and creating the **Special Brigade**, a combat unit that came to be equipped with weapons such as the **Livens projector**.

Interest in CW diminished after the war, although the United Kingdom did complete fielding of the **M Device**, an effective means of disseminating solid chemicals such as the **blue cross agents** and **adamsite**. Interest in CW was renewed during World War II, in part driven by fears that Germany would resort to CW use as it had done in World War I. As the war in Europe ended, Britain learned of Germany's discovery of **organophosphorus nerve agents** and set about conducting systematic research in this field, often in cooperation with the **United States** and Canada. This research was boosted in the 1950s by reports from the United Kingdom–based firm ICI, Ltd., of its discovery of a novel nerve agent, **Amiton**. That research culminated a few years later in the development in the United States of **VX**, which came to be regarded as the most potent of the nerve agents. Although Great Britain did produce and stockpile various nerve agents, all CW stockpiles had been destroyed by the time the **Chemical Weapons Convention** entered into force. *See also* AYRTON FAN; CACODYL CYANIDE; COCHRANE, THOMAS, LORD DUNDONALD; FOULKES, CHARLES HOWARD; PLAYFAIR, LYON.

Nuclear Weapons Program. Historically, British developments in nuclear physics and nuclear weapons have been closely linked to those of the United States. The United Kingdom set up the Military Application of Uranium Disintegration or **"MAUD" Committee** in spring 1940. Its report significantly influenced U.S. government policy toward developing nuclear weapons and spurred the creation of the **Manhattan Project**. Great Britain, along with Canada, was a close partner on this project. Outstanding British scientists such as **Robert Otto Frisch** and **Klaus Fuchs** joined the project. The contributions of Fuchs were clouded, however, by revelations of his spying for the Soviet Union during his service on the project.

In 1950, the British government created the Atomic Weapons Establishment (AWE) to be responsible for designing and assembling nuclear weapons. On 3 October 1952, the United Kingdom became the third nation to conduct a successful detonation of a nuclear device. A defining characteristic of the British nuclear weapons program, however, has been its special relationship with the United States. This relationship was formalized on 3 July 1958 when the two countries jointly concluded the Agreement for Cooperation on the Uses of Atomic Energy for Mutual Defenses Purposes. Eventually, the United Kingdom entered into a contract with a joint venture of private firms, including U.S.-based Lockheed Martin, to operate AWE. That contract, with the entity AWE Management, Ltd., is currently set to expire in 2025.

UNITED NATIONS (UN). The UN was founded on 24 October 1945 in an attempt to help prevent or limit future armed conflicts such as World War I and II. Its charter was signed on 26 June 1945 as a result of the work of a conference of representatives from 50 nations that met in San Francisco. Its forerunner, the **League of Nations**, had been established at the end of World War I under similar circumstances.

The UN structure is largely based on that of the League of Nations. Its charter, however, differs significantly. In 1980 the UN secretary-general was given the mandate to investigate allegations of use of **chemical weapons (CW)** by United Nations General Assembly Resolution 35/144C without the prior approval of the United Nations Security Council (UNSC). In 1982, this mandate was expanded to include possible violations of the **Geneva Protocol of 1925**, thereby including allegations of use of **biological weapons (BW)** within its scope. The authority given in this expanded mandate was restricted to allow for investigations of allegations raised by UN member states only. The mandate was exercised in the 1980s through the early 1990s to investigate allegations of CW and BW use in Azerbaijan, **Iran**, **Iraq**, and Southeast Asia.

The mandate has never been revoked. However, the internationally recognized legal responsibility for investigating allegations of the use of CW (including, by definition, **toxins**) currently rests with the **Organization for the Prohibition of Chemical Weapons (OPCW)**, the body that implements the **Chemical Weapons Convention (CWC)**. *See also* UNITED NATIONS MONITORING, VERIFICATION, AND INSPECTION COMMISSION (UNMOVIC); UNITED NATIONS SPECIAL COMMISSION ON IRAQ (UNSCOM).

UNITED NATIONS MONITORING, VERIFICATION, AND INSPECTION COMMISSION (UNMOVIC). UNMOVIC carried out inspections of **Iraq** in 2002 and 2003. Those inspections ceased just prior to the 2003 invasion of Iraq by coalition forces led by the **United States** and the **United Kingdom** and have never resumed. In describing the nature of Iraqi cooperation with UNMOVIC inspectors, the commission's executive chairman, Hans Blix, made a distinction between "substance" and "process." While Iraq did provide immediate access to all requested sites, its active and full cooperation was questioned.

A major unresolved issue was the failure by Iraq to account for approximately 6,500 munitions containing approximately 1,000 tons of chemical warfare agents. There was also speculation that Iraq possessed mobile **biological weapon** production facilities. Since 2003, UNMOVIC has not been allowed to visit Iraq, but it has continued to fulfill other parts of its mandate, including performing a systematic analysis of prior **United Nations Special Commission on Iraq (UNSCOM)** and UNMOVIC inspection and verification activities. This analysis is expected to provide guidance regarding lessons-learned that might be applied to future verification efforts. *See also* CURVEBALL; IRAQ SURVEY GROUP (ISG).

UNITED NATIONS SPECIAL COMMISSION ON IRAQ (UNSCOM). Following the 1991 Persian Gulf War, the **United Nations** Security Council (UNSC) adopted Resolution 687 requiring **Iraq** to verifiably end its **nuclear, biological,** and **chemical (NBC) weapons** programs. Resolution 687 also required that Iraq have no missiles with a range of more than 150 kilometers (93 miles). In concert with Resolution 687, the United Nations (UN) established the UNSCOM, which was to verify the destruction and dismantlement of prohibited weapons and associated programs. The **International Atomic Energy Agency (IAEA)** was given primary responsibility for overseeing the nuclear weapon disarmament of Iraq.

UNSCOM verified that the principal CW agents produced by Iraq were **sulfur mustard** and the **organophosphorus nerve agents cyclosarin, sarin,** and **tabun.** The main CW issue that lacked resolution was the nature and extent of Iraq's program to produce **VX.** The Iraqi government claimed to UNSCOM that it had never filled weapons with VX but had merely produced limited, pilot plant-scale quantities of the nerve agent, totaling two to three tons of poor-quality material. UNSCOM disputed this claim. In late 1998, UNSCOM was forced to leave Iraq permanently largely as a consequence of a dispute regarding allowing UNSCOM inspection teams unrestricted access to what were called "presidential sites." UNSCOM uncovered Iraq's biological weapon program largely as a consequence of the 1995 defection of **Hussein al-Kamal**, a son-in-law of Iraqi leader Saddam Hussein. UNSCOM was replaced by the **United Nations Monitoring, Verification, and Inspection Commission (UNMOVIC)** in 1999.

UNITED STATES. The United States has developed **nuclear, biological**, and **chemical (NBC)** weapons. It is the only nation to have used nuclear weapons in combat, with the successful August 1945 attacks on Hiroshima and Nagasaki, **Japan**. While the United States is a party to various nuclear arms control treaties, it retains a stockpile of nuclear weapons. There is no evidence that the United States ever used biological weapons (BW) in combat, although such weapons were developed and stockpiled. It unilaterally renounced BW in 1969 and is a party to the **Biological and Toxin Weapons Convention (BTWC)**. The United States used chemical weapons (CW) during World War I, continued to develop and stockpile CW thereafter, but never used them. It is a party to the **Chemical Weapons Convention (CWC)** and continues to dismantle and destroy its CW stockpile. *See also* BUSH, VANNEVAR; NATIONAL DEFENSE RESEARCH COMMITTEE (NDRC); OFFICE OF SCIENTIFIC RESEARCH AND DEVELOPMENT (OSRD).

Biological Weapons Program. U.S. interest in BW might be dated to World War I, when the **Chemical Warfare Service (CWS)** engaged in a successful effort to refine **ricin**, a biological **toxin** derived from seeds of the castor-oil plant. More conventional dating of the BW program, however, would place it at the time the United States entered World War II. A well-funded effort was undertaken by the CWS to develop **anthrax**-laden weapons. Small-scale production of anthrax took place at Camp Detrick (modern-day **Fort Detrick**), Maryland. A larger-scale production and weapon filling were planned for the Vigo Ordnance Plant, near Terre Haute, Indiana, but the war ended before operations began. The United States also produced BW containing the causative agent for **brucellosis**.

Interest in BW continued after the war, stimulated in part by an influential report by **George W. Merck**. BW efforts expanded and included open-air testing of BW at **Dugway Proving Ground (DPG)**, Utah, as well as bulk production of the causative agents of **Q fever** and **tularemia**. In addition, the United States prepared bulk quantities of biological agents targeted against crops rather than humans or livestock and stockpiled these **anticrop agents**. All offensive BW efforts ceased by the early 1970s, and BW stockpiles were destroyed. Thereafter, the U.S. government maintains that its BW-related efforts have been entirely defensive in nature. *See also* BIOLOGICAL WARFARE COMMITTEE (BWC); BOYLES, WILLIAM ALLEN.

Chemical Weapons Program. U.S. interest in CW dates to its April 1917 entry into World War I, when the **Bureau of Mines** was made responsible for CW activities. The work included extensive laboratory and testing grounds at **American University** in Washington, D.C. Later, the military established the CWS, the **First Gas Regiment**, and **Edgewood Arsenal**, Maryland, giving it robust capabilities for offensive and defensive CW operations. Research into novel CW continued after the war, albeit on a significantly reduced basis, and the First Gas Regiment was demobilized.

The U.S. entry into World War II brought a renewed focus on CW, and various CW were produced and stockpiled, including some containing the new **nitrogen mustards**. No combat use of these weapons occurred. After the war, the United States learned of **Germany**'s discovery and development of **organophosphorus nerve agents**, prompting research into this field and ultimately resulting in the discovery of **VX**. The United States produced and stockpiled CW containing **tabun**, **sarin**, **soman**, and VX, but none was ever used in combat. All U.S. CW either have been destroyed or are slated for destruction in accordance with the CWC. *See also* ADAMSITE; AGENT ORANGE; CATHOLIC UNIVERSITY OF AMERICA; CONANT, JAMES BRYANT; FRIES, AMOS A.; LEWISITE.

Nuclear Weapons Program. The United States began its nuclear weapons program prior to its entry into World War II, prompted in part by an appeal to President Franklin D. Roosevelt from **Albert Einstein**. That program eventually became the **Manhattan Project**, requiring the skills of thousands of scientists, engineers, and technicians and costing billions of dollars. By summer 1945, three nuclear devices were ready: "**Gadget**," which was exploded successfully on 16 July at the **Trinity Test Site**, New Mexico, and "**Little Boy**" and "**Fat Man**," which were detonated over Hiroshima on 6 August and Nagasaki on 9 August, respectively.

After the war, the United States continued to develop nuclear weapons, including the first successful **thermonuclear** device, "**George**," as well as the **Mark-9 and Mark-19 280-mm projectiles** designed for firing from a field gun such as the "**Atomic Annie**." In all, the United States conducted at least 1,030 nuclear weapon tests. The United States has now ceased such testing and is currently a party to various bilateral and multilateral agreements limiting the numbers and types of nuclear explosions and nuclear weapons, such as the **Limited Test Ban Treaty (LTBT)**, the **Nonproliferation Treaty (NPT)**, and the **Peaceful Nuclear Explosions (PNE) Treaty**. *See also* ATOMIC DEMOLITION MUNITION (ADM); ATOMS FOR PEACE; STAGG FIELD.

URANIUM. A naturally occurring element, with atomic number 92 and symbol "U." **Isotopes** of uranium find use in **nuclear weapons** as well as in nuclear power generation. The most prominent isotopes are uranium-233, uranium-234, uranium-235, and uranium-238. Uranium-233 is a man-made radioisotope, produced most often by neutron bombardment of thorium-232. It is significant largely because it is a **fissile isotope**. Uranium-234 is radioactive but is neither fissile nor **fertile**. Natural uranium contains about 0.0054 percent uranium-234.

Uranium-235 is the only naturally occurring fissile isotope of uranium. Natural uranium contains about 0.7110 percent uranium-235. It was the nuclear explosive in "**Little Boy**," the nuclear weapon dropped on Hiroshima in August 1945. "Enriched uranium"—either **low-enriched uranium** or **highly enriched uranium**—refers to uranium with higher proportions of this isotope.

Uranium-238 is the most abundant isotope of uranium, constituting approximately 99.2830 percent of natural uranium. It is not fissionable, but it is a fertile material, forming the fissile isotope **plutonium**-239 as a result of neutron bombardment.

URANIUM CLUB. In early 1939, an informal group gathered under the auspices of **Germany**'s Reich Research Council to study the possibilities of **fission** using **uranium**. Dubbed the "Uranium Club" (*Uranverein*), the group included physicists **Walther Bothe**; Peter Debye, the director of the Kaiser Wilhelm Institute for Physics,

Berlin, and winner of the 1936 Nobel Prize in Chemistry; and Hans Geiger, the codeveloper, with Walther Müller, of the Geiger counter used to measure radioactivity. This club was largely ineffective.

In September 1939, following the outbreak of hostilities in World War II, the Army Ordnance Department took over the Uranium Club, pushing aside the Reich Research Council. Kurt Diebner organized its first meeting, held in Berlin on 16 September. Attendees included Bothe and Geiger from the first Uranium Club, plus Paul Harteck and **Otto Hahn**. Later this same month, a second meeting was held at the Army Ordnance Department, with the newly conscripted **Werner Heisenberg** attending. The Uranium Club recommended pursuing research into nuclear fission, with an emphasis on technical applications, such as energy production and nuclear explosives. The club continued to meet throughout the war, but its influence on Germany's **nuclear weapons** program is difficult to measure.

URANIUM COMMITTEE. Wall Street economist Alexander Sachs met with President Franklin Delano Roosevelt, his longtime friend, in October 1939 to discuss a letter sent to the president by **Albert Einstein** in August. That letter alerted the president to the potentials of **chain reactions** of **uranium**. Einstein wrote of the possibilities for "extremely powerful bombs" and warned of **Germany**'s likely lead in research in this area. After meeting with Sachs, Roosevelt decided to set up a committee to study uranium. He advised Einstein of this decision on 19 October. Two days later, the Advisory Committee on Uranium, commonly referred to as the Uranium Committee, held its initial meeting. National Bureau of Standards chief Lyman J. Briggs chaired the committee, whose formal members included representatives from the U.S. Army Ordnance Department and the U.S. Navy Bureau of Ordnance. Sachs and several prominent physicists, including Leo Szilard and Edward Teller, became informal members of the committee. The Uranium Committee became part of the **National Defense Research Committee (NDRC)** when that body was formed in June 1941. Later, with the establishment of the **Office of Scientific Research and Development (OSRD)**, the Uranium Committee was placed under it as the OSRD Section on Uranium. Its existence was kept secret, and it was referred to broadly as Section One or, simply, **S-1**. *See also* FIFTH WASHINGTON CONFERENCE ON THEORETICAL PHYSICS.

URCHIN. The **Manhattan Project** scientists and engineers designing the first **nuclear weapons** recognized in 1943 that a source of neutrons would be needed to initiate the **chain reaction**. They constructed such initiators out of **polonium** and beryllium, giving the final product the nickname "urchin." The scheme for generating neutrons was straightforward. First, polonium, in the form of polonium-210, would undergo natural **radioactive decay** into lead and an **alpha particle**. Second, when this alpha particle hit a beryllium atom (in this case, beryllium-9), that atom would emit a neutron. A barrier within the urchin separated the polonium and beryllium until the moment a **critical mass** was formed.

The urchins functioned as designed, but they had shortcomings. Polonium-210 has a half-life of only 138 days, meaning that it had to be replaced and replenished frequently. To work properly, each urchin had to be inserted into the center of the **fissile material** within the nuclear bomb, an operation that was inconvenient at best. Eventually, an externally mounted neutron generator having a longer life was developed, allowing use of the urchins to be discontinued.

USTINOV, NIKOLAI VASIL'YEVICH (1944–1988). Russian virologist. Ustinov perished from Marburg virus, contracted from a needle prick during experiments at **Vektor**. His exposure to this virus is rumored to have become the basis for a special strain of the Marburg virus that might be used in a **biological weapon (BW)**.

In spring 1988, Ustinov was working with a colleague in a facility having a designation for the highest level of safety around biological pathogens—**Biosafety** Level 4 (BSL-4). They were injecting guinea pigs with Marburg virus. While Ustinov was holding a guinea pig, his colleague attempted to make the injection, but missed. The needle penetrated two layers of rubber gloves on Ustinov's hand and entered his finger. He received what proved to be a lethal dose of virus. Following this injection, Ustinov was taken to Vektor's BSL-4 hospital, where he remained until his death on 30 April. His wife, also a scientist working at Vektor, visited him there, but the two were always separated by the protective suit she was forced to wear to avoid becoming infected herself.

After Ustinov's death, an autopsy was performed on his body. It is rumored that his blood and other body parts were collected so that the strain of Marburg virus could be isolated and harvested for possible use in developing a BW. Colleagues at Vektor named the strain that killed him "Variant U" in his memory. That variant is alleged to have been the basis for a larger-scale production of the virus, which was treated to enhance its ability to be dispersed as an **aerosol**. Proof of this allegation is lacking, and the accusation has been routinely denied by **Russian** officials.

– V –

VARICOLORED CROSS; VARIEGATED SHOOT. During World War I, **Germany** adopted the battlefield tactic of firing a mix of **chemical weapons (CW)** containing **blue cross agents**, **green cross agents**, and **yellow cross agents**. Various terms were applied to this tactic, the most common ones being varicolored cross (*Buntkreuz*) and variegated shoot (*Buntshiessen*). The terms refer to the multicolored effect seen on a map displaying two or more colors of crosses for a single impact area. Germany used such colored crosses on their military maps to denote the type of chemical munition to be used. Development of this tactic is attributed to Lt. Col. Georg Bruchmüller, although the tactic was developed independently during the war by the **United Kingdom** and **France**.

VECTOR. Any carrier that transmits a pathogen from one host to another. The vector is itself a living organism and may or may not ultimately be affected by the pathogen. For example, *Xenopsylla choepis* fleas can be a vector for spreading the bacteria responsible for **plague**. These bacteria are ingested by a flea when it bites an infected animal, and then are transferred to another animal when the flea moves to another animal and bites it. Similarly, mosquitoes are vectors for various diseases, such as the yellow fever virus. Other common vectors for biological pathogens include rodents and ticks. Some **biological weapon (BW)** programs have used or tested vectors as a means of propagating a pathogen. *See also* OPERATION PX; UNIT 731.

VEDDER, EDWARD BRIGHT (1878–1952). U.S.-born physician and scientist. From 1925 to 1929, Vedder served as the chief of medical research for the U.S. Army **Chemical Warfare Service (CWS)**. He authored *Medical Aspects of Chemical Warfare* (1925), which became a standard work on the effects of **chemical weapons (CW)**.

VEKTOR. "Vector" is the name used by the **Russians** to designate the State Research Center of Virology and Biotechnology "Vector," Koltsovo, Novosibirsk region. Its full name in Russian is *Gosydarstvennyy Nauchnyy Tsentr Virusologii i Biotekhologii "Vektor."* Vektor houses one of the two internationally sanctioned repositories of **smallpox** virus (the other resides at the U.S. Centers for Disease Control and Prevention in Atlanta, Georgia). It was founded in 1974 as a part of the **Biopreparat** complex and became a center both for openly promoted research on virology and biotechnology and for classified work on **biological weapons (BW)**, including an effort to create substantial stockpiles of smallpox virus for use in such weapons. *See also* USTINOV, NIKOLAI VASIL'YEVICH.

VELA INCIDENT. The **United States** began deploying Vela satellites in the late 1950s as a means of detecting a nuclear detonation. On 22 September 1979, one of these satellites, Vela 6911, detected a double-flash signal of a type known to occur during a nuclear explosion. The flash occurred somewhere in an area approximately 3,000 miles in diameter, encompassing the southern tip of Africa, the Indian Ocean, the South Atlantic Ocean, and part of Antarctica. President Jimmy Carter convened a panel to investigate what became known as the Vela Incident. In May 1980, this panel issued a report, announcing its conclusion that the flash was likely to have been caused by a meteorite hitting the satellite, with sunlight then reflecting off particles as they spread around the satellite following the collision. This conclusion was not universally accepted in the United States. Other groups, including the Defense Intelligence Agency (DIA), believe that the data are sufficient to indicate that a **nuclear weapon** was detonated. The incident led to speculation that **Israel** and **South Africa** had jointly tested a nuclear weapon as part of suspected cooperation between the nations in the nuclear field. The actual cause of the September 1979 detection remains a matter of speculation. *See also* BHANGMETER; PROJECT VELA.

VEREX. VEREX is the shortened name for the Ad Hoc Group of Governmental Experts to Identify and Examine Potential Verification Measures from a Scientific and Technical Standpoint. The Third Review Conference to the **Biological and Toxin Weapons Convention (BTWC)**, held 9–22 September 1991, tasked VEREX to investigate possible ways to strengthen the BTWC. Concern had been expressed that an **anthrax** outbreak in and around Sverdlovsk, a city in the Ural Mountains of the **Russian** Soviet Federated Socialist Republic (RSFSR), in 1979 had resulted from release of *Bacillus anthracis* spores from a Soviet **biological weapon (BW)** production facility. VEREX met four times and identified 21 potential measures to promote assurance of compliance with the BTWC. These measures formed the basis of work for an ad hoc group (AHG) of BTWC parties that met between January 1995 and August 2001 to negotiate a legally binding protocol to strengthen BTWC compliance. However, the work of the AHG effectively ended when the U.S. delegation tabled a motion to end the group's mandate during the Fifth Review Conference to the BTWC during a meeting held from 19 November to 7 December 2001.

VESICANT. A substance that causes redness and blisters ("vesicles"), typically on contact with the skin or mucous membranes of the eyes, airways, and lungs. A synonym is *blister agent* or *blistering agent*. The sun and certain plants, especially poison ivy, have vesicating properties. Examples of vesicants used for military purposes in **chemical weapons (CW)** include **lewisite**, **nitrogen mustard**, and **sulfur mustard**.

V-GAS. A term used by the **Russians** and others for the variant of **VX** developed by the Union of Soviet Social Republics (USSR). VX and V-gas (Cyrillic: В-газ) are isomers; they share the same chemical formula ($C_{11}H_{26}NO_2PS$) and molecular mass, but their structures differ. Their chemical and physical properties are nearly identical.

VITRIFICATION. A method for the disposal of waste by immobilizing it in a type of leach-resistant glass. This method is sometimes used to dispose of waste **radioactive materials**, such as spent nuclear fuel. It can also be used to dispose of soil that has been contaminated with lead, iron, cadmium, mercury, or other so-called heavy metals. The technique is sometimes used for the disposal of nuclear weapons and soil contaminated by chemical and conventional munitions.

VOMITING AGENT. A substance that irritates the nose and throat, producing intense sneezing, often leading to nausea and uncontrolled and prolonged vomiting. Because exposure to vomiting agents initially produces intense sneezing, such agents were also known as sneeze gases or sternutators. However, the vomiting induced by such agents turned out to be the more important effect, and the agents were categorized for this effect.

The importance of vomiting agents as **chemical weapons (CW)** comes from the incompatibility of vomiting and wearing a gas mask. If someone wearing a gas mask needs to vomit, he must either take off the mask or vomit into the mask. If he does the former, he risks exposing himself to a toxic atmosphere. If he does the latter, he risks filling his mask with vomit, ruining the mask and any protection the mask might afford. In either case, the affected party is in trouble. His troubles worsen if the toxic atmosphere includes other, more hazardous chemicals released in addition to the vomiting agent. Examples of vomiting agents include **adamsite**, **arsine**, and the **blue cross agents**.

VOMITOXIN. *See* TRICHOTHECENE MYCOTOXINS; YELLOW RAIN.

VOROSHILOV, KLIMENT YEFREMOVICH (1881–1969). Soviet military leader. Voroshilov was an early Bolshevik activist who later served as military commander during the **Russian Civil War**. From 1925 to 1934 he was the people's commissar for military and naval matters and the chairman of the Soviet Revolutionary War Council in the Union of Soviet Socialist Republics (USSR). In 1926 Voroshilov became a Politburo member of the Soviet Communist Party's Central Committee and, nine years later, was named a marshal of the Soviet Union. From 1934 to 1940, he was the peoples' commissar for defense. During World War II, he served as chief of staff for a number of fronts. Unlike many other Soviet military leaders, Voroshilov was never purged and died in retirement in 1969.

During the 1920s and 1930s Voroshilov was involved in the military cooperation activities conducted with **Germany** under the terms of the Treaty of Rapallo, including those related to **chemical weapons (CW)**. He apparently played a key role in the establishment of MosKhim, a Moscow-based organization established to promote chemistry for national defense reasons. He is also known for his lectures and public statements on Soviet military doctrine. However, the nature and degree of influence attributed to Voroshilov over the development of the Red Army may be overrated, at least in his later years. While Voroshilov may not have been involved in CW matters at the operational level, his name was nevertheless associated with CW matters at the higher, political level, and many of his lectures are still studied. *See also* BERSOL; TOMKA.

VOZROZHDENIYE ISLAND. An island in the Aral Sea that was the principal **biological weapon (BW)** field test facility of the Union of Soviet Socialist Republics (USSR). The facility was established as early as the late 1920s. **Smallpox** may have been released there during field trials in the early 1970s. Following the collapse of the USSR in 1991, **anthrax** spores were dumped into pits and treated with a strong alkaline in an attempt to destroy the spores. The U.S. government recovered and analyzed samples of the treated spores as part of **Cooperative Threat Reduction (CTR) Program** activities with Kazakhstan. Shortly after the **Russian** withdrawal from the island, parts of the facility were stripped by scavengers for scrap metal and other valuables.

There is concern that the island may pose a continuing health and environmental health risk to the region, partly because the Aral Sea essentially no longer exists (due to Soviet-era water diversion projects). Contaminated soil can more easily become airborne and travel to the former mainland. The island's animal population, which is descended from animals exposed to various biological agents, could spread disease to animals on the mainland and, perhaps, to the human population. These concerns are being partly addressed by regional programs to improve human and environmental health. They are partly funded by the CTR Program.

VX. In the early 1950s, at least three chemical firms independently discovered a group of organophosphate esters that were substituted 2-aminoethanethiols and had important insecticidal properties. These discoveries included that of **Amiton**, reported openly by Imperial Chemical Industries (ICI), Ltd., in a 1955 publication, but secretly reported earlier by ICI to the British government. These discoveries resulted in intense research into organothiophosphate esters for both peaceful purposes and military use. By the late 1950s, the **United States** and the **United Kingdom** had synthesized O-ethyl S-(2-diisopropylaminoethyl) methylphosphonothiolate ($C_{11}H_{26}NO_2PS$). Originally designated "EA 1701" by the United States and "T.2445" by the United Kingdom, this **organophosphorus nerve agent** became known by the military code name "VX." Its formula was revealed in 1972 following the release of a previously secret British patent for its synthesis. *See also* AUM SHINRIKYO; BIGEYE; SHIFA PHARMACEUTICAL INDUSTRIES FACTORY, EL-; V-GAS.

– **W** –

W. *See* RICIN.

WAITT, ALDEN HARRY (1892–1981). American military officer. Waitt served in combat with the U.S. Army **Chemical Warfare Service (CWS)** during World War I. He continued to serve in the CWS after the war and eventually headed that service following the end of World War II. In 1948 he was promoted to the rank of major general and was named to head the newly designated **Chemical Corps (CmlC)**, the successor to the CWS. Waitt is the author of *Gas Warfare: The Chemical Weapon, Its Use and Protection against It* (1942), which draws upon his World War I experience as a combat "gas officer," as the position of chemical warfare advisor was known.

WASSENAAR ARRANGEMENT. A multilateral export control arrangement based in Vienna, Austria. Its full name is the Wassenaar Arrangement on Export Controls for Conventional Arms Control and Dual-Use Goods and Technologies. Established in 1996, the Wassenaar Arrangement is designed to act, among other things, as a transparency measure to ensure that arms and related transfers do not result in the misuse of dual-purpose technology, equipment, and materials. Decisions are made by consensus. The arrangement is partly modeled on the **Coordinating Committee for Multilateral Export Controls (COCOM)**, which was established in 1949 by Western states to prevent the transfer of sensitive military technologies and equipment to Communist-bloc countries. As of November 2006, 40 states were participating in the arrangement.

WEAPONS-GRADE MATERIAL. Those forms of **special nuclear material (SNM)** most suitable for direct use in a **nuclear weapon**. The term usually connotes either high-purity **plutonium** whose isotopic content is greater than 90 percent plutonium-239 and less than 7 percent plutonium-240 or high-purity **uranium** enriched to at least 90 percent uranium-235 ("weapons-grade **highly enriched uranium**" is a synonym for the latter). All weapons-grade material is SNM, but not all SNM is weapons-grade material.

WEAPONS OF MASS DESTRUCTION (WMD). A term used frequently in the context of **nuclear**, **biological**, and **chemical (NBC) weapons**. The term is associated with several definitions, however, and its precise meaning is open to interpretation. Some authorities include large explosions caused by conventional means within the meaning of WMD. Others note that the casualties and destruction of infrastructure caused by the release of certain toxic chemicals and biological pathogens fall short of qualifying as mass destruction; instead, these substances might more accurately be viewed as weapons of "mass distraction" or "mass disruption." The Criminal Code of the **United States** includes use of explosives, radiological and nuclear materials, toxic chemicals, and biological pathogens and **toxins** in the definition afforded for "Use of a WMD" (Title 18 U.S.C. §2332A).

A term analogous to WMD is known to have been used in an official document as early as 15 November 1945; earlier uses are likely. On that date, a communiqué sent over the signatures of U.S. president Harry S. Truman, British prime minister Clement Attlee, and Canadian prime minister W. L. MacKenzie King recommended establishing an international committee to consider proposals for eliminating **nuclear weapons** and, in the language of the communiqué, "weapons adaptable to mass destruction." The term appeared shortly thereafter (1 January 1946) in a resolution presented before the **United Nations** General Assembly (UNGA), proposing ways to eliminate nuclear weapons and all other major weapons adaptable to mass destruction. Greater clarity to the term emerged in August 1948 when the United Nations Commission for Conventional Armaments defined WMD as nuclear weapons, **radioactive material** weapons, lethal chemicals, and biological weapons (BW), and any weapons developed in the future that have characteristics comparable in destructive effect to those of the nuclear weapons or the other weapons mentioned.

This definition prompted opposition within the U.S. government, which wished to exclude BW. A July 1949 report by the secretary of defense's Ad Hoc Committee on Biological Warfare said there was reasonable doubt that BW "can be classified realistically as means of mass destruction." The uncertainty by U.S. officials over inclusion of BW within the meaning of WMD might be attributed to various factors. First, many noted that detecting a BW attack was difficult and differentiating a natural outbreak of a biological pathogen from a deliberate release was problematic, casting doubt on the ability to clearly establish that a weapon was implicated. Additionally, some felt that while the United States had superiority over the Soviet Union with respect to nuclear weapons, it was unclear whether this superiority extended to the field of BW.

WEISSKREUZKAMPFSTOFFE. *See* WHITE CROSS AGENT.

WHITE CROSS AGENT. During the period between the World Wars, **Germany** referred to chemical warfare (CW) agents whose principal physiological effect was to cause tearing of the eyes (i.e., **lachrymators**) as white cross agents (*Weisskreuzkampfstoffe*). Examples of such CW agents include bromoacetone, bromobenzyl cyanide, **chloroacetophenone**, and xylyl bromide. The term arose from the German practice of marking such munitions with a white cross. The practice was carried out inconsistently, however, as not all munitions containing lachrymators were marked in this way. *See also* BLUE CROSS AGENT; GREEN CROSS AGENT; YELLOW CROSS AGENT.

WORLDWIDE NUCLEAR TESTS. The number of worldwide nuclear tests that have been conducted is estimated to be between 2,053 and 2,069, but a precise figure is lacking owing to certain debates over issues such as what qualifies as an individual test. U.S. government sources provide a figure of 2,069, which are distributed as follows:

- **United States**, first test 16 July 1945, 1,030 tests
- Union of Soviet Socialist Republics (USSR) and **Russia**, first test 29 August 1949, 715 tests
- **United Kingdom**, first test 3 October 1952, 57 tests (including 24 joint U.S.-UK tests)
- **France**, first test 3 December 1960, 210 tests
- **China**, first test 16 October 1964, 44 tests
- **India**, first test 18 May 1974, 6 tests
- **Pakistan**, first test 28 May 1998, 6 tests
- **North Korea**, first test 9 October 2006, 1 test

Of these 2,069 tests, approximately two-thirds have been conducted underground, with the remainder either in the atmosphere or underwater. The largest nuclear device ever tested was detonated by the USSR on 30 October 1961. Its yield was estimated to be 58 megatons **TNT-equivalent**. The last atmospheric test was conducted by China on 16 October 1980. The last U.S. nuclear test was conducted 23 September 1992. The most recent test was that conducted by North Korea on 9 October 2006.

– X –

X-BASE. *See* GRUINARD ISLAND.

X PILE. A graphite reactor was built at **Site X**, Oak Ridge, Tennessee, to produce **plutonium** for the **Manhattan Project**. The original intent was to prove the feasibility for scale-up from the laboratory level prior to undertaking full-scale plutonium production at **Site W**, Hanford, Washington. This reactor, known variously as the "X Pile," "X-10 Pile," and "Clinton Pile," was the world's first continuously operated nuclear reactor. It operated for 20 years, from 4 November 1943 until 4 November 1963. After World War II, the reactor became the world's single largest source of radioisotopes for use in research, industry, and medicine. *See also* NUCLEAR PILE.

X UNIT. The high-voltage, capacitor-based system developed by the **Manhattan Project** to fire the "**Fat Man**" **nuclear weapon** detonators simultaneously. The design of Fat Man involved an **implosion** that initiated a **fission chain reaction**. Precise control of the timing and sequence of detonation events was essential to ensure proper functioning of this design.

– Y –

YELLOW CROSS AGENT. The **Germans** used the designation "yellow cross agent" (*Gelbkreuzkampfstoffe*) to refer to chemical warfare (CW) agents whose principal physiological effect was to cause blistering (i.e., **vesicants**). Examples include **sulfur mustard** and **lewisite**. The term came from the early practice by the Germans of marking such munitions with a yellow cross, although not all such munitions were marked in this way. *See also* BLUE CROSS AGENT; GREEN CROSS AGENT; VARICOLORED CROSS; WHITE CROSS AGENT.

YELLOW RAIN. A term reportedly used for the first time in the U.S. press on 20 August 1979 to describe an alleged **chemical weapon (CW)** attack in Laos. According to a *Washington Post* article by Stanley Karnow, a Hmong tribesman described a 1978 attack by jet aircraft as spraying a yellow rain over his village. On 13 September 1981, Secretary of State Alexander Haig gave a speech in which he alleged that the Soviet Union and its allies were using "lethal chemical weapons in Laos, Kampuchea, and Afghanistan." Haig went on to state that "physical evidence from Southeast Asia . . . has been analyzed and found to contain abnormally high levels of three potent **mycotoxins**." These substances would eventually be identified by the U.S. government as the **trichothecene mycotoxins** deoxynivalenol, nivalenol, and T-2. Autopsy results for one supposed victim of a yellow rain attack would reveal T-2 plus two other trichothecene mycotoxins: diacetoxyscirpenol and HT-2.

The validity of the analytical results has been challenged, as has the entire allegation of Soviet use of mycotoxins in Southeast Asia and Afghanistan. A 1994 U.S. government assessment of the investigations concluded the following: "The investigation of the 'Yellow Rain' allegations is a prime example of how *not* to conduct an investigation . . . the evidence was weak, unconfirmed, and based on classified sources not releasable to the public." An alternative explanation has been offered for the yellow rain episodes. This explanation holds that "mycotoxins occur naturally in Southeast Asia and that the alleged victims had confused chemical attacks with harmless showers of yellow feces released by swarms of honeybees" (Jonathan B. Tucker, "The 'Yellow Rain' Controversy: Lessons for Arms Control Compliance," *Nonproliferation Review*, Spring 2001).

YEMENI CIVIL WAR. On 26 September 1962, Egyptian-supported military forces overthrew the governing imam in Yemen (Sanaa), a country along the southwestern coast of the Arabian Peninsula. Fighting would continue for at least eight years before the Yemen Arab Republic was firmly established. Periodic reports alleging use of chemical weapons (CW) emerged during the ensuing Yemeni Civil War. The validity of the reports is questionable, because the reporting was mainly from groups hostile to the Egyptian-supported forces and loyal to the imam. But many authorities now accept that some use of CW did occur, with supplies coming from Egypt and, perhaps, the Soviet Union, which was then aligned with Egypt. The toxic chemicals thought to have been used include **phosgene** and **sulfur mustard**, perhaps from British supplies abandoned in Egypt following World War II. Whether CW use proved decisive in the civil war remains uncertain.

YPRES. The Belgian town of Ypres (modern-day *Ieper*) witnessed two historic events regarding use of **chemical weapons (CW)**. On 22 April 1915, **Germany** ushered in the modern age of chemical warfare during the second Battle of Ypres when its forces released approximately 160 tons of **chlorine** from nearly 6,000 cylinders. Earlier uses of CW had been ineffective. This release, though, proved different. A poisonous cloud spread over the 45th Algerian (Colonial) Division and the 87th French Territorial Division. These French troops were wholly unprepared for CW, and the suffocating chlorine fumes caused them to abandon their positions or die in place, opening a large hole in the defensive lines around Ypres. British and Canadian troops in the Ypres salient bordering the French positions were spared the majority of the chlorine gas cloud and held their position. While the Germans did advance and gain some ground, they had failed to make plans to exploit fully the breakthrough that resulted from the first large-scale release of chemical warfare agents.

On 11–12 July 1917, the German forces in the Ypres salient fired artillery shells filled with **sulfur mustard**, marking the first use of this agent in battle. Unlike previous CW, where the effects were largely transitory and immediate, sulfur mustard behaved differently. Sulfur mustard exposure might produce some noticeable effects, especially where the concentration was high, but this chemical continued to exert its effects long after a victim had left the affected area, producing blisters to the eyes, skin, and mouth and constricting the lungs and air passageways. The impact of the use of sulfur mustard at Ypres was sufficient that the substance came to be known by many as "Yperite." *See also* HABER, FRITZ; NI-SHELL; T-SHELL; YELLOW CROSS AGENT.

– Z –

Z DIVISION. During the **Manhattan Project**, **Site Y** (the Los Alamos Laboratory, New Mexico) was the main facility for designing and producing **nuclear weapons**. As its work proceeded, the site became crowded with people and experiments. Laboratory space, family housing, and water were insufficient. By summer 1945, the situation was sufficiently critical that the newly designated "Z Division," created to perform production engineering and final weapons assembly, was transferred physically from Los Alamos to Sandia Base, the former Oxnard Field, site of an airport outside Albuquerque, New Mexico. Earlier in 1945, this airfield had been transferred from the Army Air Corps to the Manhattan Project. Z Division became the predecessor to the present-day Sandia National Laboratory.

ZERO POINT. The center of a **nuclear weapon** explosion is its zero point. Depending on whether the weapon explodes in the air, underwater, on the surface, or underground, the zero point will likely differ from *ground zero*, which is the point on the surface of the Earth directly above or below the explosion.

ZHUKOV-VEREZHNIKOV, NIKOLAI NIKOLAEVICH (1908–1981). Russian-born microbiologist and immunologist. Zhukov-Verezhnikov played an important role in **biological weapon (BW)** activities of the Union of Soviet Socialist Republics (USSR) from the 1930s until the 1950s. From 1938 to 1947, he headed the Anti**plague** Department at the "Microb" Institute, Saratov, **Russia**. Thereafter, he became deputy director of the Rostov Antiplague Institute and, in 1948, was elected to full membership in the USSR Academy of Sciences. In 1950 he was named vice president of the USSR Academy of Medical Sciences. Zhukov-Verezhnikov served as deputy minister of the Health Ministry in Moscow from 1952 to 1954. Although in his various capacities, his work appeared related to public health and legitimate medical research, it also involved direct support to the **antiplague system** that served as a cover for much of the BW activities of the USSR. Zhukov-Verezhnikov testified as a medical expert at the 1949 Khabarovsk judicial proceedings against Japanese captured in China by advancing Soviet forces at the end of World War II who had been involved in BW-related activities, including those involved with **Unit 731**.

ZUBAIDY DEVICE. During the course of its work, the **United Nations Special Commission on Iraq (UNSCOM)** learned of a helicopter-borne spraying system known as the Zubaidy device. This apparatus, named for an **Iraqi** military officer associated with its development, had been modified by Iraq in the late 1980s to disperse biological warfare (BW) agents. As such, it showed the extent to which Iraq was taking steps to bolster its capabilities for offensive BW.

ZYKLON. Zyklon is a **German** trademark granted on 8 April 1920 and used for assorted formulations of toxic substances used initially as disinfectants, fumigants, and rodenticides but later used as a means of mass killings of humans. While no Zyklon formulation is known to have been used in combat as a **chemical weapon (CW)**, the development of Zyklons was a direct outgrowth of Germany's World War I CW program. Furthermore, the continued development of

Zyklons in the 1920s and 1930s was an effort by Germany to circumvent prohibitions on CW imposed by the **Treaty of Versailles**.

The earliest known Zyklon formulation is Zyklon A, a mix of methyl cyanoformate and methyl chloroform. It was developed during or immediately after World War I at the Kaiser Wilhelm Institute of Physical Chemistry and Electrochemistry by Ferdinand Flury (1877–1947), whose work was directed by **Fritz Haber**. Zyklon A was shortly replaced by Zyklon B, a mix of hydrogen cyanide absorbed onto the diatomaceous earth kieselguhr. This mix retarded the release of hydrogen cyanide, a highly volatile substance used extensively by **France** during World War I in CW and referred to as a **blood agent**. Zyklon B afforded a ready means of releasing hydrogen cyanide slowly, thereby increasing the chances that an exposed person or animal would inhale a lethal dose. In the absence of this time-released method, the lighter-than-air gaseous hydrogen cyanide would rapidly float away.

The original intended use of both Zyklon A and Zyklon B was as a fumigant and disinfectant, especially in controlling **typhus**. This historical use would be perverted during World War II when Zyklon B was used in the Nazi concentration camp gas chambers. While no one has ever been identified conclusively as being responsible for selecting Zyklon B for use in the gas chambers, German chemist Bruno Emil Tesch (1890–1946) was convicted and hanged for his role in promoting and supplying it for this purpose. Tesch had received his doctorate in 1914, and then spent World War I working for Haber on CW problems. Flury, the German chemist and toxicologist central to the development of the Zyklons, was never charged with any war crimes.

Bibliography

CONTENTS

I. INTRODUCTION

The information contained in this work is taken from unclassified primary or other authoritative sources. Most research in the nuclear, biological, and chemical (NBC) warfare field has focused on a limited number of mainly Western nations. This focus partly reflects the states that have been most active in the NBC field, as well as our language constraints as authors and availability of authoritative source material generally. An attempt has been made to provide a balance of sources covering standard historical works, semitechnical studies, arms control and disarmament, and recent works that consider contemporary issues of concern such as bioterrorism and so-called nonlethal weapons.

In order to better understand the strengths and weaknesses of NBC-relevant information, it is important to consider differences in the quality and type of information available according to weapon type. A great deal of authoritative information is available on most nuclear programs, including those of the United States, the United Kingdom, and the Union of Soviet Socialist Republics (USSR)—now Russia. There is less, but nevertheless significant, information about most major chemical weapon (CW) programs. Perhaps the least amount of information that is publicly available pertains to biological weapon (BW) programs. This is partly because the fewest resources were devoted to BW programs and states have tended to be most hesitant about publicizing any past offensive BW work. Of the NBC weapon types, BW arguably has had the greatest degree of opprobrium attached to it.

The type and quantity of NBC-related information that is made available is also to some degree based on the ease with which such information can be used to support a weapon development program. The technical challenges for developing a nuclear weapon are much higher than those for a chemical or biological weapon (CBW). A successful nuclear weapon development program requires a high degree of engineering skills and computational expertise. In addition, the challenges of designing, building, and operating a uranium enrichment facility and successfully designing, building, and testing an implosion warhead are very high and quite noticeable to the outside world. It can therefore be argued, to an extent, that making public some types of technical information about nuclear weapon development is not problematic from a proliferation standpoint because making use of such information to develop a weapon is beyond the capability of individuals and groups (i.e., nonstate actors), as well as most countries.

Broadly speaking, the NBC field can be divided according to academics, government employees, international civil servants, defense contractors, and the news media. All can produce excellent and insightful work. As a general rule, all published material contains inaccuracies and omissions (significant or otherwise). The field is rather specialized, sometimes highly so, according to weapon type and legal, political, and technical aspects. For example, some individuals working at CW destruction facilities know a great deal about the design and operation of glove boxes used by technicians to open and drain CW bulk storage containers, but they are not so concerned with keeping up on developments in other areas. Many academics and government officials working on arms control and disarmament issues lack a scientific or technical background. Former government employees sometimes continue their work as private contractors. Defense contractors must often prepare reports on tight deadlines and do not always make the necessary effort to ensure that their work is rigorous. In fulfilling contracts, a major objective for defense contractors is to ensure that the customer or purchasing agency is satisfied with the work and will wish to fund contracts in future. Academia, the government, defense contractors, and the news media periodically, and not infrequently, revamp previously completed work, with varying results in terms of quality. A rough generalization is that the prime motivation for defense contractors is the sale of contracts, while the prime motivation for academics is to publish respected publications. Those working in the media are perhaps most affected by the constraints of tight submission deadlines that can be a significant factor affecting the quality of the output. Without referring to an original source, mistakes can be repeated and subsequently become increasingly accepted as fact. The awareness of such factors, as well as an understanding of our specific background as authors, can assist with achieving a better understanding of the strengths and weaknesses of NBC-relevant information.

The work produced by academia tends to be strongly influenced by political science theory. As such, some of the work done in this area is not necessarily focused on the details of NBC per se, but is rather more concerned with testing the viability of models of international relations regime theory. Most academics are largely unaware of operational-level detail, as opposed to those working in government and international organizations who are much more likely to deal with such detail routinely. Academics do, however, tend to possess an advantage in that they often have more time to consider longer-term problems and trends than do officials in government or international organizations. Government officials and international civil servants may be largely unaware (and perhaps disinterested) in what is occurring in their field more broadly. For example, diplomats usually rotate into a different field every three to five years and must therefore undergo a learning routine that typically imposes limitations in terms of the scope and level of detail that they are able to absorb. Diplomats are specialists in the sending of signals to each other and the process of agreeing on issues by consensus. Therefore, much of their work is focused on the crafting of language (often ambiguous) and the legal and political implications of the agreed text. Researchers who work in think tanks are sometimes able to help bridge the gap between those working in universities and those in government. This is partly because individuals with experience in both areas are more likely to be found in think tanks and because think tanks are more likely to have the influencing of the policy process as part of their mandates. Think tanks can, therefore, be quite sensitive to the challenges of the policymaking and policy implementation process, both at the national and international levels.

Another background factor to understanding the strengths and weaknesses of NBC-relevant information is achieving a better understanding of how files with politically and technically sensitive information relevant to NBC weapons are handled. Information can be open, yet still be considered "sensitive." This is especially true when the information is collected and presented systematically in a "user-friendly" format. Currently, there is a trend in the United States, and to a generally lesser extent in some other countries, to restrict access to so-called sensitive but unclassified (SBU) information. U.S. government policy regarding SBU information is currently evolving and is under, at times, heated discussion. Finally, reports are occasionally classified because their quality is so poor that to make them public would prove embarrassing.

A related issue is how sensitive information should be handled by an organization within the framework of the United Nations (UN), such as by the United Nations Special Commission on Iraq (UNSCOM) and the United Nations Monitoring, Verification, and Inspection Commission (UNMOVIC). This includes how Iraqi declarations and political and technical assessments of them are to be shared within the respective organizations, with individual UN member states, and with members of the United Nations Security Council (UNSC) (including distinctions made between the P-5 and other members of the UNSC). For example, the final declaration submitted by Iraq in 2003 to try to satisfy obligations deriving from UNSC Resolution 687 was deemed to be proliferation sensitive and was not shared fully with most UN member states. In addition, UNSCOM documentation contains the names of companies that provided equipment, matériel, and technology to Iraq in violation of international and national legal obligations. Some of this information was provided to UNSCOM by the companies or by governments. In view of the fact that several Iranian organizations have been pursuing options to identify and bring lawsuits against such companies, access to this kind of information by the general public is considered to be problematic by some. Also, some information was provided by national intelligence services on the understanding that it would not go further. UNSCOM had a number of internal "firewall" procedures to restrict internal access to such information, partly to help maintain an element of surprise when carrying out inspections. Information-handling procedures will also be affected by a loss of institutional memory as UNMOVIC gradually loses personnel.

A final background factor to understanding the strengths and weaknesses of NBC-relevant literature pertains to allegations of NBC acquisition and CBW use. The often subtle distinctions between determining whether a CBW program is "offensive" or "defensive" and the possible role of political factors in influencing the characterization of such a program are sometimes ignored by the media and researchers working in the field. With respect to CBW development and use, the sampling and analysis procedures and chain-of-custody protocols for samples (such as the case of el-Shifa Pharmaceutical's plant in Sudan) have not always been given adequate attention by those analyzing whether a CBW program is being undertaken or a CBW attack has occurred. Allegations of CBW use are of three main types: disinformation, misunderstanding (e.g., the presence of toxic fumes on the battlefield is mistaken for being the result of the use of CW), and actual use. Caveats in threat assessments generally leave open the possibility that a state or nonstate actor that is believed to have an NBC program may not in fact have one. Such caveats may disappear in subsequent analyses, however, whether they appear in the news media or in academic publications.

A basic introduction to nuclear arms control and semitechnical aspects of nuclear weapon development and design is provided by Paul B. Craig and John A. Jungerman's *Nuclear Arms Race: Technology and Society.* For a basic introduction to the fundamentals of nuclear weapon design and early development, one can still usefully refer to Henry DeWolf

Smyth's *Atomic Energy for Military Purposes: The Official Report on the Development of the Atomic Bomb under the Auspices of the United States Government, 1940–1945.* A standard introductory work on CBW is the Stockholm International Peace Research Institute's (SIPRI) six-volume study *The Problem of Chemical and Biological Warfare.* The reader is also referred to the World Health Organization's (WHO) *Public Health Response to Biological and Chemical Weapons: WHO Guidance, 2004* (www.who.int/csr/delibepidemics/biochemguide/en/index.html). For information on detection and protection against NBC weapons, the reader is advised to consult the most recent edition of *Jane's Nuclear, Biological and Chemical Defence*, which is produced every other year. For information on disease surveillance and response, the reader is referred to the ProMed and WHO websites (www.promedmail.org; www.who.int/en/). The former is an email listserve used by doctors, epidemiologists, and other health care providers worldwide. Those on the listserve are often aware of the nature and type of disease outbreaks (whether naturally occurring or deliberate) sooner than governments. An important resource for mainly CBW-related developments is the Geneva-based BioWeapons Prevention Project (BWPP)'s email listserve (www.bwpp.org). For general background on pathogens, their effects, and treatments, the reader is referred to the U.S. Centers for Disease Control and Prevention (CDC) (www.cdc.gov) and WHO websites.

For recent arms control and disarmament–related developments, the following periodicals are recommended: *Arms Control Today, Bulletin of the Atomic Scientists, Disarmament Diplomacy, Jane's Intelligence Review, Nucleonics Week*, and the United Nations Institute for Disarmament Affairs's *Disarmament Forum*. Academic and scholarly journals include *Foreign Affairs, International Affairs, International Security, Nonproliferation Review, Orbis*, and occasional *Chaillot Papers* produced by European Union Institute for Security Studies (EUISS) (a list of the titles is available at www.iss-eu.org/public/content/chaile.html). The *CBW Conventions Bulletin* (formerly *Chemical Weapons Convention Bulletin*), produced by Sussex University's Science Policy Research Unit (SPRU) as part of the Harvard-Sussex Program on Chemical and Biological Weapons, is an indispensable source for staying abreast with CBW-related legal and political developments and general news (copies of the *Bulletin* may be downloaded at www.sussex.ac.uk/Units/spru/hsp/pdfbulletin.html). The quarterly publication *CBIAC Newsletter* from the Chemical and Biological Defense Information Analysis Center is an unclassified U.S. Department of Defense (DOD) publication that also reviews recent publications in the CBW field and provides overviews of CBW defense establishment activities and historical articles (copies of the newsletter may be downloaded at www.cbiac.apgea.army.mil/products/newsletters.php).

Publications more oriented toward the defense contractor and government threat analysis communities include *Defense News*, *RUSI Journal*, and *NBC International*. Applied Science and Analysis's *ASA Newsletter* provides a rather eclectic range of information, including on the letting of some U.S. defense contracts; reviews of recent, primarily CBW, publications; scientific and technical developments; and historical pieces. For biosecurity and bioterrorism developments, the reader is referred to the journal *Biosecurity and Bioterrorism: Biodefense Strategy, Practice, and Science* (www.biosecurityjournal.com).

A one-stop source for annual developments in arms control and disarmament is the SIPRI yearbooks on armaments, disarmament, and international security. The volumes provide updated lists of types and quantities of nuclear weapon holdings. The fact that they have been produced since 1968 also facilitates cross-checking of developments over a period. A number of past chapters can be downloaded free from individual SIPRI research project websites accessible via www.sipri.org.

For insight into the specific challenges posed by implementing export control regimes and the associated problems of determining whether a state is pursuing an NBC weapon program, the reader is referred to the U.S. DOD's Militarily Critical Technologies Lists (MCTL) (www.dtic.mil/mctl/MCTL.html). Parts of the lists are open to the public in order to assist industry with understanding their legal obligations, while other sections of the list are restricted. For a better understanding of how export controls are implemented and violations prosecuted, the reader is referred to the U.S. Department of Commerce's Bureau of Industry and Security website (www.bis.doc.gov).

A number of general observations can be made regarding libraries, archives, and major collections of NBC-relevant material. National defense research establishments generally maintain libraries and other collections of technical information, regardless of whether the countries have pursued NBC weapon programs. Most of these materials are not publicly accessible, both because the information may be classified and because defense establishments were never meant to serve as a research resource for academic researchers or the public. In addition, the level of importance that a government places on a particular type of information can change due to evolving threat perceptions and funding restrictions. Some defense research establishment materials are periodically destroyed as part of "housecleaning." Governments can also experience a loss of institutional memory as key individuals retire and priorities shift. Libraries and archives sometimes remove items from their collections to make room for further materials. Material may also be lost inadvertently as older materials are digitized.

The following is a sample of the type and range of NBC-relevant materials in various collections, libraries, and archives. Most are in English and are located in the United States. George Washington University's National Security Archive contains a wealth of primary declassified U.S. archival policy and technical material that is relevant to the NBC field. The materials are typically collected into briefing books, and interested individuals may register to receive an automatically generated email to alert them as they become available (www.gwu.edu/~nsarchiv/). All U.S. presidential libraries for presidents who were in office since World War II contain NBC-relevant policy material, including, in many cases, partially declassified National Intelligence Estimates (NIEs). The presidential archives are administered by the U.S. National Archives and Records Administration (www.archives.gov). Many Soviet and Russian materials with NBC relevance are held by Russian State Military Archive (www.rusarchives.ru/federal/rgva/). The British Library and the U.S. Library of Congress both hold extensive NBC-relevant literature of all kinds. Parts of their holdings are searchable online (www.bl.uk; www.loc.gov). The U.S. Army Military History Institute, located at Carlisle Barracks, Pennsylvania, and the Hoover Institution's Library and Archive, located at Stanford University in California, are recommended (www.carlisle.army.mil/ahec/;www.hoover.org/hila/). The single best collection of unclassified CBW-related material is held by the Harvard-Sussex Program office at SPRU. The archives of the negotiations of the Conference on Disarmament are located at the UN office in Geneva (www.unog.ch). The UN Department of Disarmament Affairs (DDA), located in New York, is the official repository for instruments of ratification to arms control and disarmament treaties and related documentation such as the annual information submissions provided by member states to the Biological and Toxin Weapons Convention (BTWC) to serve as confidence-building measures. The documentation at DDA is made available to states only. It is possible, however, to access some official documentation, including that produced by international organizations, through some national libraries.

Additional Internet sites of interest include the Russian BW Monitor (www.russianbwmonitor.com), the U.S. Department of Energy (www .energy.gov), the Lawrence Livermore National Laboratory (www.llnl .gov), the Monterey Institute of International Studies's Center for Non-proliferation Studies (http://cns.miis.edu), and Bradford University's Bradford Non-Lethal Weapons Research Project (www.bradford.ac.uk/acad/nlw/).

Websites listed were accurate as of August 2006.

II. BIOLOGICAL WEAPONS

A. General

Balmer, Brian. "How Does an Accident Become an Experiment? Secret Science and the Exposure of the Public to Biological Warfare Agents." *Science as Culture* 13, no. 2 (June 2004): 197–228.

Centers for Disease Control and Prevention. *Select Agent Program*. http://www.cdc.gov/od/sap/.

Cohen, Hillel, Robert Gould, and Victor Sidel. "The Pitfalls of Bioterrorism Preparedness: The Anthrax and Smallpox Experiences." *American Journal of Public Health* 94, no. 1 (October 2004): 1667–71.

Cole, Leonard A. *The Anthrax Letters: A Medical Detective Story*. Washington, D.C.: Joseph Henry Press, 2003.

Graysmith, Robert. *Amerithrax: The Hunt for the Anthrax Killer*. New York: Berkley Books, 2003.

Guillemin, Jeanne. *Anthrax: The Investigation of a Deadly Outbreak*. Berkeley: University of California Press, 2001.

———. *Biological Weapons: From the Invention of State-Sponsored Programs to Contemporary Bioterrorism*. New York: Columbia University Press, 2004.

Häggström, Britta, Åke Forsberg, and Lena Norlander. *Conversion of a Former Biological Weapon Establishment*. Report no. FOI-R-1316-SE. Umeå, Sweden: Swedish National Defense Research Establishment (FOI), September 2004. http://www.foi.se.

Kuhn, Jens H. "Experiences of the First Western Scientist with Permission to Work inside a Former Soviet Biowarfare Facility." Doctoral diss., Charité-University (Berlin), 2004.

Leitenberg, Milton. "Distinguishing Offensive from Defensive Biological Weapons Research." *Critical Reviews in Microbiology* 29, no. 3 (2003): 223–57.

——. *The Problem of Biological Weapons.* Stockholm: Swedish National Defence College, 2004.

Lindler, Luther E., Frank J. Lebeda, and George W. Korch, eds. *Biological Weapons Defense: Infectious Diseases and Counterterrorism.* Totowa, N.J.: Humana Press, 2005.

Martinetz, Dieter, and Karlheinz Lohs. *Poison: Sorcery and Science, Friend and Foe.* Trans. Alistair Wightman and Alison Wightman. Leipzig, East Germany: Edition Leipzig, 1987.

Miller, Judith, Stephen Engelberg, and William Broad. *Germs: Biological Weapons and America's Secret War.* New York: Simon & Schuster, 2001.

Naff, Clay Farris, ed. *Biological Weapons.* New York: Thomson Gale, 2006.

Pilch, Richard F., and Raymond A. Zilinskas, eds. *Encyclopedia of Bioterrorism Defense.* Hoboken, N.J.: Wiley-Liss, 2005.

Preston, Richard. "Annals of Biowarfare: The Bioweaponeers." *New Yorker* (9 March 1998), 52–65.

Rimmington, Anthony. *Russia's Biowarriors: A Who's Who of Biodefence Scientists in the Soviet Union and Russian Federation, 1917–2005.* Birmingham, England: Russian BW Monitor, 2005.

Rimmington, Anthony, and Rod Greenshields. *Technology and Transition: A Survey of Biotechnology in Russia, Ukraine and the Baltic States.* Westport, Conn.: Quorum Books, 1992.

Rosebury, Theodor. *Peace or Pestilence: Biological Warfare and How to Avoid It.* New York: Whittlesey House, 1949.

Russian BW Monitor. http://www.russianbwmonitor.com.

Thompson, Marilyn W. *The Killer Strain: Anthrax and a Government Exposed.* New York: HarperCollins, 2003.

Tucker, Jonathon. *Scourge: The Once and Future Threat of Smallpox.* New York: Atlantic Monthly Press, 2001.

Westerdahl, Kristina S., and Roger Roffey. "Vaccine Production in Russia: An Update." *Nature Medicine Vaccine Supplement* 4, no. 5 (May 1998): 506.

Whitby, Simon M. *Biological Warfare against Crops.* Chippenham, Wiltshire, England: Palgrave, 2002.

World Health Organization. http://www.who.int/en.

Zilinskas, Raymond A., ed. *Biological Warfare: Modern Offense and Defense.* London: Lynne Rienner, 2000.

B. Historical

Alibek, Ken, and Stephen Handelman. *Biohazard: The Chilling True Story of the Largest Covert Biological Weapons Program in the World—Told from the Inside by the Man Who Ran It*. London: Hutchinson, 1999.

"Anniversary Dates: Nikolai Nikolaivich Zhukov-Verezhnikov (on His 70th Birthday)." *Zhurnal Mikrobiologii, Epidemiologii i Immunologii* [Journal of Microbiology, Epidemiology and Immunology] 11 (1978): 149–50.

Balmer, Brian. *Britain and Biological Warfare: Expert Advice and Science Policy, 1930–65*. New York: Palgrave, 2001.

Birstein, Vadim. *The Perversion of Knowledge: The True Story of Soviet Science*. Boulder, Colo.: Westview Press, 2001.

Cooper, Simon. "Life in the Pursuit of Death." *Seed* (January/February 2003): 67–72, 104–7.

Geissler, Erhard. *Anthrax und das Versagen der Geheimdienste* [Anthrax and the failure of the Secret Service]. Berlin: Kai Homilius Verlag, 2003.

———. *Biologische Waffen—nicht in Hitlers Arsenalen: Biologische und Toxin-Kampfmittel in Deutschland von 1915 bis 1945* [Biological Weapons—Not in Hitler's Arsenal: Biological and Toxin War Materials in Germany from 1915 through 1945]. Münster: LIT Verlag, 1998.

———. *Hitler und die Biowaffen* [Hitler and the Bioweapons]. Münster: LIT Verlag, 1998.

Geissler, Erhard, and John Ellis van Courtland Moon, eds. *Biological and Toxin Weapons: Research, Development and Use from the Middle Ages to 1945*. SIPRI Chemical & Biological Warfare Studies no. 18. Oxford: Oxford University Press, 1999.

Gold, Hal. *Unit 731 Testimony*. Tokyo: Yen Books, 1996.

Hammond, Peter M., and Gradon Carter. *From Biological Warfare to Healthcare: Porton Down, 1940–2000*. New York: Palgrave, 2001.

Hansen, Friedrich. *Biologische Kriegsführung im Dritten Reich* [Biological Warfare in the Third Reich]. Frankfurt: Campus Verlag, 1993.

Harris, Sheldon H. *Factories of Death: Japanese Biological Warfare, 1932–1945, and the American Cover-up*. London: Routledge, 1994.

Landau, Henry. *The Enemy Within: The Inside Story of German Sabotage in America*. New York: G. P. Putham's Son's, 1937.

Lexow, Wilton E., and Julian Hoptman. "The Enigma of Soviet BW." *Studies in Intelligence* 9 (1965): 15–20.

Mangold, Tom, and Jeff Goldberg. *Plague Wars: The Terrifying Reality of Biological Warfare*. New York: St. Martin's Press, 1999.

Mayor, Adrienne. *Greek Fire, Poison Arrows, and Scorpion Bombs*. London: Overlook Duckworth, 2003.

Microbe Culture at Bukarest: Discoveries at the German Legation from the Rumanian Official Documents. London: Hodder & Stoughton, 1917.

National Security Archive. *Volume III: Biowar; The Nixon Administration's Decision to End US Biological Warfare Programs*. National Security Archive Electronic Briefing Book no. 58, updated 7 December 2001. http://www.gwu.edu/~nsarchiv/NSAEBB/NSAEBB58.

Ochsner, Herman. *History of German Chemical Warfare in World War II. Part I: The Military Aspect*. Washington, D.C.: Historical Office, U.S. Chemical Corps, 1949.

Raginsky, M. Yu., S. Ya. Rozenblit, and L. N. Smirnov. *Bakteriologicheskaya Voina—Prestupnoe Orudie Imperialisticheskoi Agressii (Khabarovsky Protsess Yaponskhikh Voennikh Prestupnikov)* [Bacteriological War: The Criminal Weapon of Imperial Aggression (The Khabarovsk Proceedings of Japanese Criminals)]. Moscow: USSR Academy of Sciences Publisher, 1950.

U.S. Congress. Senate. Committee on Human Resources. Subcommittee on Health and Scientific Research. *Biological Testing Involving Human Subjects by the Department of Defense, 1977*. 95th Cong., 1st sess., 8 March and 23 May 1977.

Wallace, David, and Peter Williams. *Unit 731: The Japanese Army's Secret of Secrets*. London: Hodder & Stoughton, 1989.

Wheelis, Mark, Lajos Rózsa, and Mark Dando, eds. *Deadly Cultures: Biological Weapons since 1945*. Cambridge, Mass.: Harvard University Press, 2006.

C. Technical

Banks, H. Thomas, and Carlos Castillo-Chavez, eds. *Bioterrorism: Mathematical Modeling Applications in Homeland Security*. Philadelphia: Society for Industrial and Applied Mathematics, 2003.

Beecher, Douglas J. "Forensic Applications of Microbial Culture Analysis to Identify Mail Intentionally Contaminated with *Bacillus anthracis* Spores." *Applied and Environmental Microbiology* 72, no. 8 (August 2006): 5304–10.

De Clerq, Erik, and Earl R. Kern, eds. *Handbook of Viral Bioterrorism and Biodefense*. Amsterdam: Elsevier Science, 2003.

DelVecchio, Vito G., and Vladimir Krcmery, eds. *Applications of Genomics and Proteomics for Analysis of Bacterial Biological Warfare Agents*. Amsterdam: IOS Press, 2003.

Institute of Medicine. *Assessment of Future Scientific Needs for Live Variola Virus*. Washington, D.C.: National Academy Press, 1999.

Layne, Scott P., Tony J. Beugelsdijk, and C. Kumar N. Patel, eds. *Firepower in the Lab: Automation in the Fight against Infectious Diseases and Bioterrorism*. Washington, D.C.: John Henry Press, 2001.

III. CHEMICAL WEAPONS

A. General

Harnly, Caroline D. *Agent Orange and Vietnam: An Annotated Bibliography.* London: Scarecrow Press, 1988.

Kelly, Len, Dale Dewar, and Bill Curry. "Experiencing Chemical Warfare: Two Physicians Tell Their Story of Halabja in Northern Iraq." *Canadian Journal of Rural Medicine* 9, no. 3 (summer 2004): 178–81.

Witten, Benjamin. *The Search for Toxic Chemical Agents.* Edgewood Arsenal, Md.: Department of the Army, November 1969.

B. Historical

Antonov, Nikolai. *Khimicheskoe Oruzhie na Rubezhe Dvukh Stoletii* [Chemical Weapons at the Turn òf the Century]. Moscow: Progress Publisher, 1994.

Balfour, Sebastian. *Deadly Embrace: Morocco and the Road to the Spanish Civil War.* Oxford: Oxford University Press, 2002.

Brophy, Leo P., and George J. B. Fisher. *The Chemical Warfare Service: Organizing for War.* Washington, D.C.: Office of the Chief of Military History, U.S. Army, 1959.

Brophy, Leo P., Wyndham D. Miles, and Rexmond C. Cochrane. *The Chemical Warfare Service: From Laboratory to Field.* Washington, D.C.: Office of the Chief of Military History, U.S. Army, 1959.

Cook, Tim. *No Place to Run: The Canadian Corps and Gas Warfare in the First World War.* Vancouver: UBC Press, 1999.

Del Boca, Angelo. *The Ethiopian War, 1935–1941.* Trans. from Italian by P. D. Cummins. Chicago: University of Chicago Press, 1969.

Evans, Rob. *Gassed: British Chemical Warfare Experiments on Humans at Porton Down.* London: House of Stratus, 2000.

Fishman, Yakov M. *Khimizatsiya i vozdushno-khimicheskaya oborona SSSR (doklad na II vsesoyuznom sezde OSOAVIAKhIMA)* [Chemicalization and Chemical Air Defense of the USSR (Report on the Second All-Union Meeting of OSOAVIAKhIM]. Moscow: "OSOAVIAKhIM" Publishers, 1930.

Fries, Amos A., and Clarence J. West. *Chemical Warfare.* New York: McGraw-Hill, 1921.

Gilchrist, Harry Lorenzo. *A Comparative Study of World War Casualties from Gas and Other Weapons.* Washington, D.C.: GPO, 1928.

Haber, Ludwig Fritz. *The Poisonous Cloud: Chemical Warfare in the First World War.* Oxford, England: Clarendon Press, 1986.

Infield, Glenn B. *Disaster at Bari.* New York: MacMillan, 1971.

Johnston, Harold. *A Bridge Not Attacked: Chemical Warfare Civilian Research during World War II.* London: World Scientific, 2003.

Jones, Daniel Patrick. *The Role of Chemists in Research on War Gases in the United States during World War I.* Ann Arbor, Mich.: UMI Dissertation Services, 1993.

Kleber, Brooks E., and Dale Birdsell. *The Chemical Warfare Service: Chemicals in Combat.* Washington, D.C.: Office of the Chief of Military History, U.S. Army, 1966.

Krause, Joachim, and Charles K. Mallory. *Chemical Weapons in Soviet Military Doctrine: Military and Historical Experience, 1915–1991.* Boulder, Colo.: Westview Press, 1992.

Lindsay-Poland, John. *Emperors in the Jungle: The Hidden History of the U.S. in Panama.* Durham, N.C.: Duke University Press, 2003.

Manning, Van. H. *War Gas Investigations: Advance Chapter from Bulletin 178, War Work of the Bureau of Mines.* Washington, D.C.: GPO, 1919.

Mellor, David P. *The Role of Science and Industry.* Adelaide, Australia: Griffen Press, 1958.

Plunkett, Geoff. *Chemical Warfare Agent (CWA) Sea Dumping off Australia.* 3rd ed. Canberra: Australian Ministry of Defence, 2003. Available at http://www.hydro.gov.au/n2m/dumping/cwa/cwa.htm.

Sawyer, Ralph D. *Fire and Water: The Art of Incendiary and Aquatic Warfare in China.* Boulder, Colo.: Westview Press, 2004.

Schmaltz, Florian. "Neurosciences and Research on Chemical Weapons of Mass Destruction in Nazi Germany." *Journal of the History of Neurosciences* 15, no. 3 (September 2006): 186–209.

Sloan, Roy. *The Tale of Tabun.* Llanrwst, Wales: Gwasg Carreg Gwalch, 1998.

Stoltzenberg, Dietrich. *Fritz Haber: Chemiker, Nobelpreisträger, Deutscher, Jude.* Weinheim, Germany: VCH, 1994. English ed., *Fritz Haber: Chemist, Nobel Laureate, German, Jew.* Philadelphia: Chemical Heritage Press, 2004.

Thomas, Andy. *Effects of Chemical Warfare: A Selective Review and Bibliography of British State Papers.* SIPRI Chemical & Biological Warfare Studies no. 1. London: Taylor & Francis, 1985.

Tu, Anthony T. *Chemical Terrorism: Horrors in Tokyo Subway and Matsumoto City.* Fort Collins, Colo.: Alaken, 2002.

Tucker, Jonathan B. *War of Nerves: Chemical Warfare from World War I to Al-Qaeda.* New York: Pantheon Books, 2006.

Vilensky, Joel A. *Dew of Death: The Story of Lewisite, America's World War I Weapon of Mass Destruction.* Bloomington: Indiana University Press, 2005.

C. Technical

"Analytical Methods for Chemical Warfare Agents." Special issue. *Journal of Analytical Toxicology* 28, no. 5 (July/August 2004).

Arms Control and Disarmament Agency. *Special Study on the Sea Disposal of Chemical Munitions*. Washington, D.C.: Arms Control and Disarmament Agency, 1993.

Board on Army Science and Technology and National Research Council. *Analysis of Engineering Design Studies for Demilitarization of Assembled Chemical Weapons at Pueblo Chemical Depot*. Washington, D.C.: National Academy Press, 2001.

Bunnett, Joseph, and Marian Mikoajczyk, eds. *Arsenic and Old Mustard: Chemical Problems in the Destruction of Old Arsenical and "Mustard" Munitions*. Dordrecht, Netherlands: Kluwer Academic, 1998.

Crippen, James B. *Explosives and Chemical Weapons Identification*. Boca Raton, Fla.: CRC Press, 2006.

Danon, Yehuda L., and Joshua Shemer, eds. *Chemical Warfare Medicine, Aspects and Perspectives from the Persian Gulf War*. New York: Geffen, 1994.

Federal Maritime and Hydrographic Agency. *Chemical Munitions in the Southern and Western Baltic Sea: Compilation, Assessment and Recommendations*. Hamburg: German Federal Government Working Group "Chemical Munitions in the Baltic Sea," May 1993.

Franke, Siegfried. *Lehrbuch der Militärchemie* [Textbook of Military Chemistry]. 2 vols. Berlin: Deutscher Militärverlag, 1967. 2nd ed., Berlin: Deutscher Militärverlag, 1977.

Hanaoka, Shigeyuki, Koji Nomura, and Takeharu Wada. "Determination of Mustard and Lewisite Related Compounds in Abandoned Chemical Weapons (Yellow Shells) from Sources in China and Japan." *Journal of Chromatography A* (2006): 268–77.

Heyl, Monica, and Raymond McGuire, eds. *Analytical Chemistry Associated with the Destruction of Chemical Weapons*. Dordrecht, Netherlands: Kluwer Academic, 1997.

Institute of Medicine. *Veterans and Agent Orange: Update 1996*. Washington, D.C.: National Academy Press, 1996.

Kaffka, Alexander V., ed. *Sea-Dumped Chemical Weapons: Aspects, Problems, and Solutions*. Dordrecht, Netherlands: Kluwer Academic, 1996.

Marrs, Timothy C., Robert L. Maynard, and Frederick R. Sidell. *Chemical Warfare Agents: Toxicology and Treatment*. New York: John Wiley & Sons, 1996.

MEDEA. *Ocean Dumping of Chemical Munitions: Environmental Effects in Arctic Seas*. McLean, Va.: MEDEA, 1997.

Missiaen, Tine, and Jean-Pierre Henriet, eds. *Chemical Munition Dump Sites in Coastal Environments*. Brussels: Federal Office for Scientific, Technical and Cultural Affairs (OSTC) and Federal Ministry of Social Affairs, Public Health and the Environment, 2002.

National Research Council. *Alternative Technologies for the Destruction of Chemical Agents and Munitions*. Washington, D.C.: National Academy Press, 1993.

Olajos, Eugene J., and Woodhall Stopford, eds. *Riot Control Agents: Issues in Toxicology, Safety and Health.* Boca Raton, Fla.: CRC Press, 2004.

Prentiss, Augustin M. *Chemicals in War: A Treatise on Chemical Warfare.* New York: McGraw-Hill, 1937.

Sartori, Mario. *The War Gases.* London: J. & A. Churchill, 1940.

Somani, Satu M., and James A. Romano Jr., eds. *Chemical Warfare Agents: Toxicity at Low Levels.* Boca Raton, Fla.: CRC Press, 2001.

Sun, Yin, and Kwok Y. Ong. *Detection Technologies for Chemical Warfare Agents and Toxic Vapors.* Boca Raton, Fla.: CRC Press, 2004.

Trapp, Ralf. *The Detoxification and Natural Degradation of Chemical Warfare Agents.* SIPRI Chemical & Biological Warfare Studies no. 3. London: Taylor & Francis, 1985.

Vedder, Edward B. *Medical Aspects of Chemical Warfare.* Baltimore, Md.: Williams & Wilkins, 1925.

IV. NUCLEAR WEAPONS

A. General

Cochran, Thomas B., William M. Arkin, and Milton M. Hoenig. *U.S. Nuclear Forces and Capabilities.* Nuclear Weapons Databook, vol. 1. Cambridge, Mass.: Ballinger, 1984.

Cochran, Thomas B., William M. Arkin, Robert S. Norris, and Milton M. Hoenig. *U.S. Nuclear Warhead Facility Profiles.* Nuclear Weapons Databook, vol. 3. Cambridge, Mass.: Ballinger, 1987.

———. *U.S. Nuclear Warhead Production.* Nuclear Weapons Databook, vol. 2. Cambridge, Mass.: Ballinger, 1987.

Cochran, Thomas B., William M. Arkin, Robert S. Norris, and Jeffrey I. Sands. *Soviet Nuclear Weapons.* Nuclear Weapons Databook, vol. 4. Grand Rapids, Mich.: Harper & Row, 1989.

Craig, Paul B., and John A. Jungerman. *Nuclear Arms Race: Technology and Society.* 2nd ed. New York: McGraw-Hill, 1990.

Norris, Robert S., Andrew S. Burrows, and Richard W. Fieldhouse. *British, French, and Chinese Nuclear Weapons.* Nuclear Weapons Databook, vol. 5. Boulder, Colo.: Westview Press, 1994.

Podvig, Pavel, ed. *Russian Strategic Nuclear Forces.* Cambridge, Mass.: MIT Press, 2001.

Sagan, Scott D. *The Limits of Safety: Organizations, Accidents, and Nuclear Weapons.* Princeton, N.J.: Princeton University Press, 1993.

B. Historical

Allison, Graham T., and Philip Zelikow. *Essence of Decision: Explaining the Cuban Missile Crisis.* 2nd ed. New York: Longman, 1999.

Avery, Donald A. *The Science of War: Canadian Scientists and Allied Military Technology during the Second World War.* Toronto: University of Toronto Press, 1998.

Gibson, James N. *Nuclear Weapons of the United States: An Illustrated History.* Atglen, Pa.: Schiffer, 1996.

Gosling. F. G. *The Manhattan Project: Making the Atomic Bomb.* Washington, D.C.: Department of Energy, 2001.

Groves, Leslie R. *Now It Can Be Told: The Story of the Manhattan Project.* New York: Harper, 1962.

Rhodes, Richard. *The Making of the Atomic Bomb.* New York: Simon & Schuster, 1986.

Richelson, Jeffrey T. *Spying on the Bomb: American Nuclear Intelligence from Nazi Germany to Iran and North Korea.* New York: Norton, 2006.

Schwartz, Stephen I., ed. *Atomic Audit: The Costs and Consequences of U.S. Nuclear Weapons since 1940.* Washington, D.C.: Brookings Institution Press, 1998.

United States. Department of Energy. Office of History and Heritage Resources. *The Manhattan Project: An Interactive History.* http://www.mbe.doe.gov/me70/manhattan/index.htm.

Weinstein, Allen, and Alexander Vassiliev. *The Haunted Wood: Soviet Espionage in America—the Stalin Era.* New York: Random House, 1999.

C. Technical

Gibson, James N. *Nuclear Weapons of the United States: An Illustrated history.* Atglen, Pa.: Schiffer, 1996.

Moody, Kenton J., Ian D. Hutcheon, and Patrick M. Grant. *Nuclear Forensic Analysis.* Boca Raton, Fla.: CRC Press, 2004.

Smyth, Henry DeWolf. *Atomic Energy for Military Purposes: The Official Report on the Development of the Atomic Bomb under the Auspices of the United States Government, 1940–1945.* Princeton, N.J.: Princeton University Press, 1945. Revised and reprinted, Stanford, Calif.: Stanford University Press, 1989.

Szasz, Ferenc M. *The Day the Sun Rose Twice: The Story of the Trinity Site Nuclear Explosion, July 16, 1945.* Albuquerque: University of New Mexico Press, 1984.

Wilson, Peter D., ed. *The Nuclear Fuel Cycle: From Ore to Waste*. Oxford: Oxford University Press, 1996. Reprinted in 2001.

V. NUCLEAR, BIOLOGICAL, AND CHEMICAL WEAPONS

A. General

Baldwin, Ralph Belknap. *The Deadly Fuze: The Secret Weapon of World War II*. San Rafael, Calif.: Presidio Press, 1980.

Burger, Marléne, and Chandré Gould. *Secrets and Lies: Wouter Basson and South Africa's Chemical and Biological Warfare Programme*. Cape Town: Zebra Press, 2002.

Eldridge, John, ed., *Jane's Nuclear, Biological and Chemical Defence, 2005–2006*. Coulsdon, Surrey, England: Jane's Information Group, 2005.

Lawrence Livermore National Laboratory. http://www.llnl.gov.

Lindblad, Anders, et al. *Russian Biological and Chemical Weapons Capabilities: Future Scenarios and Alternatives of Action*. Report no. FOI-R-1561. Umeå, Sweden: Swedish National Defense Research Establishment (FOI), FOI, January 2005. http://www.foi.se.

Los Alamos National Laboratory. http://www.lanl.gov.

Rothschild, Jacquard H. *Tomorrow's Weapons: Chemical and Biological*. New York: McGraw-Hill, 1964.

World Health Organization. *Public Health Response to Biological and Chemical Weapons: WHO Guidance (2004)*. Geneva: World Health Organization, 2004. Available at http://www.who.int/csr/delibepidemics/biochemguide/en/index.html.

B. Historical

Agrell, Wilhelm. *Svenska Förintelsevapen: Utveckling av kemiska och nukleära stridsmedel 1928–70* [Swedish Weapons of Mass Destruction: The Development of Chemical and Nuclear War Materials, 1928–70]. Lund, Sweden: Historiska Media, 2002.

Carr, Edward Hallet. *German-Soviet Relations between the Two World Wars, 1919–1939*. Baltimore, Md.: Johns Hopkins University Press, 1951.

Carter, Gradon B., *Chemical and Biological Defence at Porton Down, 1916–2000*. London: HMSO, 2000.

Gould, Chandré, and Peter Folb. *Project Coast: Apartheid's Chemical and Biological Warfare Programmes*. Geneva: United Nations Institute for Disarmament Research, 2002.

Hirsch, Walter. *Soviet BW and CW Capabilities* ["The Hirsch Report"]. Declassified. Washington, D.C.: U.S. Army Chemical Intelligence Branch, 1951.

Manchenko, V. D., et al., eds. *70 let Na Sluzhbe Otechestvu* [Seventy Years in the Service of the Fatherland]. Moscow: Fourth Military Branch of the Military Publisher, 2002.

Mountcastle, John Wyndham. *Flame On! U.S. Incendiary Weapons, 1918–1945*. Shippensburg, Pa.: White Mane, 1999.

Orlov, V. N., et al., eds. *My Zashchitily Rossiyu: Istoricheskii Ocherk o Sozdanii i Deyatel'nosti Nauchno-Tekhnicheskogo Komiteta, Upravleniya Zakazov, Proizvodstva i Snabzheniya i Upravleniya Biologicheskogo Zashchity UNV RKhB Zashchity MO RF* [We Defended Russia: Historical Outline on the Establishment and Activities of the Scientific-Technical Committee, the Directorate of Orders, Production and Supply and the Directorate of Biological Defense of the Directorate of Radiological, Chemical and Biological Defense Forces Command of the Russian Federation Ministry of Defense]. Moscow: Ministry of Defense of the Russian Federation, 2000.

Pash, Boris. *The Alsos Mission*. New York: Award House, 1969.

Truth and Reconciliation Commission (South Africa). http://www.doj.gov.za/trc.

C. Technical

Arkin, William M. *Code Names: Deciphering U.S. Military Plans, Programs, and Operations in the 9/11 World*. Hanover, N.H.: Steerforth Press, 2005.

Carey, Christopher T. *U.S. Chemical and Biological Defense Respirators: An Illustrated History*. Atglen, Pa.: Schiffer, 1998.

Hooshang, Kadivar, and Stephen C. Adams. "Treatment of Chemical and Biological Warfare Injuries: Insights Derived from the 1984 Iraqi Attack on Majnoon Island." *Military Medicine* 156 (April 1991): 171–77.

Militarily Critical Technologies List. http://www.dtic.mil/mctl.

National Research Council. *Making the Nation Safer: The Role of Science and Technology in Countering Terrorism*. Washington, D.C.: National Academy Press, 2002.

———. *Toxicologic Assessment of the Army's Zinc Cadmium Sulfide Dispersion Tests*. Washington, D.C.: National Academy Press, 1997.

Taylor, Eric R. *Lethal Mists: An Introduction to the Natural and Military Sciences of Chemical, Biological Warfare and Terrorism*. Commack, N.Y.: Nova Science, 2001.

U.S. Congress. Office of Technology Assessment. *Technologies Underlying Weapons of Mass Destruction*. Report no. OTA-BP-ISC-115. Washington, D.C.: GPO, 1993.

VI. MEMOIRS

Barton, Rod. *Weapons Detective: The Adventures of Australia's Top Weapons Inspector*. Melbourne, Australia: Black Inc. Agenda, 2006.

Blix, Hans. *Disarming Iraq: The Search for Weapons of Mass Destruction*. London: Bloomsbury, 2004.

Burgasov, Pyotr N. *Ya Veril* [I Believed]. Moscow: GEOTAR Meditsina, 2000.

Domaradsky, Igor Valerianovich. *Troublemaker; or, The Story of an "Inconvenient" Man*. Moscow, 1995. Available in Russian at http://domaradsky.h1.ru/ [accessed 18 November 2006].

Domaradsky, Igor V., and Wendy Orent. *Biowarrior: Inside the Soviet/Russian Biological War Machine*. Amherst, N.Y.: Prometheus Books, 2003.

Graham, Thomas, Jr. *Disarmament Sketches: Three Decades of Arms Control and International Law*. Seattle: University of Washington Press, 2002.

Lukina, R. N., and E. P. Lukin, eds. *Dostoiny Izvestnosti: 50 let Virusologicheskomu Tsentru Ministerstva Oborony* [Worthy of Fame: Fifty Years of the Ministry of Defense's Virology Center]. Sergiev Posad, Russia: Ves' Sergiev Posad Publisher, 2004.

Madariaga, Salvador de. *Disarmament*. London: Oxford University Press, 1929.

Mirzayanov, Vil. *Vyzov* [The Call]. Kazan', Russia: "Dom Pechati" Publisher, 2002.

Sinclair, David. *Not a Proper Doctor*. Cambridge: Cambridge University Press, 1989.

Smirnov, Efim Ivanovich. *Voina i Voennaya Meditsina* [War and Military Medicine]. Moscow: Meditsina Publisher, 1979.

Vorobyov, Anatoly A. *Ne Podvodya Cherty* [Without Drawing a Line]. Moscow: Meditsinskoye Informatsionnoye Agenstvo, 2003.

Zhukov, G. A. *Vospominaniya Voennogo Khimika* [Recollections of a Military Chemist]. Moscow: Military Publishers, 1991.

VII. ARMS CONTROL AND DISARMAMENT

Arbatov, Alexei, and Vladimir Dvorkin. *Beyond Nuclear Deterrence: Transforming the U.S.-Russian Equation*. Washington, D.C.: Carnegie Endowment for International Peace, 2006.

Arms Control Association. http://www.armscontrol.org.

Australia Group. http://www.australiagroup.net.

Biological and Toxin Weapons Convention Website. http://www.opbw.org.

Brauch, Hans Günter, and Rolf-Dieter Müller. *Chemische Kriegsführu— Chemische Abrüstung: Dokumente und Kommentare* [Chemical Warfare—Chemical Disarmament: Documents and Commentary]. Berlin: Berlin Verlag Arno Spitz, 1985.

Bulletin of the Atomic Scientists. http://www.thebulletin.org/index.htm.

Burck, Gordon M., and Charles C. Flowerree. *International Handbook on Chemical Weapons Proliferation.* New York: Greenwood Press, 1991.

Central Intelligence Agency. *Iraq's Weapons of Mass Destruction Programs.* October 2002. https://www.cia.gov/cia/reports/iraq_wmd/Iraq_Oct_2002.htm.

Dittmer, Lowell, ed. *South Asia's Nuclear Security Dilemma: India, Pakistan, and China.* London: M. E. Sharpe, 2005.

Ekéus, Rolf. "Reassessment: The IISS Strategic Dossier on Iraq's Weapons of Mass Destruction." *Survival* 46, no. 2 (Summer 2004): 73–88.

Frisina, Michael E. "The Offensive-Defensive Distinction in Military Biological Research." *Hastings Center Report* 20, no. 3 (May/June 1990): 19–22.

Harvard-Sussex Program on Chemical and Biological Weapons (CBW). http://www.sussex.ac.uk/Units/spru/hsp.

"Impact of Scientific Developments on the Chemical Weapons Convention." Proceedings of International Union of Pure and Applied Chemistry (IUPAC) workshop, Bergen, Norway, 30 June–3 July 2002. *Pure and Applied Chemistry* 74, no. 12 (12 December 2002).

International Atomic Energy Agency. http://www.iaea.org.

International Institute for Strategic Studies. *Iraq's Weapons of Mass Destruction: A Net Assessment.* London: IISS, 2002.

International Union of Pure and Applied Chemistry. *Impact of Scientific Developments on the Chemical Weapons Convention.* Report to the Organization for the Prohibition of Chemical Weapons. Research Triangle Park, N.C.: IUPAC, 2002.

Kalinowski, Martin B. *International Control of Tritium for Nuclear Nonproliferation and Disarmament.* Science and Global Security Monograph Series. Boca Raton, Fla.: CRC Press, 2004.

Kelly, David. "The Trilateral Agreement: Lessons for Biological Weapons Verification." In *Verification Yearbook 2002*, ed. Trevor Findlay and Oliver Meier, 93–109. London: VERTIC, 2002.

Krasno, Jean E., and James S. Sutterlin. *The United Nations and Iraq: Defanging the Viper.* Westport, Conn.: Praeger, 2003.

Krutzsch, Walter, and Ralf Trapp. *A Commentary on the Chemical Weapons Convention.* Dordrecht, Netherlands: Martinus Nijhoff, 1994.

Larsen, Jeffrey A., and James M. Smith. *Historical Dictionary of Arms Control and Disarmament.* Lanham, Md.: Scarecrow Press, 2005.

Lewer, Nick, ed. *The Future of Non-Lethal Weapons: Technologies, Operations, Ethics and Law*. London: Frank Cass, 2002.

Littlewood, Jez. *The Biological Weapons Convention: A Failed Revolution*. Aldershot, England: Ashgate, 2005.

Lundin, S. Johan, ed. *Non-Production by Industry of Chemical-Warfare Agents: Technical Verification under a Chemical Weapons Convention*. SIPRI Chemical & Biological Warfare Studies no. 9. Oxford: Oxford University Press, 1988.

————. *Verification of Dual-Use Chemicals under the Chemical Weapons Convention: The Case of Thiodiglycol*. SIPRI Chemical & Biological Warfare Studies no. 13. Oxford: Oxford University Press, 1991.

Mauroni, Albert J. *Chemical Demilitarization: Public Policy Aspects*. Westport, Conn.: Praeger, 2003.

Mesilaakso, Markku, ed. *Chemical Weapons Convention Chemicals Analysis: Sample Collection, Preparation and Analytical Methods*. Chichester, England: John Wiley & Sons, 2005.

Meyrowitz, Henri. *Les Armes Biologiques et le Droit International (Droit de la Guerre et Désarmement)* [Biological Weapons and the International Law (Law of War and Disarmament)]. Nancy: Grandville, 1968.

Missile Technology Control Regime. http://www.mtcr.info.

Monterey Institute Center for Nonproliferation Studies. http://cns.miis.edu.

Organisation for the Prohibition of Chemical Weapons. http://www.opcw.org.

Pearson, Alan. "Incapacitating Biochemical Weapons: Science, Technology, and Policy for the 21st Century." *Nonproliferation Review* 13, no. 2 (July 2006): 151–88.

Pearson, Graham S. *The UNSCOM Saga: Chemical and Biological Weapons Non-Proliferation*. New York: St. Martin's Press, 1999.

Perkovich, George. *India's Nuclear Bomb: The Impact on Global Proliferation*. Berkeley: University of California Press, 1999.

Preparatory Commission for the Comprehensive Nuclear-Test-Ban Treaty Organization. http://www.ctbto.org.

Pugwash Conferences on Science and World Affairs. http://www.pugwash.org.

Rappert, Brian. *Non-Lethal Weapons as Legitimizing Forces? Technology, Politics and the Management of Conflict*. London: Frank Cass, 2003.

Report on the Inquiry into Australian Intelligence Agencies [the "Flood Report"]. Canberra: Department of the Prime Minister and Cabinet, 2004. Available at http://www.pmc.gov.au/publications/intelligence_inquiry.

Rimmington, Anthony. "From Offence to Defence? Russia's Reform of Its Biological Weapons Complex and the Implications for Western Security." *Journal of Slavic Military Studies* 16, no. 1 (March 2003): 1–43.

Roffey, Roger. "Biological Weapons and Potential Indicators of Offensive Biological Weapon Activities." In *SIPRI Yearbook 2004: Armaments, Disarmament and International Security*, 557–71. Oxford: Oxford University Press, 2004.

Sims, Nicholas A. *The Evolution of Biological Disarmament*. SIPRI Chemical & Biological Warfare Studies no. 19. Oxford: Oxford University Press, 2001.

Six-Party Talks, Beijing, China. http://www.state.gov/p/eap/regional/c15455.htm.

Stockholm International Peace Research Institute. http://www.sipri.org.

Stockholm International Peace Research Institute. *The Chemical Industry and the Projected Chemical Weapons Convention*. 2 vols. SIPRI Chemical & Biological Warfare Studies nos. 4–5. Oxford: Oxford University Press, 1986.

———. *The Problem of Chemical and Biological Warfare*. 6 vols. Stockholm: Almqvist & Wiksell, 1971–1975.

Tabassi, Lisa. "Impact of the CWC: Progressive Development of Customary International Law and Evolution of the Customary Norm against Chemical Weapons." *CBW Conventions Bulletin* no. 63 (March 2004): 1–7.

Thakur, Ramesh, and Ere Haru, eds. *The Chemical Weapons Convention: Implementation Challenges and Opportunities*. Paris: United Nations University Press, 2006.

United Kingdom. *Iraq's Weapons of Mass Destruction: The Assessment of the British Government*. London: HMSO, 2002. Available at http://www.number 10.gov.uk/output/Page271.asp.

United Kingdom. Butler Committee. *Review of Intelligence on Weapons of Mass Destruction* ["The Butler Report"]. London: HMSO, 2004. Available at http://www.butlerreview.org.uk.

United Nations. *The United Nations and the Iraq-Kuwait Conflict*. United Nations Blue Books Series, vol. 9. New York: United Nations Department of Public Information, 1996.

United Nations. Security Council. Resolution 1540. http://disarmament2.un .org/Committee1540.

United Nations Institute for Disarmament Research. http://www.unidir.org.

United Nations Monitoring, Verification, and Inspection Commission (UNMOVIC). *Unresolved Disarmament Issues: Iraq's Proscribed Weapons Programmes*. 6 March 2003. http://www.un.org/Depts/unmovic/documents/cluster6mar.pdf.

Wassenaar Arrangement on Export Controls for Conventional Arms and Dual-Use Goods and Technologies. http://www.wassenaar.org.

Weapons of Mass Destruction Commission [the "Blix Commission"]. http://www .wmdcommission.org.

About the Authors

Benjamin C. Garrett serves as a senior scientist in the Federal Bureau of Investigation (FBI) Laboratory, located in Quantico, Virginia. He holds an undergraduate degree in chemistry from Davidson College, Davidson, North Carolina, and a doctorate in analytical chemistry from Emory University, Atlanta, Georgia. He served with the U.S. Army Chemical Corps (1975–1978) and spent two decades working on defense, environmental, and intelligence programs prior to joining the FBI.

John Hart is a researcher at the Stockholm International Peace Research Institute (SIPRI). He has worked at the Verification Research, Training and Information Centre (VERTIC) in London and at the Monterey, California–based Center for Nonproliferation Studies (CNS). He was also an intern in the Verification Division of the Provisional Technical Secretariat to the Preparatory Commission (PrepCom) to the Organization for the Prohibition of Chemical Weapons (OPCW), where he contributed to the drafting of the OPCW's *Declarations Handbook* and prepared draft chairmen's papers, discussion papers, and Expert Group (Working Group B) reports. He coedited *Chemical Weapon Destruction in Russia: Political, Legal and Technical Aspects* (1998) and is the author of "The ALSOS Mission, 1943–1945: A Secret U.S. Scientific Intelligence Unit" (2005) and "The Soviet Biological Weapons Program" (in *Deadly Cultures: Biological Weapons since 1945*, 2006).